Studies on the History of Behavior
Ape, Primitive, and Child

STUDIES ON THE HISTORY OF BEHAVIOR
Ape, Primitive, and Child

L. S. Vygotsky
A. R. Luria

edited and translated by

Victor I. Golod
Harvard University

Jane E. Knox
Bowdoin College

with Introduction by Jane E. Knox

LAWRENCE ERLBAUM ASSOCIATES, PUBLISHERS
1993   Hillsdale, New Jersey   Hove and London

26220100

Lawrence Erlbaum Associates, Inc., Publishers
365 Broadway
Hillsdale, New Jersey 07642

Library of Congress Cataloging-in-Publication Data
Vygotskiĭ, L. S. (Lev Semenovich), 1896–1934.
    [Etiudy po istorii provedeniia. English]
    Studies on the history of behavior : ape, primitive, and child
/ L.S. Vygotsky, A.R. Luria ; edited and translated by Victor I. Golod
and Jane E. Knox : with introduction by Jane E. Knox.
        p. cm.
    Translation of Etiudy po istorii povedeniia.
    Includes bibliographical references and index.
    ISBN 0-8058-1014-5 (cloth)
    1. Psychology, Comparative.   2. Behavior evolution.   3. Genetic
psychology.   I. Luria, A. R. (Aleksandr Ramanovich), 1902–1977.
II. Golod, Victor I., 1946–1991.   III. Knox, Jane E., 1940-   .   IV.   Title.
    [DNLM: 1. Behavior.   2. Behavior, Animal.   3. Psychology.   BF 121
V996s]
BF767.V9413   1993
156—dc20
DNLM/DLC
for Library of Congress   92-23404
                                                                          CIP

Books published by Lawrence Erlbaum Associates are printed on acid-free paper, and their
bindings are chosen for strength and durability.

Printed in the United States of America
10 9 8 7 6 5 4 3 2

Dedicated in loving memory of my friend and
guide to life, Victor I. Golod (1946–1991).

Contents

CHAPTER 3
The Child and Its Behavior

Foreword*

James V. Wertsch
Clark University

The theoretical perspective outlined by Lev Semenovich Vygotsky can be understood in terms of three general themes that run throughout his writings: (a) the use of a genetic, or developmental method; (b) the claim that higher mental functioning in the individual emerges out of social processes; and (c) the claim that human social and psychological processes are fundamentally shaped by cultural tools, or mediational means. The surge of contemporary interest in Vygotsky's approach has focused largely on the second of these two themes, especially as it is manifested in his notion of the "zone of proximal development" (e.g., Cole, 1985; Moll, 1990; Rogoff, 1990; Rogoff & Wertsch, 1984). In my view, the third theme concerning mediation is the most interesting and uniquely Vygotskian of the three, yet it is only beginning to receive the attention it deserves (e.g., Cole, 1990; Wertsch, 1991).

In the end, however, our understanding of the second and third themes is limited until we have a more elaborated notion of his genetic method because all three themes were interdefined in Vygotsky's thinking. Therefore, an account of each depends on advances in our understanding of the others. This interconnectedness should not be underestimated. In my own writings (e.g., Wertsch, 1985, 1991), I have differentiated the themes in an attempt to introduce Vygotsky's approach, but I have also noted that, in the end, the meaning of each can be understood only by understanding its relationship to the others. It is worth noting that Vygotsky himself never outlined his approach by laying out these three discrete themes.

---

*The writing of this foreword was assisted by the Spencer Foundation. The statements made and the views expressed are solely the responsibility of the author.

Studies on the History of Behavior: Ape, Primitive, and Child is one of the most important documents we have for understanding Vygotsky's claims about a genetic or developmental method, the theme in his approach that has probably received the least attention. Although this volume was co-authored with Vygotsky's student and colleague Aleksandr Romanovich Luria, Vygotsky's guiding voice emerges clearly throughout the text. This is not surprising as it was written at a time when he was in the midst of his short, yet prolific career and when Luria was heading a research team. This in no way detracts from the brilliant contributions Luria made to other areas of psychology ranging from neurolinguistics to cross-cultural psychology; it is more in the spirit of recognizing the relationship that existed between Vygotsky and Luria in the late 1920s and early 1930s.

The ideas sketched out in Vygotsky's and Luria's introduction and then elaborated in the following three chapters present the most extensive single view we have of their general developmental method. Their starting assumption is that any adequate account of human behavior must be grounded in genetic analysis. In this view, a developmental or genetic approach is not just one among many methods, rather it grounds all others. Vygotsky made this point in other works such as *Mind in Society* (1978), where he argued that "the historical [that is in the broadest sense of 'history'] study of behavior is not an auxiliary aspect of theoretical study, but rather forms its very base. As P.P. Blonsky has stated 'Behavior can be understood only as a history of behavior' " (p. 65).

With this general commitment to genetic method as a starting point, Vygotsky and Luria went on to identify *"three main lines* in the development of behavior—evolutionary, historical, and ontogenetic." By incorporating all three lines, or "genetic domains" (Wertsch, 1985, 1991) into their approach, Vygotsky and Luria outline vision that differs markedly from that of most contemporary scholars under the rubric of developmental psychology.

Today, the term *developmental psychology* is applied almost exclusively to the genetic domain of ontogenesis, and typically even more narrowly to the periods of childhood and adolescence. In contrast to this narrowed focus, Vygotsky and Luria argue that a thorough genetic analysis must address the ways in which knowledge about all three genetic domains contributes to our understanding of behavior and mental functioning. Therefore, in addition to considering how a particular form of mental functioning reflects the ontogenetic transitions leading up to it, one must also take into consideration the forces of phylogenesis and sociocultural history that have shaped it. In this respect, the genetic method outlined here parallels, in many ways, other genetic theorists such as Werner (1926), whom Vygotsky frequently cited.

In mapping out the domains of phylogenesis, sociocultural history, and ontogenesis, Vygotsky and Luria take a very strong anti-recapitulationist position. They reject claims about simple parallels between genetic domains in the developmental processes at work. In their introduction, they argue that each domain represents a new era in the evolution of behavior: "one process of development dialectically prepares for the next one, transforming and changing into a new type of development." The key to this is their recognition of *"changes in the type of developmental itself,"* a claim that precludes any notions of straightforward parallelisms, positing instead that different principles of development are at work in different domains.

With this in mind, Vygotsky and Luria focus on the critical turning points in the development of behavior. In their view, these were "for the behavior of apes—the use of tools, for the behavior of man—labor and the use of psychological signs, and for the behavior of the child—the split of the developmental line into natural psychological and cultural psychological." In this view, developmental processes in each genetic domain are governed by forces and properties unique to that domain. For example, Darwinian evolutionary principles apply to phylogenesis, whereas a version of Lamarckianism accounts for the transitions of sociocultural history.

As others have noted (e.g., Wertsch, 1985), the boundaries between genetic domains are, in fact, not so neat as Vygotsky and Luria assumed. Recent findings in physical anthropology and archaeology indicate that hominidization involved an extended period of overlap (something on the order of 2 million years) between phylogenesis and sociocultural history. This contrasts with the view generally accepted when Vygotsky and Luria were writing. In their view, phylogenesis is assumed to have culminated with a final qualitative transition giving rise to the organism of homo sapiens, and this, in turn, allowed sociocultural history to begin. The massive overlap now generally accepted as existing between these two genetic domains means that cultural or proto-cultural development provided part of the context for, and hence influenced organic evolution during hominidization. This upating of Vygotsky and Luria's perspective, however, in no way refutes their general claims about the differences in developmental processes at work in the various genetic domains, which disallow reductionistic or recapitulationistic assumptions that still continue to creep into psychology and related disciplines.

Other aspects of the argument Vygotsky and Luria propose in this volume are dated as well. For example, many advances have been mode in cultural and social anthropology since 1930, and some current findings would challenge many of the particulars of their argument. The fact that we now know a great deal more than was known in 1930 about languages of the world, for example, indicates that some of the authors' generalizations about levels of linguistic complexity are no longer accepted. The same critique applies to many of their general statements about cultural complexity as well.

In addition to advances, there are simply differences between 1930 and today that count as legitimate and interesting areas of inquiry. There has been something of a paradigm shift away from evolutionary approaches toward cultural analyses, and from linguistic analysis toward linguistic and cultural relativism. Figures such as Boas (1916, 1966), Sapir (1921, 1931), and Whorf (1956) led the way in rejecting the kind of evolutionary ranking of languages and cultures that plays such an essential role in the authors' argument. In the end, however, this shift is not simply in the form of some progression toward an ultimate truth (a claim that would be difficult for a relativist to defend in any case). Instead, it represents a paradigm shift associated with structuralist analyses, which are notoriously difficult to reconcile with accounts of cultural and psychological change.

Thus, although some of the specifics of the claims of Vygotsky and Luria about culture may be outdated, this does not call into question the basic genetic approach that they were seeking to outline. We still have not come to grips with how one accounts for the complex structural properties of cultures and language on the one hand, and genetic transitions on the other. For example, as Wertsch and Tulviste (in press) note, there is very little attention paid in contemporary developmental psychology to historical factors and historical change. One manifestation of this general state of affairs is that, at a time of increasing traffic between psychologists and anthropologists, there still continues to be little productive contact between psychologists and historians. For all of these reasons, the attempt by Vygotsky and Luria to outline a "new genetic psychology" touching on multiple domains of development retains great contemporary relevance.

This book is a critical text for understanding these and a host of other issues. By making such a work by two of the 20th century's greatest psychologists available to readers of English, the translators and editors have made a major contribution. Furthermore, it should be noted that this is no ordinary translation. The knowledge of languages and the material that Golod and Knox brought to bear in completing their work make this book one of the best translations we have of Vygotsky's and Luria's writings. This is more than an accurate translation, it is an elegant one that retains much of the feel of the authors' own styles. Furthermore, thanks to their energetic and ingenious bibliographic sleuthing, Golod and Knox have provided us with insights into the sources of the authors' ideas that come to light here for the first time. Some of these findings are reviewed in Knox's introduction, and others are in evidence throughout the text. This undertaking has resulted in an accurate, complete, and elegant translation of a very important work in psychology and its related fields.

REFERENCES

Boas, F. (1916). *The mind of primitive man.* New York: Macmillan.
Boas, F. (1966). Introduction. In, F. Boas (Ed.), *Handbook of American Indian Languages* (pp. 1–79). Lincoln, NE: University of Nebraska Press.

Cole, M. (1985). The zone of proximal development: Where culture and cognition create each other. In J. V. Wertsch (Ed.), *Culture, communication, and cognition: Vygotskian perspectives* (pp. 146–161). New York: Cambridge University Press.

Cole, M. (1990). Cultural psychology: A once and future discipline? In J. Berman (Ed.), *Nebraska Symposium on Motivation: Cross-cultural perspectives,* Vol. *37,* pp. 379–335.

Moll, L. (Ed.). (1990). *Vygotsky and education: Instructional implications and applications of sociohistorical psychology.* New York: Cambridge University Press.

Rogoff, B. (1990). *Apprenticeship in thinking: Cognitive development in social context.* New York: Oxford University Press.

Rogoff, B., & Werstch, J. V. (Eds.). (1984). *Children's learning in the "zone of proximal development,"* (Monograph No. 23). In *New directions for child development* (pp. 1–102). San Francisco: Jossey-Bass.

Sapir, E. (1921). *Language: An introduction to the study of speech.* New York: Harcourt Brace.

Sapir, E. (1931). Conceptual categories in primitive languages. Science, 74, p. 578.

Vygotsky, L. S. (1978). *Mind in society: The development of higher psychological processes* (M. Cole, V. John-Steiner, & E. Souberman, Eds.). Cambridge, MA: Harvard University Press.

Werner, H. (1926). *Einführung in die Entwicklungspsychologie* [Introduction to developmental psychology]. Leipzig, Germany: J.A. Barth.

Wertsch, J. V. (1985). *Vygotsky and the social formation of mind.* Cambridge, MA: Harvard University Press.

Wertsch, J. V. (1991). *Voices of the mind: A sociocultural approach to mediated action.* Cambridge, MA: Harvard University Press.

Wertsch, J. V., & Tulviste, P. (in press). L.S. Vygotsky and contemporary developmental psychology. Developmental Psychology.

Whorf, B. L. (1956). *Language, thought, and reality: Selected writings of Benjamin Lee Whorf* (J. B. Carroll, Ed.). Cambridge, MA: MIT Press. (Original works written 1927–1941).

Preface

Studies on the *History of Behavior: Ape, Primitive, and Child* was first published in 1930 and has not since then appeared again in Russian for reasons discussed in the introduction to this book. The renewed interest in the work of both L.S. Vygotsky and A.P. Luria both in Russia and in the West makes the appearance of this book a timely contribution to scholars in many fields: psychology, education, psycholinguistics, and cultural anthropology.

As in the case for many of his works, Vygotsky here uses many obscure references that were not identified. We have, to the best of our knowledge, supplied those missing references for chapter 1 and chapter 2 to which Vygotsky himself supplied none. A.R. Luria contributed the references and footnotes to chapter 3, unless otherwise indicated.

ACKNOWLEDGMENTS

We wish to express our gratitude and thanks to those many people who helped us research this missing information. In particular, Peeter Tulviste (Psychology Department, Tartu University, Estonia), James V. Wertsch (Psychology Department, Clark University), Robert LeVine (Graduate School of Education, Harvard University), Lena Moskovichyute (Boston University, School of Medicine, Behavior Neurology), Bencie Woll (Department of Education, Bristol University, England), Victor Shnirelman (Institute of Ethnology and Anthropology, Moscow), Alex Kozulin (Boston School of Medicine), Mary Towle (Russian Research Center, Harvard

University), and Jaan Valsiner (University of Carolina, Chapel Hill). We wish to thank in particular Catherine Snow (Dean of the Harvard Graduate School of Education) for her suggestions with respect to the section on child speech.

Grants and fellowships that supported an excellent research environment for the preparation of this text both in the Soviet Union and in the United States came from IREX (International Research Exchange), The National Academy of Sciences, The Russian Research Center of Harvard University, and Bowdoin College.

Our special thanks go to the Foundation for American Communications in Los Angeles for its support during the final stages of this book, Charles Banks of the Bowdoin College Computer Center who helped print out this text, and to the many Bowdoin college students and other associates who helped with this manuscript, in particular to Amanda Bichsel, Jennifer Andich, and Vladimir Kitaigorodsky. Lastly, I would like to thank close friends who supplied the devotion and support for the completion of this manuscript after the untimely death of Victor Golod, my beloved colleague, friend, and the co-editor of this book, namely to Alexander and Svetlana Rosin, Tatyana Gorlina, Slava Gaufberg, Lee Russell, Vida and Dean Johson, Vladimir Voina, and my son, Robert Knox.

Jane E. Knox

Translator's Introduction

Jane E. Knox
Bowdoin College

INTELLECTUAL AND SOCIAL SETTING

In order to fully understand and appreciate the contribution of Lev Semenovich Vygotsky and Alexander Romanovich Luria to the field of modern psychology, their work must first be seen within the framework of its time, within the context of the prevalent theories and ideas with which these two scholars had to grapple in order to arrive at a new orientation befitting a new Soviet psychology; a psychology that must correspond to the needs and principles of a society newly emerging from a revolution that affected all layers and areas of Russian culture.

Among the ideological frameworks that shaped 20th-century thought perhaps none had such an influential impact as that provided by Darwin's theories of evolution of the species. In this book, Vygotsky and Luria extend Darwin's theories of biological evolution to a theory of cultural and ontogenetic change, arguing for the existence of *developmental* historical stages of mental phenomena as the mind develops from ape to primitive man to cultural man. From Darwin comes the idea of development from *lower to higher* stages, whereby "primitive people," for example, are at a lower or, in other words, earlier stage in the historical evolution of man.

This book represents an important milestone in the general search by modern psychologists for general principles "that govern the nature and development of human intellectual capacities, and that determine how these are organized, tapped, and transformed over a lifetime," to use the words of Gardner (1985, p. 32) in his book describing modern theories of intelligence. However, Vygotsky and Luria were interested in development

1

not only over a life time (ontogenesis) but *over the course of all human development* (phylogenesis). In the strict sense of the word they offer not just a *cross-cultural approach* where various ethnic groups of preliterate people are compared, but a *cross-historical approach* that examines the different stages of development through which the human species passes from its original beginnings in the anthropoid apes. For Vygotsky's theory of human development, the terms *cultural* and *historical* are important, however, more emphasis is placed on historical differences. As Wertsch (1991) pointed out, "Building on the ideas of Hegel, Marx, Lévy-Bruhl, and others, he (Vygotsky) tended to see what we would now term cross-cultural differences as cross-historical differences . . . this is a major point that distinguishes Vygotsky's ideas from those developed in American anthropology by Franz Boas, Edward Sapir, and Benjamin Lee Whorf" (p. 16). (For a full description of Vygotsky's cross-historical approach, one should read Puzyrei [1986], Van der Veer [1991], and Van der Veer & Valsiner [1988, 1991].)

The cross-historical approach that Vygotsky and Luria present here corresponds to a new orientation spreading through all branches of the sciences at the beginning of the 20th century, an orientation that rejected the prevailing 19th-century attitude, for example, toward language. According to Roman Jakobson, this orientation grew as a reaction "against the naturalistically oriented scientist who dissected his material into a multitude of parts" (Jakobson, 1939/1989, p. 1).

> Everywhere there appeared a new orientation towards organizing unities, structures, forms whereby not the multitude or sum of successive elements but the relationship between them determined the meaning of the whole. . . . Speech sounds, which until the beginning of the 20th century had been merely the subject of sensory psychology and sensory physiology, were finally in the truest sense of the words incorporated into linguistics, i.e., speech sounds began to now be examined as to their sign value and especially as to their *function* of imparting meaning. (Jakobson, 1939/1989, p. 2, italics added)

In this book, this focus on actual symbolic vehicles of thought created historically *over generations* is directed not only at oral and written symbols, but also at gestures, systems of counting, systems of remembering, and other human symbols.

The notion of signs and sign value is the underlying principle in Vygotsky and Luria's investigation of the use of "psychological tools" by ape, primitive man, and child. This notion was incorporated into the study of behavior on a large scale: Both *ape and human forms of behavior* are seen here in terms of *semiotic activity,* that is, activity that organizes and transforms objects (sticks, rope, paint, pieces of colored paper, cards, etc.)

into meaningful, cultural signs or tools to be used to manipulate or mediate the environment and then to communicate with others about it.

As Cole pointed out, "Developmental and historical approaches to the study of human nature were not unique to Vygotsky in the Soviet Union in the 1920s. Within psychology, an older colleague, Blonsky, had already adopted the position that an understanding of complex mental functions requires developmental analysis." From Blonsky, Vygotsky adopted the notion that "behavior can be understood only as the history of behavior." Moreover, "Blonsky was also an early advocate of the view that the technological activities of people were a key to understanding their psychological makeup, a view that Vygotsky exploited in great detail" (Cole, Scribner, John-Steiner, & Souberman, 1978, p. 8).

Activity or "action" with tools becomes the very point of analysis in the history of human development. As Wertsch (1991) pointed out, "human begins are viewed as coming into contact with, and creating, their surroundings as well as themselves through the actions in which they engage. Thus action, or rather interaction, not human beings in isolation, provides the entry point into the analysis" (p. 8).

The Vygotsky–Lurian approach embraces two opposing schools of thought about human development: that which has become known today as the American behaviorist school (stemming from Pavlov's stimulus–response paradigm, whereby the individual is treated primarily as a *passive* recipient of information from the environment) and the Cartesian line of reasoning that views "the human mind largely in terms of universal, innate categories and structure," whereby the environment plays a secondary role, "serving merely as a device to trigger certain developmental processes" (Wertsch, 1991, p. 8).

According to Kozulin (1990c) Vygotsky's earlier work, *Educational Psychology,* presents "Pavlov's theories in rather apologetic terms, claiming that reflexes ought to become the foundation of the new psychology" (p. 67). Moreover, that text seems "peppered with quotations from the influential party leader and theoretician, Leon Trotsky" so that "at times the text is so un-Vygotsky that it looks like a page lifted from a popular communist propaganda brochure" (Kozulin, 1990c, p. 69).

However, although in this book Vygotsky pays tribute to the theory of conditional reflexes, he now goes beyond them, focusing on Pavlov's later ideas. Namely, Vygotsky stresses and expands Pavlov's notion of the goal-oriented reflex as the major impetus for driving a work-oriented society of laborers. People must always have a goal toward which they strive. All human thought develops precisely from this striving; the greater the difficulty in reaching this goal the greater the "psychic" energy expended in achieving it, a view Vygotsky shared both with Bühler and Dewey.

It seems Vygotsky borrowed the term *psychic* from the German *Gestalt* psychologists or "mentalists" and used it repeatedly throughout his works beginning with *Psychology of Art* (Vygotsky, 1925/1971). The term has been translated differently by American scholars. Some use the term *mental* and others the term *psychological,* as in the expression, "the higher psychological functions" (Cole, Scribner, John-Steiner, & Souberman, 1978; Kozulin, 1990b, 1991; van der Veer, 1991), or "the higher mental functions" (Wertsch, 1985).

On the Soviet home front, where training of reflexes became the cornerstone of the ideology for forming the new Soviet man, Vygotsky was closer to Anokhin, the "first Pavlovian to start thinking about 'dialectical materialism' and the problem of the 'psychic' " (Joravsksy, 1989, p. 394). Trying to bridge the gap between Pavlovian orthodoxy and "world thought in neurology," Anokhin carried out experiments that showed that "the *Gestalten* . . . persist" even when "the reflex arcs are drastically altered," that is "experiments which made it impossible to go on thinking of all behavior as chains of reflexes. . . ." (Joravsky, 1989, p. 396).

It is precisely at this point that Vygotsky departs from the officially accepted Pavlov who seethingly derided German *mentalism* and particularly the experiments to test intelligence in chimpanzees (Pavlov, 1955, pp. 551-604). In this book, Vygotsky makes almost a quantum leap to the position of Köhler and Bühler, affirming that although a conditional reflex arises as a "result of instruction or training—a slow gradual process," in those difficult new situations where an ape suddenly happens upon a solution to a problem by creating a new tool, form (configuration), path, or, in the case of primitive man or child, a new word, he often does so without instruction and adapts to this new demand or new circumstance precisely when "instinctive and trained movements are no longer of use to him." As Vygotsky writes in the current text, "The work of the intellect begins at the point where the activity of instinct and conditional reflexes stops or is blocked."

Vygotsky was also influenced by the work of Western European psychologists, sociologists, and anthropologists. From such Western psychologists as Bühler, Vygotsky took the notion of functioning or, more precisely, tool creation as the primary unit of human behavior. "Bühler considered Freud's emphasis on the pleasure of satisfaction to be but one third complete: He added the pleasure of functioning and the pleasure of creating" (Corsini, 1984, p. 175). The seeds of this creativity are traced by Bühler back to animal behavior. In the first chapter of *The Mental Development of the Child,* Bühler (1919/1930) analyzed the beginnings of language and art going back to their beginnings: Instinct, Training, and Intellect. He drew heavily on a comparative psychology and the research done by Köhler with apes, chickens, and other animals. Much of what Bühler and Köhler said finds its way into Vygotsky's first chapter.

Moreover, in chapter 2 of this text, Vygotsky follows in the tradition of August Comte, who maintained that "the highest mental functions remain unintelligible as long as they are studied from the individual." Acknowledging Lévy-Bruhl's descriptions of "primitive" thought, Vygotsky argues that if we are to understand the highest mental functions, we must take into consideration the development of differing types of human societies. Throughout this book it is clear that Vygotsky and Luria share Lévy-Bruhl's (1965) view that "In man's mental life everything which is not merely the reaction of the organism to the stimuli it receives is necessarily of social character" (p. 15).

Like Thurnwald and Lévy-Bruhl, Vygotsky and Luria were interested in the history of mental processes as reconstructed from anthropological evidence of the intellectual activity of primitive peoples. The development of "primitive" mental processes understood historically receives special attention in this book and is discussed at greater length later.

As elsewhere in Vygotsky's works (1986, 1983/in press), the idiosyncratic style of this book is characteristic for many writers and thinkers of the 1920s where great significance is attributed to the role of dialogue with others and to *the interiorization* of that dialogue as the structure of one's own inner speech. For example, Vygotsky's contemporary, the literary critic and philosopher of language Bakhtin (1895-1975), proposed that all our thoughts are forms of internalized dialogues with others, whose voices are internalized, reworked, and incorporated into our own: In other words, one person's voice "gives the illusion of unity to what [he or she] says;" but in fact, this person is "constantly expressing a plenitude of meanings, some intended, others of which [the person is] unaware" (Holquist, 1981, p. xx). According to this line of thinking, " 'Two minds' 'intermingled' in one head and in one expanded dialogic consciousness (EDC), are mutually transparent; each has penetrated the other to its depths, yet they do not merge, but remain two different voices" (Radzikhovskii, 1986-1987, p. 14).

This concept of double or multiple voices or centers of *one* consciousness *found* its reflection in the real-life practice of writing collaborative works; it is at the very core, for example, of the whole controversy surrounding the identity of three of Vygotsky's contemporaries—Voloshinov, Medvedev, and Bakhtin—whose voices for many merged into one, that is, that which became known as Bakhtin's.[1] This serves as an extreme example of dialogic or collaborative thinking, writing, and creativity at a time when the cult of

---

[1]Holquist (1981) explained, "There is a great controversy over the authorship of three books that have been ascribed to Bakhtin: *Freudianism* (1927) and *Marxism and the Philosophy of Language* (1929; 2nd ed. 1930), both published under the name of V. N. Voloshinov, and *The Formal Method in Literary Scholarship* (1928) published under the name of P. N. Medvedev" (p. xxx).

the individual was scorned, a time when writers or groups were encouraged to work collectively and present themselves in one voice, that is "we" — a phenomenon that has survived in scholarship in the former Soviet Union until today.

"Double voicing" is very characteristic of the style in which this book was written. We often see here, to use Bakhtin's definition, another person's words as if "they have wedged their way into his [here Vygotsky's] speech . . . and their influence brings about a radical reorganization" so that "sometimes the speech of another person, in addition to its influence on the accentual and syntactical structure, leaves behind a word or two, and sometimes a whole sentence. . . . The word is present with such a strong accent of the speech of another that from time to time, it suddenly breaks through and takes on the form of the direct speech of the other person" (Bakhtin, 1973, pp. 172–173).

There are times when it is very difficult to tell whether indeed the voice is that of Vygotsky or someone else. The Bakhtinian phenomenon of reported or indirect speech just described is evident here; for example, what begins as Vygotsky's words will end up as Lévy-Bruhl's without any clear demarcation indicating where one voice ends and the other begins. In many passages, a whole thought previously expressed by Lévy-Bruhl appears in the current text without reference to that specific passage in *How Natives Think*. For example, when describing the concrete image-laden nature of primitive speech, Vygotsky writes:

> The Tasmanians do not have words to specify such qualities such as sweet, bitter, hard, cold, long short, and round. Instead of "hard," they say, "like a stone," in place of "tall" — "high feet," "round" — "like a ball," "like a moon," and they also add a gesture which explains this. (p. 170)

If we compare this with Lévy-Bruhl's (1910/1926) text we find there a similar passage:

> The Tasmanians had no words to represent abstract ideas, and though they could denote every variety of gum-tree or bush, by name, they had no word for tree. They could not express qualities, such as hard, soft, hot, cold, round, tall, short, etc. To signify "hard" they would say: like a stone; for tall, big legs; round, like a ball; like the moon; and so on, always combining their words with gestures, designed to bring what they were describing before the eyes of the person addressed. (p. 179)

More complicated or problematic is a passage where Vygotsky switches from indirect reporting of Lévy-Bruhl's text to direct reporting. Vygotsky writes:

That is why in cases where a European may use one or two words a primitive man utters sometimes ten, eg., the phrase "a man killed a rabbit": in the language of the Ponka Indian tribe would literally be rendered as "man he one alive (nominative case) standing killed intentionally to shoot an arrow a rabbit him one alive (accusative case) sitting." (p. 140)

The analogous text in Lévy-Bruhl's (1910/1926) *How Natives Think* reads as follows:

> Perhaps the most salient characteristic of most of the North American Indians is the care they take to express concrete details which our languages leave understood or unexpressed. "A Ponka Indian in saying that a man killed a rabbit, would have to say: the man, he, one, animate, standing (in the nominative case), purposely killed by shooting an arrow the rabbit, he, the one, animal, sitting (in the objective case). . . . (p. 140)

It must be pointed out that in both examples the first of each of the two passages is a double translation, that is, a translation from Vygotsky's Russian text based on his knowledge or *recall* of a Russian translation of Lévy-Bruhl, hence this is a translation of a translation of the original. Moreover, the passages from Lévy-Bruhl's French text of *Les Fonctions Mentales Dans des Sociétés Inférieures* have been given here from the published English translation, *How Natives Think*. This makes it difficult to make a word-for-word comparison of the two different renditions of the previously cited texts. It is clear that in Vygotsky's texts Lévy-Bruhl's words flow over and beyond the demarcation boundaries, that is, the quotation marks designating the latter's voice. The same phenomenon can be found in chapter 1 if you compare Vygotsky's text with passages from Köhler's (1921/1926) *The Mentality of the Apes.*

Many Vygotskian scholars regard this characteristic of Vygotsky as sloppy scholarship excused perhaps only by the very serious nature of his prolonged illness (tuberculosis), which took his life in 1934, as inevitable negligence due to the feverish haste at which he had worked to produce what he could before death. According to Joravsky (1989), "the incredibly young genius . . . had to do his enormous work at great speed, while tuberculosis was pushing him to periodic bed rest and early death (1934, aged thirty-seven)" (p. 255).

Moreover, the difficult times of the Russian Revolution, the ensuing years of the Civil War, and political unrest did not make the job of a research scientist an easy one and much of such work had to be directed at solving actual social problems, for example the growing number of bands of orphaned or disabled children who needed to be educated and transformed into productive members of the new Soviet society. The fact that Vygotsky himself had no apartment for several years, lived in the basement room of the Institute of Psychology, and received "almost symbolic pay—lecturing in different colleges and conducting research at a number of laboratories and research stations . . . almost a norm in those days" made a detached theoretical progression of ideas and classical scholarship in the Western sense of the word very difficult" (Kozulin, 1990c, p. 111).

However, there may be still other factors involved. First, Luria is reported to have said that Vygotsky was a speed reader with a photographic memory who could recall verbatim passages from any book that had particularly struck him. During those times one did not have easy access to original sources or have a personal library. It was difficult to return to those sources, so Vygotsky may have had to recall them by memory alone. It is plausible that the wealth of material that Vygotsky had read over the years was maintained photographically in his memory, merging with his own voice. Moreover, many of his *own* notions in earlier works often reoccur verbatim *in later works,* as if from memory; for example, the now often quoted passage about the two stages of child speech development (interpersonal, intrapersonal,), which almost every Vygotskian scholar can recall exactly. It is of great interest that much of chapter 2, as well as sections of other works, is devoted to the phenomenon of extraordinary photographic memory.

Second, because of Vygotsky's illness, some of his manuscripts were compiled and worked on by his students, including Luria whose name is given as the author of chapter 3. Many of the volumes were composed from various materials, only later collectively compiled and made ready for publication. Initially, a "troika" formed including Luria and Leontiev, but eventually expanding into a group of eight with the addition of Bozhovich, Levina, Morozova, Slavina, and Zaporozhets. As Kozulin (1990c) pointed out, "The work of the group was truly collective. All of the members accepted Vygotsky's theoretical leadership and each was free to use Vygotsky's ideas in his or her own research. This commune-like attitude toward intellectual property creates a number of problems for a historian and a critic"[2] (p. 111).

Therefore the compilers of recent Vygotsky editions have been faced with the problem of missing notes or citations to original sources of views voiced by other scholars. For example, this has been a major difficulty for both Soviet and American editors of recent publications of Vygotsky's works.

---

[2]As an example of this problem, Kozulin (1990c) pointed out that, "On the one hand it is clear that such a large work as *The History of the Development of Higher Psychological Functions,* which was completed in 1931, was based on a number of studies done by different members of the group, theoretically integrated by Vygotsky. There are, however, less clear cases, such as Luria's article "Problems of the cultural behavior of the child" (p. 111).

Throughout this book, we have tried consistently to indicate all passages from the works of other scholars that Vygotsky used, but, for what ever reason, remained uncited.

TERMINOLOGY: "PRIMITIVE" AND "CULTURAL"

These terms must be defined not from today's perspective, but from the context of the first two decades of the Soviet Union, and particularly from the time around the Russian Revolution. At that time there was an attempt to throw culture "off the ship of modernity,"[3] to look back at and restore to their rightful place the natural abilities of human nature that cultural habits and customs of a stagnating aristocracy had stifled, or, even worse, atrophied. Primitivism became a major movement in art. Moreover, in some studies by the Soviet linguists known as the Formalists, child perception was heralded as superior to that of the cultural adult. This was believed because at this point of development, perception had not yet become automatic, all the physical sensations from interaction with the world were still maintained in the memory merged with the emotional or affective elements, and "habitualization" had not yet devoured life—not taken the "stony" out of the stone (Shklovsky, 1965, p. 12).

Futurist poets of this period used the language of "zaum" (transense) to revitalize and create language anew, thereby escaping the relics of modern language that had lost contact with life and human essence. With the rise of science and technology, the fear arose that words were becoming but abstract tools, x-rays without the brilliant wealth of content found in child or early primitive language.

In short, early 20th-century literature and art considered the "primitive" to be natural and superior, and "cultural" as something *artificial,* removed from the primary and natural. Indeed, in his description of the development of primitive people Vygotsky refers to the "Baldwin effect" whereby evolution is always accompanied by involution (chapter 2).

Against this popularized notion of primitivism, Vygotsky himself redefined these terms in the light of his own theory of development: As man progresses over history and a child through stages of development in his or her life time, the primitive or natural stage is not replaced by later cultural

---

[3]The thrust of this attack was expressed in the December 1912 Futurist manifesto "A slap in the face of public taste," written by Burlyuk, Kruchenykh, Mayakovsky, and Khlebnikov:
The past constricts. The Academy and Pushkin are less intelligible than hieroglyphics. Pushkin, Dostoevsky, Tolstoy, etc., etc., must be thrown overboard from the Ship of Modernity. . . . We decree that the following *rights* of poets be respected:. . . . to feel insuperable hatred for the language that existed before them. . . . (Proffer, Proffer, Meyer, & Szporluk, 1987, p. 542).

stages, rather the latter was superimposed like scaffolding on top of the former, changing, restructuring, and adapting these natural processes. Thus, the psychology of a cultural man is not superior or inferior but *different* than that of a primitive man, just as the psychology of an adult is different from that of a child, particularly a child without schooling.

Vygotsky's approach to "primitive" or "primary" abilities found both in children and in so-called "primitive," uneducated, or "semi-illiterate" people is clearly an extension of Lévy-Bruhl's similar approach to the thinking of primitive people. In *How Natives Think* Lévy-Bruhl (1910/1926) said, for example, "Let us abandon the attempt to refer their mental activity to an inferior variety of our own" (p. 78). Vygotsky relates Lévy-Bruhl's dispute with the British school in anthropology, accepting his criticism of Tylor and Frazer: They confused "simple" with "undifferentiated." Lévy-Bruhl's influence is clearly discernible in Vygotsky's discussion of "primitive" languages, and namely the former's view that "primitive does not mean simple. . . . 'least developed' languages such as those used by the Australian aborigines, Abipones, Andaman Islanders, Fuigians, etc. exhibit a good deal of complexity. They are far less 'simple' than English, though much more primitive" (Lévy-Bruhl, 1910/1926, p. 22).

As van der Veer (1991) pointed out, Vygotsky merited Lévy-Bruhl for his claim that the higher mental processes in "primitive" people were not inferior but *different* from those in "cultural" or "civilized" people (pp. 9–10). The fundamental idea of cultural–historical theory was not necessarily a ranking of various ethnic groups but a description of the developmental different stages of the higher mental processes in relationship to the different stages and conditions of historical development.

Kozulin gave the following interpretation of Vygotsky's concept of higher or cultural processes and lower or natural mental processes:

> Higher mental processes in their turn include more primitive and more advanced processes, depending on the form of mediation. Second, higher mental processes have a mediate nature, the role of mediator being played by semiotic systems that could be as simple as gesture and as complex as literary discourse. Finally, the development and composition of human higher mental processes depends on culturally and historically specific forms of semiotic mediation. (Kozulin, 1991, p. 342, see also, Vygotsky, 1986, Wertsch, 1985)

Moreover, although mechanisms of mental activity *differ* with stages, within groups, depending on the acquisition of cultural tools, the *underlying primary or innate capacities do not.* This idea was furthered and more explicitly stated by Vygotsky (1983/in press) in his description of experimental work with "handicapped" and abandoned children: for example, a deaf child is not a child with a "minus" development but one who develops *differently,* according to the different cultural tools that are used to circumvent weakness (here deafness) and to build on intact innate capacities.

As van der Veer (1991) pointed out, "The implication of this view was that one should not confront people from other cultures with tasks taken from our culture and then draw conclusions from their possibly 'poor' performance. For this would be judging them by our Western standards and seeing their thinking as a rudimentary form of ours, an approach that Lévy-Bruhl explicitly condemned" (p. 11). Similarly, in *Fundamentals of Defectology,* Vygotsky criticizes the assessment of handicapped children solely on the basis of a quantitative measuring of tasks completed within the culture of the hearing, that is, tests based on the cultural tools created for the hearing. Such testing only measures weakness and results in a label of inferiority. In both *Studies on the History of Behavior* and *Fundamentals of Defectology,* the central idea is that there exist different psychological or mental approaches to a task depending on the cultural context or domain in which the task is given.

Vygotsky expands this view of primitive language, pointing out that the two stages that Lévy-Bruhl described can also be seen in child language development. Vygotsky takes exception with Lévy-Bruhl's view of magic as a primary, independent feature in primitive thinking and agrees with Thurnwald that magic develops only at a later stage, once substantial enculturation has occurred allowing the primitive to merge his or her "fantasy" or mystical (magical) character with the external worlds of signs. This discussion of magic is echoed in Vygotsky's (1991) later study of fantasy in adolescence when, similar to magic at the second stage of the development of primitive mentality, "fantasy is not regarded as a primary, independent, or leading function" and its development is a consequence of the formation of concept (p. 73).

For Vygotsky in both the development of the primitive and the adolescent, "The primitive forms were of interest primarily because they help to explain the dynamics of the emergence of the mediated type of mental process from the syncretic one" (Kozulin, 1990c, p. 118).

A point of departure for Vygotsky's theories is Lévy-Bruhl's description of the primitive thought process, not as *anti-logical* or *alogical,* but rather *prelogical* activity; this means, above all, that such mental activity "does not bind itself down, as our thought does, to avoiding contradictions" (Kozulin, 1990c, p. 78). Accordingly, primitive thought follows "the law of participation:" "prelogical mentality is essentially synthetic" (Kozulin, 1990a, p. 108). It combines, by free association, a wealth of undifferentiated, varied, diffuse, and concrete perceptions that are stored in the memory in eidetic form.

However, culturally adopted sign systems, such as systems of writing, begin to rearrange, structure, and systematize this wealth of raw material, developing "higher" or later mental functions (attention, will, etc.), which can free memory from an overload of individual elements, details, and so on. Vygotsky's treatment of the higher stage of cultural development is, however, essentially Eurocentric: he follows the lead of other Western psychologists who saw Europe's enlightened, rational, or scientific thought as the latest and most advanced (hierarchically speaking) step in psychological development. Still, he did not ignore the importance of the type of thinking characteristic of the "primitive" mentality that can still be found in cultural adults in differing degrees, a notion that in some ways corresponds to and compliments Gardner's (1985) theories of multiple intelligences.

Many scholars have paid close attention to these different types of *thought structure*. According to the Estonian Vygotskian scholar Tulviste (1987, p. 14), "the idea of the heterogeneity of human thought within one culture and one individual mind, together with the idea that thought undergoes qualitative transformations during the course of its evolution, must be considered one of Lévy-Bruhl's 'important discoveries.'" As Tulviste (1987) reported, the foreword to the Russian edition of Lévy-Bruhl's *Primitive Thought* illuminates the nature of this heterogeneity:

> There are not two forms of thinking for mankind, one logical, the other prelogical, separated from each other by an impenetrable wall. They are different thought structures that exist in the same society and often, perhaps always, in one and the same mind. (pp. 14–15)

Vygotsky took as his point of departure Lévy-Bruhl's view that these two types of thinking–prelogical and logical–are not incompatible and one does not necessarily cancel out the other. Accordingly, "In the mentality of primitive peoples, the logical and prelogical are not arranged in layers and separated from each other like oil and water in a glass. They permeate each other, and the result is a mixture which is very difficult matter to differentiate" (Tulviste, 1987, p. 106).

This view is expanded at length in chapter 2, and then later given more generalized form in other Vygotsky works. For example, in *Fundamentals of Defectology,* the major framework for the discussion of handicapped children is the notion of two levels of development, "the natural, physiological, or biological, on the one hand, and the historical–cultural, on the other" (Vygotsky, 1983/in press). The cultural–historical line is internalized through the use of psychological tools, the most important of which is language. This second line of development is superimposed on and radically transforms natural behavior, but does not replace the former, which becomes embedded in the structure of the personality as a whole.

CHILD AND ADULT EXPERIMENTAL SUBJECTS

The most crucial moments in the development of the cultural historic or social historical theory of development worked out by Vygotsky and his colleagues occurred at the beginning of the 1930s. The first point they addressed was the social determination of the higher psychological functions. They were very interested in experimental proof of this fact and they found an interesting and unique opportunity to experimentally perform a psychological study of people in the Soviet Union who were still illiterate at that period.

To this end, two populations were of particular interest to Vygotsky and Luria and served as experimental subjects to test their principles, namely: (a) the growing population of homeless, unnurtured orphans, victims of the Civil War and famines of the early 1920s; and (b) those semi-illiterate populations of various remote regions of the Soviet Union that had still not been industrialized.

The first category of children served as the basis for Vygotsky's (1983/in press) observations in *Fundamentals of Defectology*. The second group represented various ethnic groups in remote Soviet Central Asia who did not undergo, so to say, the usual industrial development that all the modern countries at that time had undergone. Because it was Stalin's aim to collectivize and industrialize all populations, experiments turning attention to semi-illiterate populations were often seen, and still are by some Soviet scholars today, in a negative light. These views were often misjudged as a type of "racism," whereby some nationalities or folk cultures were thought to be judged not as *different, but inferior.* As has been shown earlier, this is a clear misreading of the Vygotsky-Luria terms *primitive, primary,* or *natural.*

According to Cole, Scribner, John-Steiner & Souberman (1978), *Studies on the History of Behavior* "served as the impetus for Luria's two expeditions to Central Asia in 1931 and 1932, the results of which were published long after Vygotsky's death" (p. 9). These expeditions were organized and headed by A. Luria because Vygotsky himself was too ill with tuberculosis to travel to the Soviet Asian republic of Uzbekistan. The aim of the experiment was to see how the influence of culture, how social influences, modify the state of the psychological functions such as perception, memory, verbal memory, and so on.

The test sites that Luria's team chose for their psychological experiments in Soviet Middle Asia (Uzbekistan) varied, including such cities as Samarkand, very remote villages of the Alaiskii mountain range, and state farm villages where collectivization had already begun to take place. A. Luria wrote that, as test subjects, he chose: (a) "illiterate cloistered women who lived in the women's half of the house, who were covered with a *yashmak* [italics added] and who spoke with no one but their husbands"; (b) state farm activists"; and (c) "young people who had completed short courses" (cited in L. Luria, 1991, p. 86).

It was obvious to A. Luria that the psychological tests could not be conducted in the traditional fashion, but instead must be carried out, as he wrote in his dairy, "by specially devised means," the underlying theme of this book. Such means corresponded to the circumstances and the customs of these test subjects and therefore could not but seem meaningful to them, and more adequately reflect the "specific structure of their cognitive activity." Thus, these tests, wrote A. Luria, "always began with conversations in the natural, unrestrained environment of the tea hut where most of the local residents spent most of their free time or around the evening campfire in the mountain pastures. . . . Gradually certain riddles prepared in advance, were entered into the conversation" (cited in L. Luria, 1991, p. 86). These riddles were among the "specific means."

One of the greatest obstacles in the path of the researchers was the reticence that many of the residents of these remote villages *(kishlak)* naturally felt in their interaction with members of the expeditions. As A. Luria wrote, "it was even more difficult to engage the mountain shepherds, particularly the Kirgizian women who would shout, 'DON'T BEWITCH MY CHILD!' (cited in L. Luria, 1991, p. 85). Female assistants from the Uzbek Scientific Research Institute conducted the tests in the women's sector of the house *(ichkara)*.

The goal of these psychological expeditions was to demonstrate directly in a "concrete experiment that all psychological processes have a historical character" (cited in L. Luria, 1991, p. 84). A. Luria chose Central Asia for the reason that Uzbekistan is country with an extensive cultural heritage that "Produced such geniuses as Ulugbek, Ala Burini, Avitsenna, but this culture belonged to a very narrow layer of intellectuals, and all the rest [of the people] were illiterate" (cited in L. Luria, 1991, p. 85). But under Stalin's official policy promoting universal literacy, this was expected to change, and therefore, the expeditions had a certain immediacy to study the psychological changes in a population that was historically moving from illiteracy to literacy before Luria's very eyes. He wrote:

> This was a particular period when a backward, illiterate people, brought to bay by Moslemism, had just fallen into conditions of another culture: collectivization was underway, illiteracy was being liquidated, all before our very eyes. . . . We could see to what degree culture was influencing the formation of the psychological processes. (cited in L. Luria, 1991, p. 85)

In other words, all the concepts and ideas argued in this book were to be tested by these expeditions. Luria's team of 14 researchers collected almost

600 individual protocols and built their experiments around 11 themes, among which the most important were:

[1] thought as a function subjected to historical changes (and namely, the process of word usage, deduction, comprehension of metaphors and symbols, logical thought, etc.) [2] the structure of individual psychological processes (in particular, perceptions: the perception of form and color in connection with visual [pictoral] thought, optical geometrical illusions, drawings, the features of remembering, counting, and so forth). (cited in L. Luria, 1991, p. 89)

As a result of this data, A. Luria came to the conclusion that "all the categories, which we had become accustomed to think of as natural, in fact are social" (cited in L. Luria, 1991, p. 87).

The fate of these data and of this book is closely connected with Stalin's official policies on collectivization and universalism as well as his war on illiteracy. At the beginning of the first expedition, Luria sent a telegram back to Vygotsky in Moscow, marking a very crucial moment in the development of this theory. They had started with experiments devoted to an assessment of perceptual illusions. The telegram, which Luria sent back to Moscow—and you can imagine, how difficult that was at this time because they were somewhere in the mountains of Uzbekistan—contained just three words: "u uzbekov net illiuzii" (Uzbeks do not have illusions).

As one might imagine, this telegram caused A. Luria considerable hardships: Members of the KGB were awaiting Luria as he exited the train on his return to Moscow. According to report, these words had been interpreted in a totally political vein to mean that the Uzbeks had no illusions about Soviet power or authority in that area. This is perhaps only one of the reasons why those data were published only in 1973–1974 (cf. A. Luria, 1974a, 1974b).

Alexander Luria was not allowed to continue this extremely important and interesting research on the cultural or ethnographical uniqueness of these remote people of Central Asia. In his own words, "I was accused of all mortal sins right down to racism, and I was forced to leave the Institute of Psychology" (cited in L. Luria, 1991, p. 98).

After the second expedition, the Commission MKK RKI (International Consultive Committee for Inspection of Workers and Peasants) set to work at the Institute and left no stone unturned, striking a strong blow at the cultural historical theory of psychology proposed by Vygotsky and A. Luria. This routing of the Vygotskian cultural–historical school greatly affected the course of the Luria's next 40 years of research and the fate of this book, causing him to abandon further investigations of this type. Luria's plea by letter to the Commission proved fruitless so that he had little choice but to put aside for some 40 years the material he had collected on his expeditions and to change the direction of his research undertaking a new program of clinical investigations of aphasia in Kharkov at the Ukrainian Psychoneurological Academy in Kharkov (A. Luria, 1974a, p. 267; L. Luria, 1991, p. 101).

A scathing official attack on the cultural historical theory was published in a 1934 issue of the journal *The Book and the Proletarian Revolution,* and, according to A. Luria, goes as follows:

> The cultural–historical theory has only just been created, but it already has succeeded in causing much harm to the psychological sector of the theoretical front, cleverly disguising its pseudo-scientific aspects — foreign to Marxism — with quotations from the works of the founders of Marxism. . . . Instead of showing the process of development and the cultural growth of the workers in Uzbekistan, they search for justifications for their "cultural–psychological theory" and "find" identical forms of thought in the adult Uzbek woman and a five year old child, dangling before us under the banner of science ideas, which are harmful to the cause of the national cultural construction of Uzbekistan. (cited in L. Luria, 1991, p. 89)

Under Stalin's campaign to "collect" all people's into State farm communities or urban centers, to liquidate illiteracy, and force a universal culture, any attempts to study the cultural or ethnic traits of different ethnic groups was seen as "bourgeois nationalism" carrying with it the danger that individual groups would take greater pride in those ethnic differences and resist being transformed into examples of the new Soviet man. Ethnographical research within the Soviet Union thus all but died out, until the recent era of "glasnost' " which has brought with it the vary sweeping nationalistic uprisings which Stalin feared.

MAJOR ASPECTS OF THEORY
OF CULTURAL TOOLS

In spite of the fact that upon a hasty glance one might conclude that this work is a rehash of the views proposed by others (Lévy-Bruhl, Thurnwald, Köhler, etc.), it is hoped that these observations will encourage the reader to see how Vygotsky and Luria selectively use their material to reinforce their own theories and how they transfer those components of the views of others needed to build and support their own.

The major contribution of this book is that it lays out Vygotsky's notion of the evolution of development from its roots (embryonic form) in the use of objects as tools by anthropoid apes. The notion of the use of "psychological tools" (the internalization of these tools) as the basic force pushing forward the various developmental stages is no where as clearly and strongly argued as in this book.

In short, as has been said earlier, the crux of this development is not the tools in and of themselves but in *the way in which they are used, in the meaning which they acquire.* The outline of this book is as follows:

1. Apes use objects to satisfy their needs, particularly when something stands in the way of their goal—such an object may be a branch of a tree used to get fruit hanging out of reach, that is, in the ape's natural habitat. The ape is then able to transfer this "knowledge" to the use of a stick in a cage to get fruit hanging up too high. What is indicative of "intelligence" for Vygotsky is that in a difficult experimental situation, the ape is finally able to take or select a component or element from one structure (a box that was always used for *sitting in a certain place*), and put it *to use in another structure,* as something to climb up on in a *different place* in order to get food. This ability to take *or transfer* a part of a whole and assign it to another plane (to another use for achieving a goal) is, in Vygotsky's view, the first step in the evolution of the higher mental/nervous processes that culminated in humans.

2. Similarly, a primitive man who begins to use "knots" in order not to tie something (the natural primary use) but to remember something (a secondary symbol system) is a similar step in the development of man and his ability to both control the environment and regulate his own behavior (to control and organize his memory). Vygotsky advances these "tools" (the ape's box or the primitive man's knots) as artificial signs, as "technology," used to mediate the environment and give it new meaning—they are artificial in that they have acquired meaning not from their natural setting or from instinctive use (a child moving a spoon to its mouth to eat), but from an arbitrary meaning assigned to the tool by man (or, in the case of the box, by the ape) for use in achieving some goal. Using a box to get food requires much more mental activity from the ape than using a stick—that is, an extension of his earlier habit in the woods of using a branch to get fruit. The box or boxes when piled on top of each other are use to *reconstruct* the environment for a goal or purpose for which the box was not naturally intended. Thus, for example, the "knot" when used to remember is a more highly advanced psychological sign than a spoon, Vygotsky argues. The knot is here used to regulate mental activities, whereas the spoon is used to satisfy basic instincts (hunger), hence the former is called a "psychological" tool.

3. Vygotsky strongly argues both in chapter 1 and chapter 3 that this use of "artificial" tools for psychological or mental development is passed on or communicated to others; once one ape masters the use of the box for

various goals, other apes quickly acquire this same use of the object and are then able to do those tasks that they could not do before. Similarly, as is seen in chapter 3 when school children are given "words" by adults to help remember and solve certain tasks the children are able to complete those memory tasks that until then they had not been able to do. Any Vygotsky scholar will easily recognize this as the embryo of the concept that has become known as the Zone of Proximal Development, whereby any function first develops interpersonally and then intrapersonally.

4. Vygotsky builds on Levy-Bruhl's discussion of various stages of thinking and shows how these stages are also visible in child language development. Unlike Werner, Volkelt, and Kretschmer who used the term *complex* to describe preverbal thinking and thinking in animals, Vygotsky shows here as well as in his later works, how thinking in complexes is a very important stage in the development of *verbal thinking* and *word meaning*. Chapter 3 of this book is then an important prelude to *Thought and Language,* where Vygotsky (1986) wrote that "words also fulfill an important, though different function in the various stages of thinking in complexes" (p. 139). After Vygotsky's death, A. Luria went on to further expand this understanding of the development of word meaning during ontogenesis (A. Luria, 1982).

In all three chapters of this book, Vygotsky and A. Luria examine how in this way "higher mental functions" emerge, and how memory, attention, and will develop as a result of "sign" or tool activity by ape, primitive man, and child.

THE STRUCTURE OF THE BOOK

The introduction by Vygotsky in this book gives a general outline for a theory of development of behavior from ape to cultural man. Three different paths that make up the history of human behavior are involved: phylogenesis, primate history, and ontogenesis.

Each of the three essays in this book focuses on the essential link connecting one developmental stage of behavior with another: the development of the use of tools. The use and "invention" of tools by apes distinguishes their behavioral development from earlier phylogenetic stages. Human development, the next stage of evolution of behavior, is distinguished by labor, and, in conjunction with it, human speech and other psychological signs used by primitive man developed to gain control over behavior. Finally, the main feature of ontogenesis (i.e., child development) is the acquisition of skills and modes of cultural thinking in a coordinated fashion with biological or organic development. Each behavioral stage more or less repeats the preceding one, reconstructing it. Such is the essence of what Vygotsky and A. Luria call *a new genetic psychology.*

In chapter 1, which deals with primate behavior, three stages of development are discussed: (a) the development of instincts, (b) the development of "conditional reflexes," and (c) the development of "visual–motor" intellect.

Much of this chapter is devoted to Köhler's attempt to look for the missing link between the development of ape and man. According to Vygotsky, Köhler finds in the ape rudiments of specifically human forms of behavior—the use of rudimentary tools to get food.

Three conditions are described as the basis of "Köhler's experiments. In order for the animal to solve the task, the ape must: (a) find *indirect* ways to reach the goal in situations where for some reason the direct solution was impossible, (b) bypass or eliminate an obstacle found on the path to the goal, and (c) use, invent, or produce tools as a means for achieving an otherwise unachievable goal.

At Köhler's experimental station, it was found that the apes' favorite toy, used for different aims, was the stick. The cleverest of the apes even invented a game of jumping from the stick. Subsequently, the other apes imitated this play, becoming surprisingly skillful at it. The apes were then able to transfer the functional meaning of the stick to other objects such as pieces of straw reeds, pieces of rope, boxes, hat rims, and shoes, which then also became tools to get food hung out of reach.

Vygotsky stresses that in this activity, the role of visual factors is most significant: "the ape must be able to take in the whole field." Here, Vygotsky introduces Bühler's assessment of these experiments along with the presupposition that they are rooted in the ape's ability to use indirect ways of solving problems in their natural habitat and that the apes possess a certain ability "to size up the situation at a glance and choose the correct path. The most difficult experiments turn out to be those where the ape must single out some object that is an element of one structure and transfer it to another new one."

Hence, the law of structure is introduced into primate behavior. Vygotsky's interpretation of the data agrees with Köhler's view: the apes' behavior in relation to potential tools is determined by the structure of the visual field. The experiments demonstrate that the discovery of the relationship of parts of the structure to its whole is often accidental and that the simplest reaction of an organism is a holistic response to the structure.

Vygotsky follows this discussion with an analysis of intellect and the natural experience of apes. Vygotsky shares with Köhler and Bühler the view that primate behavior breaks down first into what represents just an extension of the "conditional reflex" stage of behavior (replication of experiences obtained in the natural condition) and then into a complex combination or intellectual reactions, a new and later stage in behavioral development. First, Vygotsky points out that "the ape's ability to use a stick is not a sudden acquisition but the result of all his previous experience in the wild"; the ape "has to *reestablish the former situation under new conditions.*"

Vygotsky explains how Köhler's experiment allows us to understand, albeit in hypothetical terms, the inner processes occurring in the ape when it performs on experimental task. These processes begin in the most pure and simple cases when, during the solution of Köhler's experimental task two stimuli, both the stick and the fruit act simultaneously on the ape. However, these two interconnected stimuli, although in a different combination, had already long influenced the ape during its life in the wild.

Therefore, it comes as no surprise to Vygotsky that both of these stimuli, now perceived independently of one another, *recharge* independently those centers in the nervous system that had previously always acted together. At this point, Vygotsky again introduces terminology that cropped up earlier in *Psychology of Art* (1925/1971). He describes the effect of this process as "*a short circuit of the nervous current,* that is, a connecting of two rather strongly excited centers."

One of Vygotsky's most significant theoretical contributions is introduced here in his explanation of what precisely facilitates this process. In order for the ape, and subsequently for human beings, to make an advancement in intellectual behavior, the necessary condition is that both must go beyond instinctive and learned reactions that fail to overcome some difficulty. In other words, these conditions are met when either apes, or subsequently humans, find themselves in new conditions differing from those in which they have already grown accustomed or when they come across a difficulty, barrier, or obstacle.

Thus, Vygotsky points out in these experiments that the ape's intellectual reactions appear always in response to some obstacle, delay, difficulty, or barrier preventing its realization. The role that difficulties play in the process of acquiring new modes of action was made perfectly clear by Groos (1928), whom Vygotsky cites in this text: "The moment repetition of a habitual reaction is interrupted, diverted, or delayed onto other paths, immediately consciousness rushes to the scene. . . . in order to regain control over what it had before relegated to the domain of the unconscious processing of the nervous system."

Just as in his other works, such as *Fundamentals of Defectology* (Vygotsky, in press), here too Vygotsky expands Lipps' *law of damming up or stoppage,* whereby a difficulty or stumbling block activates the intellect "although still not cognition itself," when "something unusual is confronted or when the expectation of something habitual is thwarted." According to Vygotsky's Darwinian approach to the development of primate and human behavior, this law "is a type of biologically foreseen condition for the intervention of higher levels of our nervous system." A sudden abrupt change in behavior occurs when a short circuit is brought about between the excited centers in the brain. This causes first sudden increased external activity and then an abrupt suspension of action when "the amplified nervous excitement is no longer wasted on external chaotic movements but is transformed into some complex, inner process" ("The ape sits immobile his eyes fixed on the goal.").

Thus, intellect is described as the third stage in the evolution of behavior. Here Vygotsky gives an analysis of a new feature: an apparent instantaneous "Aha!" discovery followed by a considerably longer degree of subsequent generalization of the "discovery" once obtained.

In summary, chapter 1 illustrates the limited place of tool utilization by primates: It never becomes the predominant activity for achieving a goal. Most importantly, Vygotsky stresses the inability of the apes to introduce the tool into the sphere of communication, that is, the *inability to produce a symbol system.*

In chapter 2, Vygotsky turns his attention to the development of the behavior of Primitive Man. Here, he analyzes the beginnings and evolution of symbolic systems from a cultural–historical point of view. He introduces data of ethnopsychology and comparative linguistics.

Three theories of cultural–psychological growth are examined. Vygotsky reviews and criticizes the purely associationistic approach to psychological growth, where the latter is understood as a purely quantitative accumulation. He then proceeds to review Lévy-Bruhl's view that the psychological structure of an individual is a direct function of the social structure he or she belongs to ("human societies, like organisms, can present profoundly differing structures and, consequently, corresponding differences in the higher psychological functions"). Lévy-Bruhl (1910/1926) held that primitive thought is not unlogical or antilogical but rather prelogical or "alogical, having nothing in common with logical forms and lying outside or on the periphery of any logic" (pp. 9, 78).

A third theory emerges as Vygotsky modifies Lévy-Bruhl's view agreeing with the position held by Thurnwald and stating: "Primitive thought really only seems alogical" whereas "in reality, it is completely logical from the viewpoint of primitive man himself."

Although it was sometimes held that primitive man has a superiority over cultural man, that he is better armed by nature, that he has a more acute sense of smell, sight, and hearing, Vygotsky makes it clear that existing data do not give any evidence of a truly different *organic type of human being.*

As others have shown (Rivers and Meyers), the elementary or primary physiological activity that lies at the basis of our perceptions and our movements—the simplest reactions underlying all our behavior—does not differ in any substantial way in primitive and cultural people. Hence, Vygotsky advances the hypothesis that the apparent psychophysical superiority of a primitive is due to his or her interpretation of sensory inputs rather than psychophysics proper.

The major point that Vygotsky makes here is that the difference between primitive and cultural people lies in their *social* development, not in their *biological* development. Each of these two processes is subjected to its own particular laws and represents two distinct lines of development (natural and physiological, on the one hand; cultural–historical, on the other).

As an example of these two lines of development, Vygotsky examines memory in primitive man. Although at first glance it may seem that primitive man's memory is superior to that of modern cultural man because "the latter's experiences are condensed into concepts, the difference," Vygotsky asserts, "is not just quantitative, not just a difference in the *number* of things remembered" (italics added). Each type of memory (in primitive and in cultural man) has a different "tonality." As others have pointed out, Vygotsky also describes primitive memory as something photographic, eidetic, concrete — something that "stores representations with an enormous abundance of details precisely in the same order that they were presented in reality," just as does primitive man's language. Memory in the primitive has a *different function*.

Citing Jaensch's experiments with children, Vygotsky dwells on eidetism that represents the early, primitive phase in the development of memory. This is a primary undifferentiated stage of unity of perception and memory. The materials preserved in the primitive memory or memory of eidetic children is "unworked," "uncontrolled." Relying on the research of various ethnographers and anthropologists, Vygotsky examines the early tools of memory: knots tied to jog the memory or to count, reed scripts of primitive man, pierced feathers. He illustrates how memory is gradually reorganized, restructured, with these systems.

Presaging his later work, *Thought and Language,* Vygotsky's most exciting passages in the current text deal with the development of thought and language in primitive man. Vygotsky bases many of his views on the research that has come before him, namely that of Lévy-Bruhl, Jaensch, and Powers. In their field studies, these individuals discussed the most striking feature of the language of various primitive peoples, namely, the immense wealth of specific nomenclature that they have at their disposal and the paucity of general words and qualifiers (like "sweet, bitter, hard"). This language loads down thought with details and particulars, without processing the experiential data but reproducing them in the full completeness of reality. Vygotsky writes, "[this is] pictorial, colorful language that speaks with the eyes and that is dominated by the primacy of the spatial component."

At the second stage of language development, one word appears "as an associative sign not for an individual object, but for an aggregate." Here primitive thought is not subject to the "third law" of formal logic, according to which *only one* of two contradictory statements given at the same time and in the same relation can definitely be true—for the primitive man one and the same object can be a constituent in completely different connections.

The beginnings of the utilization of symbolic devices and systems for communication is examined by Vygotsky. He traces the history of writing back to the most ancient relics, such as *quipu* (knotted cords in the Peruvian language), used in ancient Peru, ancient China, Japan, and other countries as conventional auxiliary memory aids that were widespread among primitive people.

Vygotsky draws on the work of Clodd (1905) who similarly held that any sign is "a means of mnemotechnic remembering" (p. 35). This stage of development is the utilization of mnemotechnic devices "for the user," to regulate and control the memory. For Vygotsky, a skilled user of knots stands higher on the ladder of cultural development not because he has a superior natural memory but because he *has learned how to make better use of his memory with the help of artificial signs.* The historical development of human memory is then directly connected with the development and perfection of those "auxiliary means" that *social* human beings have created in their collective cultural life. Thus, here again we see the first stage of language development as an "interpsychological" process (interaction with others in the process of controlling one's environment), and the second stage as an "intrapsychological" process (interiorization of those symbols for the regulation of one's own behavior).

In general, Vygotsky's discussion of the history of writing here and elsewhere (Vygotsky, 1935, pp. 73-95) corresponds to those stages of development of writing that Clodd depicted in 1905, namely: (a) the "mnemonic, or memory aiding stage," (b) "the pictoral stage," where the picture itself tells the story, (c) the "ideographic" stage where the picture becomes representative (a symbol for something else), and finally (d) "the phonetic" stage, where the picture is a "sound-representing sign" (cf. Clodd, 1905, p. 35).

More importantly, Vygotsky outlines the progress in thought development according to a shift from the mode of using a word as a proper name to the mode where a word is a complex, and then finally "a tool or means for developing a concept."

Taking his cue from Lévy-Bruhl and Cushing, Vygotsky also examines dual languages that many primitive people possess. Specifically, he discusses oral speech and sign language (the language of gestures or "manual concepts"), showing the interaction between the two. This involves a look at the mutual influence of mind upon hand and hand upon mind: A primitive man did not speak or, even more importantly, think without his hands. Moreover, the grammar of oral speech (particularly) was inseparably tied to the movement of the hands, whereby each phrase was a complex of manual signs and words. Vygotsky gives considerable attention to Mallery's (1881/1971) studies on Indian sign languages.

Vygotsky's discussion of numeric operations in primitive man begins with the earliest stage of counting quantities by perceptual *gestalts* (complexes) such as "a group of twelve apples." This type of operation is something that Leibniz called an "unconscious mathematics" (in relation to the perception of a bar of music) or a sizing-up-at-a-glance. At the next stage, primitive man uses tools for numeric operation, first as physical objects that Vygotsky calls "concrete mnemotechnics" (use of fingers, parts of the body, later additional auxiliary aids like knotted strings, sticks, etc.) to "get beyond certain limits. Hence, like primitive man's language, these numeric signs still represent a very content-dependent notion of number, bearing a concrete and visual–optical character. However, a subsequent alienation from content occurs with the evolution of "cultural mathematics" and the interiorization of numeric tools. There follows a vast review of the emergence of complex quasi-languages based on number concepts.

Chapter 2 ends with an analysis of primitive man's· magic behavior. Vygotsky again enters into a polemic with Lévy-Bruhl as to its origin and argues that magic behavior must be understood as a certain level of sophistication of cultural behavior rather than its starting point (compare with development of fantasy in adolescence, Vygotsky, 1991). Magic is yet another system of "subjective, intuitively used psychological devices" ("psycho-technology") that the primitive man creates to control his environment and to control himself. Vygotsky uses his discussion of magic thinking as his final illustration of the third theory of cultural–psychological development, having shown that the major factors in the primitive's psychological development are "the development of technology" (systems of techniques, artificial auxiliary devices, tools) and with it, the development of a social structure.

Chapter 3, written by Luria, presents some of the original experiments of the author and his colleagues and deals with the acquisition of culturally developed symbol systems and psychological operations (speech, numeric operations, cultural memory, abstraction).

This chapter begins with a criticism of the theory that holds that an adult differs from a child only quantitatively, that is, that the child is a small adult. Luria argues that the child thinks differently because he or she is born cut off from the world and others. The world of *habitually perceived* things still does not exist for the child.

The first stage of the child's life is dominated by organic sensations and primitive drives—the visibly perceived world, although seen, is still little accessible. However, Luria asserted, "the child is not a blank sheet," but "a sheet of paper covered with letters that are not yet differentiated, or organized as they are for the adult." Luria embraces the view that "the physiological trace left on the retina by a perceived object has yet to be processed and evaluated from a *perspective of previous experience,*" which the infant still does not have. In short, the child begins his or her journey as an "organic creature" and prolonged cultural development must occur in order that this primary weak connection with the world become firmly established.

In his discussion of the emergence of a child's primitive thought, Luria, like Vygotsky (1986) in the latter's well-known work *Thought and Language,* analyzed Piaget's data on egocentric thought and speech. However, here too a hypothesis is offered that opposes certain aspects of Piaget's position on egocentric speech. Both Luria and Vygotsky hold that, based on their experiments with children, egocentric speech is not a manifestation of a rudimentary function, but is the initial, still external stage of self-regulation through language. Two fragments of child speech in the current text show that egocentric speech manifests some *obvious planning functions.* Moreover, these authors strive to show that egocentric speech is not just speech for oneself, but is in some ways socialized.

There is a striking comparison made between primitive magic and egocentric thinking or fantasy in the child: it is a way of organizing the child's world and fulfilling wishes and needs that the world itself is still unable to gratify. The live reality for the child is still the world of wishes, day dreaming, and play, representing a stage in the ability to process and make sense of the world.

The young child's lack of understanding of relations between physical objects is demonstrated through an analysis of children's drawings. A review of Piaget's as well as Vygotsky's experiments serves to show this lack of cause–consequence relations. The first stage of thinking is described as natural, spontaneous, or primary: The young child is still unable to inhibit the first solution to come to mind and it is easier for him or her to give an absurd answer.

Like the primitive, the young child perceives the world's objects concretely, holistically, seeing those aspects that affect him or her directly. Luria compared a child's drawing of a lion and a primitive (illiterate) woman's drawing of a rider on a horse to illustrate the absence of causal connections. Both still do not fully see the connections between parts, or a systemic picture of the world and its phenomena. Individual objects are glued together in additive combination and strings of individual objects. The most striking phenomenon is that a child's notions are not yet organized in a certain hierarchy. Instead, syncretism is the dominant feature. Notions known are brought together with the unknown in this additive way: no contradictions exist for the child—everything can be connected to anything. Although he took the concept of syncretism from Piaget, Luria introduced examples from Chukovsky's (1925/1968) book *From Two to Five* to demonstrate this first stage in child thinking.

In his or her first steps to culture, Luria explained, the child begins to respond instinctively or spontaneously according to his or her natural abilities ("reach instinctively for the cup or breast to satisfy his hunger"). Then the child learns how to respond indirectly, thinking in complexes or aggregates of objects linked by experience (such as "mouth," "cup," "milk," and so forth) in order to fulfill physical needs.

There follows a long analysis of the cultural growth of specific higher psychological functions: memory, attention, abstraction, and, finally, thought and language. In examining each specific function, the idea is reiterated that symbolic systems serve as self-regulatory devices for the users. Original experiments are introduced to illustrate this ability of self-regulating attention through mediating devices at different age groups.

Luria's discussion of *natural* versus *cultural* memory represents another manifestation of the interrelationship between the two lines of development, the core of the Vygotskian–Lurian approach to development both in this book and all other major works. Cultural memory is memory that is mediated by symbolic systems otherwise known as mnemotechnic devices. Luria reviews data indicating that natural memory does not undergo any considerable growth with age, however, there is a gradual shift toward the use of artificial devices such as rips in paper or cutting out shapes of numbers that parallel the tallies and notches in wood made by primitive man to augment memory.

The child first remembers by shapes, particularly number shapes, just as the primitive counted in wholes. For example, he tells even and odd not by individual numbers of parts, but by the shapes of the configurations. Similarly, children use picture prompts to help them remember. However, Luria points out, the connections must already have been made by prior experiences. Finally, they shift from such devices to coding in words and numbers, developing mediated memory. Such devices, concludes Luria, help the child "improve his/her memory several times."

In an examination of the growth of attention, Luria proposed that, at first, the strength of the stimulus caused by external physical objects controls attention. Later, voluntary attention emerges in the child with the growth of his ability to actively manipulate external physical objects (such as the "forbidden colors" in the experiments introduced here) to regulate attention. Luria's experiments show that at a still more advanced stage older children cease to use external objects as mediating devices and shift to interiorized self-commands.

Certainly, one of the most interesting sections of this book is the analysis of child speech and with it child thought. Criticism of the "speech minus sound" theory of thought is found here as well as in other works by the authors, as, for example, in *Thought and Language* (1986) and *Fundamentals of Defectology* (1983/in press). Here again, the authors point out that thought and speech have different psychological origins and can exist without each other. For example, on the one hand, at the beginning stages of thought development, planned, organized behavior can be found in primitive forms in the absence of speech: The activity of the apes and children at play demonstrate this phenomenon. On the other hand, there are many voiced reactions accompanying movements, strong emotions, and so forth that do not represent speech, that is, they do not convey or vocalize a specific message, idea or thought.

Luria gives the following description of speech development. A child suddenly and miraculously switches from vocalized reflexes and imitated sounds to sounded out thoughts ("concretization"), and then to sounds that serve a function or purpose. Once the young child has passed the imitation stage, when he or she repeated the sounds that adults have introduced, then the pragmatic function of speech emerges: the child discovers the functional use of a word as a means of naming an object, for expressing certain wishes, and getting control of those things that interest him or her. The initial one-word stage of speech production is characterized by the compression of a whole thought or wish, that is, a whole sentence, into one word that can mean many things.

The first stage of language acquisition is marked by a rapid and active accumulation of words, which the child both repeats and *invents,* when he or she comes across a situation where a previously heard words does not fit. To illustrate the child's linguistic genius, Luria introduces some wonderful examples of child speech from Chukovsky's *Two to Five.* Luria shares with Chukovsky the view that a child's communication with adults evokes a special heightened sensitivity to the meaning and significance of the elements (such as prefixes and suffixes) from which words are formed (cf. also Chukovsky, 1963, pp. 7–9). In this way speech concept formations evolve.

Attention is given to Ach (1905, 1921) and his experiments to study the process of developing absolutely new concepts in children by using words as auxiliary tools. Although the artificiality of these experiments is pointed out, Luria welcomes the conclusion to which Ach came: artificial tools can aid a child to build a new concept and master a task that they would otherwise not have been able to complete. Herein lies the major importance of schooling for a child: it introduces the child to these tools and skills.

However, Luria points out, it would be a mistake to conclude that this entire process boils down simply to a gradual, evolving accumulation of complex techniques and skills. The child at different ages represents significant *qualitative,* not *quantitative* differences, which are not rooted in purely physiological changes. The child passes through different stages of cultural development, each of which is characterized by the different ways the child relates to the world—from natural, simple reactions to more complex psychological behavior, after interiorization of symbolic mediation of discriminative behavior has occurred.

An important section of this book is Luria's discussion of the psychology of physically and mentally impaired children that parallels Vygotsky's (in press) longer, more extensive treatise of these children in *Fundamentals of Defectology.* Here too the idea is advanced that an impaired function may be reorganized so that it is able to draw on intact functions.

Finally, these theories of development are applied to special children; both retarded and gifted children. There is a review of the data indicating that retardation is not necessarily accompanied by poor psychophysical characteristics. For example, the natural memory of retarded children may be unusually strong, but they often fail to integrate symbolic systems into their behavior and hence do not develop a strong cultural memory. Experiments with normal and retarded children are introduced to illustrate this. Moreover, a review of original experimental data shows that a high IQ may not necessarily be accompanied by above-average natural memory. Yet the use of mediation, of artificial aids, may result in a more effective use of memory.

The book ends with a critical examination and assessment of various approaches to intelligence testing (e.g., those of Binet and Rossolino), because predictions made purely on the basis of these statistical results are far from adequate. Alexander Luria claims that such measurements reveal only culturally dependent dimensions and do not reflect the *natural abilities or natural line of development* that may still be *culturally* compensated, developed, or enhanced.

VYGOTSKY TODAY: EXTENSIONS AND APPLICATIONS

This book is certainly interesting historically, given the fact that Western readers until recently erroneously associated Soviet psychology almost solely with "conditional reflexes." This book is, however, important and relevant today not only because it offers a good introduction to the beginnings of modern Russian or "Soviet" psychology, but because the views expressed here by Vygotsky and Luria find many applications to contemporary research being conducted in various fields in the West: education, developmental psychology, cultural psychology, psychological anthropology, cognitive psychology, and neuropsychology.

In the field of education, where there is a critical need to reform and revitalize the philosophy and methodology of principles of child development, this book addresses the present nature/nurture debate by offering a synthesis of these two lines of development. Moreover, it offers a supportive, basic model of learning that corresponds to newly emerging approaches to schooling in the United States and in other Western countries. Vygotsky's notions of "collaborative learning" and Zone of Proximal Development have now become "household terms" for most young researchers in education. Any educators or developmental psychologists who wish to investigate child development, and particularly language development, will be considered amiss if they fail to take into account Vygotsky's discussion of child development (the focus of studies in chapter 3).

This book offers an extensive examination of Vygotsky's approach to other aspects of human development that heretofore have still received little attention. The author examines heterogeneity of thought, development of unschooled, semi-literate peoples, development of literacy and numeric operations, and development of attention and memory—all extremely important questions of early childhood development. Here, as elsewhere in Vygotsky's work, schooling proves to be a pivotal point in development because it provides many cultural tools, which allows a school child to perform tasks a preschooler cannot (see also Vygotsky, 1928, 1935).

It will immediately become obvious to the reader that Vygotsky did not have all the data on infant studies available now and therefore may not be accurate in his discussion of the first few months of infant life. Still, his general principle of collaborative learning beginning with mother–infant interaction (see earlier example of the infant's acquired understanding of "cup") and continuing with peer interaction (see "The Collective" in Vygotsky, 1983/in press) is now heralded as an important paradigm for understanding many aspects of learning. Therefore, it comes as no surprise that the author of the recent book *Knowing Children* is criticized for his failure "to integrate Vygotskian-inspired research into this thesis," that is, the point of view that "all higher mental functions initially come into being through children's social interaction with more knowledgeable adults" (Bretherton, 1991, p. 446).

Although the notion of the Zone of Proximal Development has been overworked and isolated as Vygotsky's major treatise, other notions, equally important, still need to be examined. This book brings other Vygotskian principles to the foreground, such as the notion of "natural" versus "mediated" activity and the notion of transferal of knowledge or understanding from one learning situation to another.

For example, in chapter 1 we saw how the experimenter builds on the "natural activity" of apes in their natural habitat, that is, using branches to get fruit hanging up high in the tree, and reconstructs a "mediated" activity in the new environment of the research station. This natural activity is now manipulated and organized to make the ape complete more complex tasks, first with natural tools (the stick) and then with more artificial tools (string or rope), so that the ape has to *transfer* its knowledge from one situation to another *new one*. As was pointed out above, it is this transferal of "understanding" that, according to Vygotsky, constitutes the basis of mental activity in both apes and humans.

Humans, however, do not simply acquire tools ready-made or handed down from one generation to another, rather they also *create* tools for themselves and, in turn, create a Second Symbol System, that is, words or signs to substitute for these concrete props or tools. They first use this symbol system to communicate with or control each other, then internalize it in order to regulate their own behavior in new situations. How they do this is Vygotsky's major concern. Vygotsky speaks to prominent developmental scholars today, such as Gardner (1991) in *The Unschooled Mind* or Papert (1980) in *Mind Storms*. Like them, Vygotsky emphasizes that the nature of real learning is not ritualized, mechanistic, or "behavioristic," but *generative*.

Chapter 2 of this book addresses issues that many educational researchers are now exploring in their study of the nature and origins of literacy. Moreover, it expands the notion of semiotic means to include a richness of nonverbal means — concrete tools or props (such as gestures, beads, pieces of rope, etc.) that can be used to convey meaning (both linguistic and numeric). This view supports a new approach to literacy that gives great importance to nonverbal, symbolic activity (for example, drawing, play, etc.) as a necessary and natural step in the development of learning a written code.

Moreover, chapter 2 supports and enriches the investigation of sign language as a natural means of communication and cognitive development for the deaf — work that is now being carried by linguists at Northeastern University, the University of New Mexico, and the Moscow Scientific Institute of Defectology Russian Academy of Pedagogical Sciences (cf. Zaitseva, 1990).

Vygotsky's treatment of the two lines of development — primary, natural development, and historical–cultural development, which in the educated adult becomes superimposed on top of the former but *does not replace* it — lays a foundation for those psychoanalysts today who seek to lay bare different layers or domains of psychological activity. What we have is a type of "cognitive Freudism," to use the term of Howard Gardner (1982, 1985) of Harvard University's Graduate School of Education: in nearly every individual there exists the mind of the child — those early intuitive understandings that through schooling we upgrade, cultivate, make more sophisticated, but which still underlie our mental activity. Only with time and constant application of a higher level of learning does the individual stretch and gradually change or effectively restructure that primary level.

Much of what Vygotsky says in chapter 2 on the nature of thinking in primitive man—thinking on the primary or natural level—parallels Kris's (1965, 1979) assessment of psychological activity of the creative personality. This type of thinking is not only found in "primitive" people or children. Like Vygotsky, Kris attributed great importance to primary processes that the adult has embedded in his or her personality and to which he or she still can revert. According to Kris, particularly creative individuals constantly transport themselves to early primitive stages of free associations and so on. As Kozulin (1990a) pointed out, "Kris demonstrates that it would be *incorrect* to present the primary process type of mentation as exclusively pathological or indicative of a totally "regressive" mental state" (p. 235, italics added).

"The law of participation," which Vygotsky describes in his sections on "primitive thinking," presages Rothenberg's notion of "Janusian thinking." Rothenberg (1976, 1988, 1990) described the mental activity of certain individuals as the capacity to hold in mind two opposing kinds of views. For example, we know that the artist or scientist often takes two things that were thought to be contradictory and considers them both to be valid or true. Vygotsky's interest in the levels of processing is also echoed in Arieti's (1974) notion of tertiary mental activity, whereby the more diffuse, primary, uncontrolled, irrational thinking combines with secondary thinking (organized, goal oriented, rational, or problem solving).

As Kozulin (1990a) pointed out, for Vygotsky, the interaction of levels (natural and cultural) is particularly important in the case of the "influx of sense" in inner verbal thought: "An important addition made by Vygotsky is that thought should not necessarily leave the verbal domain in order to plug into the primary process resources. . . . Social meanings of the words are thus deconstructed during the inspirational stage, then turned into idiosyncratic sense, only to be reassembled again with the help of social principles of artistic form carried by the total text" (p. 235).

This book may be appreciated by a quite unexpected readership: clinical neuropsychologists and those concerned with brain-behavior relations. Indeed, A. Luria's reputation is in these two areas. His philosophy in assessing these areas is very different from that of most American scholars. Implicitly, he utilizes all the assumptions made in this book in his approach to neuropsychology, but these assumptions are not spelled out in his books in neuropsychology that are available in English. So this book may provide the necessary background for these later works.

The sections of this book that deal with the relationship between learning and changes in brain structures address the current interest in analyzing the nature and systematicity of brain changes, particularly frontal brain changes that effect higher cognitive functions. This book is a type of predecessor for the contemporary "neuro-Darwinism," which postulates a type of pruning away of neurons or neuron selectivity occurring on the basis of experience. At birth, there is an overproduction or high density of neurons; with learning and development, certain neurons are strengthened whereas others atrophy. As pointed out elsewhere, Vygotsky shows that there is no progression without regression. As always for Vygotsky, it is not the quantity (of neurons) or size of the brain that usually matters most, but the selective use to which brain tissue is put that pushes development forward.

In short, although this book precedes by some 20 years the "revolution" that has been taking place in cognitive psychology since the 1950s, it provides strong arguments for reexamining the very basis of thought, that is, meaning as it is created from social encounters with the world in specific historical cultural settings. As we have shown, this book does not refute the importance of stimuli, responses, or biological drives and their transformation, but shifts the focus of attention to semiotic activity and meaning making (cf. Lotman, 1990).

Such an orientation closely corresponds to the fervor of activity today in psychology that has been prompted, as Bruner (1990) wrote in *Acts of Meaning,"* to join with its sister interpretive disciplines in the humanities and in the social sciences" (p. 2). Very much in the Vygotsky–Luria tradition, "today one finds flourishing centers of cultural psychology, cognitive and interpretive anthropology, cognitive linguistics, and above all, a thriving worldwide enterprise that occupies itself as never before since Kant with the philosophy of mind and language" (Bruner, 1990, p. 3). For example, the new constructionism of the cognitive psychologist Goodman (1984) at Harvard, the interpretative anthropology of Geertz (1973, 1983) and the new environmentalism of Snow and LeVine (1982) at Harvard University represent just such centers of which Bruner speaks. The current text should be a very useful resource for the research activities in these various disciplines.

Within what used to be the Soviet Union, the Vygotskian–Lurian tradition has now risen again to the forefront, particularly at the Institute of Psychology of the Academy of Pedagogical Sciences under the leadership of Davydov and others and at the Department of Psychology of Moscow State University in the work of the cognitive neuropsychologist T. Akhutina. However, the most important center of this direction in psychology is at the Estonian University of Tartu, where P. Tulviste has addressed the main questions raised by many critics of the central issues of this book — namely, in the words of Cole:

How are we to interpret the heterogeneity of human thought revealed by cross-cultural comparisons? Are there fundamental differences in human thought as a function of the culture into which one is born and are such differences, if they are shown to exist, rankable in terms of developmental level. In crude but direct terms, do primitives think like children? (cited from introduction to Tulviste, 1991, p. x).

Tulviste's (1991) work updates the current text by attempting to show that although there are "qualitative differences in human thought attributable to the cultural environment," (p. x) heterogeneity exists within individuals in any culture, and therefore a single mentality cannot be reduced to either primitive or civilized. The conclusions that Vygotsky, Luria, and then Tulviste have reached are not beyond dispute and raise deep methodological questions. However, they invite serious exploration and research at a time when diversity and cultural ethnicity are issues that challenge all existing social institutions.

REFERENCES

Ach, N. (1905). *Über die Willenstätigkeit und das Denken* [The activity of the will and thought]. Göttingen, Germany: Vandenhoeck and Ruprecht.

Ach, N. (1921). *Über die Begriffsbildung* [Development of Concepts]. Bamberg, Germany: Buhner.

Arieti, S. (1974). *Interpretation of schizophrenia.* New York: Basic Books.

Bakhtin, M. (1973). *Poetics of Dostoevsky.* Ann Arbor, MI: Ardis.

Bretherton, I. (1991, October). What children know. *Science, 25,* 446.

Bruner, J. (1990). *Acts of meaning.* Cambridge: Harvard University Press.

Bühler, K. (1930). *The mental development of the child.* New York: Harcourt, Brace. (Russian ed., 1927; original work published 1919)

Chukovsky, K. (1968). *From two to five.* (M. Morton, Trans; rev. ed.) Berkeley: University of California Press. (Original work published under the title *Little Children* in 1925/1928)

Clodd, E. (1905). *The story of the alphabet.* New York: D. Appleton and Company.

Cole, M., Scribner, S., John-Steiner, V., & Souberman, E. (1978). *L. S. Vygotsky, mind in society.* Cambridge: Harvard University Press.

Corsini, R. J. (Ed.). (1984). *Encyclopedia of psychology.* (Vols. 1–3). New York: Wiley.

Gardner, H. (1982). *Art, mind, brain.* New York: Basic Books.

Gardner, H. (1985). *Frames of mind: The theory of multiple intelligences.* New York: Basic Books.

Gardner, H. (1991). *The unschooled mind.* New York: Basic Books.

Geertz, C. (1973). *The interpretation of cultures.* New York: Basic Books.

Geertz, C. (1983). *Local knowledge: Further essays in interpretive anthropology.* New York: Basic Books.

Goodman, N. (1984). *Of mind and other matters.* Cambridge, MA: Harvard University Press.

Groos, K. (1928). *The growth of the mind.* New York: Harper.

Holquist, M. (1981). *The dialogic imagination: Four essays by M. M. Bakhtin.* Austin: University of Texas.

Jakobson, R. (1989). *On the structure of the phoneme.* (M. Shapiro, Trans.). Unpublished manuscript. (Original work published 1939)

Joravsky, D. (1989). *Russian psychology.* Cambridge, England: Basil Blackwell.

Köhler, W. (1926). *The mentality of apes.* New York: Harcourt, Brace & Company. (Original work published 1921)

Kozulin, A. (1990a). The concept of regression and Vygotskian developmental theory. *Developmental Review, 10,* 218–238.

Kozulin, A. (1990b). Mediation: Psychological activity and psychological tools. *International Journal of Cognitive Education & Medicated Learning, 1*(2), 151–159.

Kozulin, A. (1990c). *Vygotsky's psychology.* Cambridge: Harvard University Press.

Kozulin, A. (1991). Life as authoring: The humanistic tradition in Russian psychology. *New Ideas in Psychology, 9*(3), 335–351.

Kris, E. (1965). *Psychoanalytic explorations in art.* New York: International Universities Press.

Kris, E. (1979). *Legend, myth, and magic in the image of the artist: An historical experiment.* New Haven: Yale University Press.

LeVine, Robert. (1982). *Culture, behavior, and personality* (2nd ed.). Cambridge: Harvard University Press.

Lévy-Bruhl, L. (1926). *How natives think* (L. Clare, Trans.). London: George Allen & Unwin LTD. (Original work published 1910)

Lotman, Yu. M. (1990). *Universe of the mind: A semiotic theory of culture.* Bloomington: Indiana University Press.

Luria, A. R. (1974a). *A. R. Luria.* In G. Lindzey (Ed.), *A history of psychology in autobiography* (pp. 251–292). Englewood Cliffs, NJ: Prentice Hall.

Luria, A. R. (1974b). *Historical development of the cognitive processes.* Moscow: Nauka.

Luria, A. R. (1982). *Language and cognition.* (J. Wertsch, Ed.). New York: Wiley.

Luria, L. (1991). *Memoires of her father's work and life.* Unpublished manuscript.

Mallery, D. G. (1971). *Sign language among North American indians.* The Hague: Mouton. (Original work published 1881)

Papert, S. (1980). *Mindstorms.* NY: Basic Books.

Pavlov, I. P. (1955). *Selected works.* Moscow: Foreign Languages Publishing House.

Proffer, C. R., Proffer, E., Meyer, R., & Szporluk, M. A. (1987). *Russian literature of the 1920s.* Ann Arbor, MI: Ardis.

Puzyrei, A. A. (1986). *Cultural-historical theory of L. S. Vygotsky and contemporary psychology.* Moscow: Moscow University.

Radzikhovskii, L. A. (1986–1987, Winter). The dialogic quantity of consciousness in the works of M. M. Bakhtin. *Soviet Psychology, 6,* 103–116.

Rothenberg, A., Housman, C. R. (1976). *The creativity question.* Durham, NC: Duke University Press.

Rothenberg, A. (1988). *The creative process of psychotherapy.* New York: Norton.

Rothenberg, A. (1990). *Creativity and madness: New findings and old stereotypes.* Baltimore, MD: Johns Hopkins University Press.

Shklovsky, V. (1965). Art as technique. In L. A. Clare (Trans.), *Russian formalist criticism.* London: George Allen & Unwin. (Original work published 1926).

Tulviste, P. (1987, Spring). Lévy-Bruhl and the development of thought. *Soviet Psychology, 25*(3), 3–21.

Tulviste, P. (1991). *The cultural-historical development of verbal thinking* (M. J. Hall, Trans.). Commack, NY: Nova Science.

Van der Veer, R. (1991). The anthropological underpinning of Vygotsky's thinking. In *Studies in Soviet Thought, 42,* 73–91.

Van der Veer, R., & Valsiner, J. (1988). Lev Vygotsky and Pierre Janet: On the origin of the concept of sociogenesis. *Developmental Review, 8,* 52–56.

Van der Veer, R., & Valsiner, J. (1991). *The quest for synthesis: Life and work of Lev Vygotsky.* Oxford: Basil Blackwell.

Vygotsky, L. S. (1928). Problema kul'turnogo razvitiia rebenka [Problem of cultural development of the child]. *Pedologiia, 1,* 58–57.

Vygotsky, L. S. (1929). *Pedologiia pedrostka* [Pedology of the school child]. Moscow: Biuro zaochnogo obucheniia.

Vygotsky, L. S. (1935). *Umstvennoe razvitie v protsesse obucheniia* [Mental development of children in the process of schooling]. Moscow: State Academic Pedagogical Publishers.

Vygotsky, L. S. (1971). *The psychology of art.* Cambridge: The M.I.T. Press. (Original work published 1925)

Vygotsky, L. S. (1986). *Thought and language* (A. Kozulin, Trans.). Cambridge, MA: MIT Press.

Vygotsky, L. S. (1991). Imagination and creativity in the adolescent. *Soviet Psychology, 29* (3), 73-88.

Vygotsky, L. S. (in press). *Fundamentals of defectology: Collected works.* (J. Knox & C. Stevens, Trans; Vol. 2) New York: Plenum. (Original work published 1983)

Wertsch, J. V. (1985). *Vygotsky and social formation of mind.* Cambridge: Harvard University Press.

Wertsch, J. V. (1991). *Voices of the mind.* Cambridge: Harvard University.

Zaitseva, G. L. (1990). L. S. Vygotsky and studies of sign language in Soviet psycholinguistics. In S. Prillwitz & T. Vollhaber (Eds.), *Sign Language Research and Application.* (pp. 271-290). Hamburg, Germany: Signum.

Studies on the History of Behavior: Ape, Primitive, and Child

INTRODUCTION

In our book, we have collected three psychological essays on the behavior of the anthropoid ape, primitive[1] man, and the child. All three essays are united by one idea, that is, *the idea of development.* Their aim is to schematically present the path of psychological evolution from the ape to the cultural man.

Each of these essays, therefore, deals *not with the full scope of* behavior of the anthropoid ape, primitive man, and the child, but with only *one dominating feature or aspect of behavior,* namely the one that, like a compass arrow, points from a certain starting point to a new direction and path in the development of behavior. Our task was to portray *three main lines* in the development of behavior — evolutionary, historical and ontogenetic — and to show that the behavior of a cultural man is the product of these three lines of development and may be understood and explained scientifically only by analyzing *the three different paths that make up the history of human behavior.*

It was also not our aim to give a full scale description of each of these three developmental processes. Neither did we intend to dwell in full detail on all aspects of the behavior of the ape, primitive man, and the child.

---

[1](V. G., J. K.) See discussion of the term *primitive* in the introduction to the book. References and footnotes were not supplied by Vygotsky in his part of this book (chapters 1 and 2). Therefore, *all* footnotes and citations have been added by the translator–editors (i.e., V. G., J. K.)

Rather than presenting the whole process in its entirety we have attempted here to outline the main landmarks on the path of psychological evolution at its various turning points. Thus, in each essay we have revealed the essential link that serves to connect one developmental stage of behavior with the next. In doing so, we consciously limited the contents of the essays to only the evolution of the *forms of behavior.*

The structure of our essays may be outlined as follows. The use and "invention" of tools by anthropoid apes bring to an end the organic stage of behavioral development in the evolutionary sequence and prepare the way for a transition of all development to a new path, creating thereby *the main psychological prerequisite of historical development of behavior.* Labor and, connected with it, the development of human speech and other psychological signs used by primitive man to gain control over behavior signify the beginning of cultural or historical behavior in the proper sense of the word. Finally, in child development, we clearly see a second line of development paralleling the processes of organic growth and maturation, that is, we see the cultural development of behavior based on the acquisition of skills and modes of cultural behavior and thinking.

All three phenomena are symptoms of new eras in the evolution of behavior, signs *of changes in the type of development itself.* Thus, we have concentrated on the turning points, the critical stages in the development of behavior. We consider the following stages to be critical: the use of tools in apes, labor and the use of psychological signs in primitive man, the split of the developmental line into natural–psychological and cultural–psychological development in the child. Every critical turning point is viewed primarily from the standpoint of *something new* introduced by this stage into the process of development. Thus, we treated each stage as a starting point for further processes of evolution.

The first essay is based on the materials collected by Köhler (1921/1926) in his famous research;[2] the second essay includes material on ethnic psychology collected in the works of Lévy-Bruhl (1910/1926, 1923), Thurnwald (1922), Wertheimer (1912), Leroy (1927), Danzel (1912), and many others; finally, we based the third essay mainly our own material gathered in the experimental studies of child behavior.

We tried to shed light on and incorporate all the facts from one point of view, from one approach to the processes of cultural–psychological development, from the theoretical position expanded in Vygotsky's (1929b) book *Pedology of the School Child.*

What is new about this work (in addition to a certain portion of the research material) is our attempt to describe the link interconnecting all

---

[2]Wolfgang Köhler (1887–1967), a German psychologist, who investigated the use of creation of tools by anthropoid apes at a special station set up on Teneriffe Islands.

three lines of development and to define in the most general terms the character and type of this connection. Our approach to the relations existing between the different lines of the development of behavior in a certain sense contradicts the standpoint developed by the theory of biogenetic parallelism. In answer to the question about the relations existing between ontogenesis and phylogenesis, this theory asserts that one process *repeats* more or less the other and reconstructs it; our theory states that the aforementioned relation is best defined as a parallelism of the two processes.

The groundlessness of the principle of genetic parallelism was demonstrated both in the works by bourgeois researchers and even more so by Marxists. Our aim was primarily to discover the maximum specificity of each of the three paths of behavioral development, the differences in modes, and the types of development. We were interested in discerning only the distinctive, not the common, features of these processes. In contrast with the theory of parallelism, we considered that the results of studying the main distinctive features of each developmental process — the features distinguishing the process from the general notion of evolution — can shed direct light on the type and specific regularities of each of the three lines under discussion. Our main task was to show the independent, specific regularities and essence of each particular type of development. This in no way means that we completely rejected any correspondence between ontogenesis and phylogenesis. On the contrary, this theory, as it has been developed and critically described by many modern authors, may serve as a beautiful, euristic principle that we indeed used to reveal the formal correspondence among certain phenomena belonging to the different planes of development. However, we have attempted to comprehend the very connection between the three paths of development in a completely different manner.

This connection, to our mind, is materialized in the way that one process of development dialectically prepares for the next one, transforming and changing into a new type of development. We do not think that all three processes fall into a straight-line sequence. Instead, we believe that each higher type of development starts precisely at that point where the previous one comes to an end and serves as its continuation in a new direction. This shift in the direction and pattern of development in no way excludes the possibility of a connection between two the processes, but, on the contrary, it sooner presupposes this connection.

The main idea of our essays is most clearly and thoroughly expressed in the epigraph. We intended to show that, in the sphere of psychological development, there takes place something similar to that which has already long ago been established with respect to organic development. Similar to what happens in the process of historic development whereby the tools of human beings change rather than their natural organs, in the process of psychological development the human being perfects the work of the mind mainly in conjunction with the development of specific techniques or "auxiliary means" of thought and behavior. The history of human memory is impossible to understand without the history of writing, just as the history of human thinking cannot be understood without the history of speech. We have only to remember the social nature and origin of every cultural sign in order to understand that when approached from this point of view, psychological development is precisely social development conditioned by the environment. Psychological development is solidly introduced into the context of the entire social development and is revealed in its organic constituent.

We believe that by introducing the psychological development of behavior into the context of mankind's historical development we are making the first steps towards the most important issues of the *new genetic psychology*. In so doing we bring a historical perspective to psychological research, to take Thurnwald's position. We understand all the risks and the responsibility of any first step in a new direction, but only on this path do we see the possibility of genetic psychology as a science.

The first and the second chapters were written by Vygotsky, the third A. Luria. The experiments underlying our essay on child behavior were conducted by us and our colleagues in the Laboratory of Psychology at the Academy of Communist Education.

1 Behavior of the Anthropoid Ape

Nec manus nuda intellectus
sibi permissus multum valet: instruments et
auxiliis res perficitur.

—*BACO*

A bare hand and a mind by itself
are worth not that much: everything is performed
with the help of tools and auxiliary means.

—F. Bacon

THREE STAGES IN THE DEVELOPMENT OF BEHAVIOR

When analyzing the development of behavior from its simplest forms observed in the lower animals to the most complex and the highest observed in man, one can easily see that behavior taken as a whole goes through three main stages in its development.

The first stage in the development of behavior in all animals is represented by hereditary reactions or innate modes of behavior. These are usually called instincts. They serve mostly to satisfy the basic needs of an organism. Their biological function is that of self preservation and reproduction. The main distinctive feature of instinctive reactions is that they operate without being learned and are structurally inherent to the organism. Immediately after birth, a child moves his hands and legs, cries, sucks the breast, swallows milk.

But not all instincts mature as early as sucking, and not all of them are functional immediately after birth. Many of them, for example, the sexual instinct, mature much later, only when the organism itself reaches a high enough stage of maturation and development. However, even those instincts that mature later are still characterized by the same fundamental feature. This is the innate reserve of reactions at the animal's disposal as a result of its hereditary structure.

The animal does not learn instinctive reactions in the course of its life; these [instinctive reactions — J. K.] do not appear as a result of trial-and-error or of successful and unsuccessful experiences; they are also not the result of imitation. This constitutes their main distinctive feature. The biological importance of instinctive reactions is that they are useful adaptations to the environment; they are developed in the course of struggle for survival and reinforced by natural choice in the process of biological evolution.

That is why their origin is explained in the same way as is the origin of "expedient" structures and functions of any organism, that is, according to Darwin's laws of evolution. If we take the lower species, for example, insects or other invertebrates, we will easily see that their entire behavior is almost completely limited to this type of instinctive reactions. A spider weaving a web, a bee constructing a honeycomb, all such species use instinctive reactions as the main form of adaptation to the environment.

The second stage is built up and erected directly above the first and basic stage in the development of behavior. This is the so-called training stage or stage of conditional reflexes. The second class of reactions differs from the previous one in that it is not hereditary but arises from the animal's individual experience. All the reactions in this category are the result of specific learning, specific training, and individually accumulated experience. The usual conditional reflex, which is well known and described in the works Pavlov and his school, may serve as the classic example of a reaction at the second stage.

It is now important for us to note only two aspects that characterize this second stage in the development of reactions. First we have in mind the connection existing between reactions of the second stage and instinctive or hereditary reactions. Studies of conditional reflexes have shown that any primary conditional reflex appears only on the basis of the unconditional reflex or instinctive hereditary reactions.

In essence, training does not create new reactions in the animal, but only serves to combine inherent reactions, giving rise to new conditional connections between the innate reactions and environmental stimuli. Thus, the new stage in the development of behavior arises directly on top of the foundation of the previous one. A conditional reaction is nothing more than an immediate reaction altered by the conditions under which it appeared.

The second aspect characteristic for this stage of behavioral development is the new biological function created by the conditional reflexes. Although instincts serve as a means of adaptating to more or less constant, stable, and fixed environmental situations, conditional reflexes constitute a much more flexible, subtle, and refined mechanism of adaptation; in essence, this (mechanism allows) hereditary, instinctive reactions to adapt to the individual conditions of a given animal's existence. If Darwin has explained the origin of species, Pavlov has explained the origin of the individual, that is, the biology of the individual, particular experience of an animal.

Complete development of this second stage of behavior is found only in vertebrate animals, although some more primitive forms of conditional reactions may be seen already in ants, bees, and crabs. However, vertebrates are the first to demonstrate a shift in behavior. In spite of all the success achieved in training lower animals, the dominating, overpowering form of their behavior still remains the instinct. In contrast, in higher animals we note a shift toward the dominance of conditional reflexes in the overall system of reactions.

These animals are the first in which the plasticity of innate abilities is found; "childhood" in the proper sense of the word and, linked with it, "child" play emerge. Itself being a type of instinctive activity, play is also an exercise for other instincts, the young animal's natural school, its self-instruction or training. According to Bühler,[1] "Young dogs, cats, and the human child play, whereas beetles and insects, even the highly organized bees and ants, do not. This cannot be mere chance, but must rest upon an inner connection: *play supplements the plastic dispositions*" (Bühler, 1919/1930, p. 9).

Finally, it is necessary to also note that the second stage has a reverse influence on the first. Conditional reflexes, being overlaid on top of unconditional reflexes, change the latter profoundly, and very often in the individual experience of an animal we observe "a perversion of instincts,"[2] that is, a new direction taken by an innate reaction due to the conditions in which it appeared.

The classic example of such a "perversion of instinct" is demonstrated by Pavlov's experiment where a conditional reflex is developed in a dog by

---

[1]Bühler considered Freud's emphasis on the pleasure of satisfaction to be but one third complete: He added the pleasure of functioning and the pleasure of creating (Corsini, 1984, p. 175). The seeds of this creativity are traced by Bühler back to animal behavior. In the first chapter of *The Mental Development of the Child,* Bühler analyzed the beginnings of language and art going back to their beginnings: "Instinct, Training, and Intellect." He drew heavily on a comparative psychology and the research done by Köhler with apes, chickens, and other animals. Much of what Bühler says here finds its way into Vygotsky's text.

[2]For more information on this phenomenon in development, see Kozulin (1990a). There, the concept of regression and Vygotskian developmental theory is discussed at length.

cauterizing its skin with an electric current. The animal's first response to pain is a violent defensive reaction; it strains against its harness, it bites the device with its teeth, and it fights with all its might. But as a result of a long series of experiments, where pain stimulation was accompanied by food, the dog's response to burns on the skin began to be that very same reaction with which it usually responded to food. The famous English psychologist Sherrington,[3] who was present at these experiments, said, looking at the dog, "Now I understand the joy with which martyrs ascended the fire." With these words he pointed out the enormous perspective revealed by this classic experiment. In this simple experiment he saw the prototype of those profound changes in our nature that are produced by enculturation (education)[4] and by the environment's influence on us.

Ukhtomskii (1945) stated:

> Our nature is cultivatable, the foundation itself, though slowly, has to necessarily be altered in the course of the appearance of still newer and newer Pavlovian conditional connections. That is why *instincts are not a stable and permanent stock, but an expanding and transforming property of man.* The fact that under normal conditions higher achievements quite readily disintegrate, whereas the most primary instincts do not, means that the latter make up 'the basis of man's behavior,' not the newer and higher ones.

> The behavior of the modern normal human being can no more be explained by the most ancient animal instincts than it can by the characteristics of the ovum or the embryo. One can say that *the entire scope of man's pursuits and behavior boils down to the formation and cultivation of new instincts.* I am convinced that the most important and inspiring idea of Pavlov's doctrine is the notion that the reflex apparatus functions not by treading in place but by constantly transforming and pushing forward in time.

On top of this second stage in the development of behavior, there arises the third and, apparently for the animal kingdom, last stage, which is, however, not the last for man. The presence of this third stage has been established with undoubted scientific certainty only in the behavior of the higher anthropoid apes. Darwin's theory stimulated precisely this search for and discovery of the third stage in these very animals.

According to data on comparative anatomy and comparative physiology, it has been established with absolute reliability that anthropoid apes appear

---

[3]C. S. Sherrington later conducted the same experiments with apes (see A. Luria, 1963, p. 12).

[4]The word "vospitanie" means here not just instruction but moral upbringing whereby society's values and goals as well as its knowledge is instilled in the child. The two other words that Americans often translate as "education" are "obrazovinie" (the whole system of education) and "obuchenie" (instruction).

to be our close relatives in the evolutionary progression. Until most recently, however, one link in this evolutionary chain that connects man with the animal world has remained missing, namely the psychological link. Up until now, psychologists have not succeeded in showing that the behavior of apes bears the same relationship to man as their anatomy does.

Köhler undertook the task of finding this missing psychological link in Darwin's theory and of showing that, like biological development, psychological development also proceeded along the same evolutionary path — from the highest animals to man. To this end, Köhler (1921/1926) tried to find in the ape rudiments of those specifically human forms of behavior that are usually referred to by the general term *rational behavior* or *the mind*.

In doing so, Köhler proceeded along the same path, as did all the comparative sciences in their time. "The anatomy of man," says Marx, "is the key to the anatomy of the ape. Traces of the higher forms (of behavior) present in the lower animal species can be understood only when these higher [forms — J. K.] are already known." Köhler chose to use this very approach in his analysis of ape behavior. He considered the invention and use of tools to be the most essential and distinctive characteristics of human behavior. That is why he undertook the task of showing that the rudimants of these forms of behavior could already be found in anthropoid apes.

Köhler (1921/1926) conducted his experiments from 1912 to 1920 on the Island of Teneriffe at the anthropoid station that the Prussian Academy of Sciences specially organized for this purpose. Nine apes (chimpanzees) were under his observation and served as experimental subjects.

The importance of Köhler's experiments is not limited to the discovery of the missing psychological link in the evolutionary chain. We will easily find in them yet other significance that is of our immediate interest. It is in these very experiments with anthropoid apes where intellectual reactions appeared in that simple, clear cut, transparent form that we have never been able to observe in the developed behavior of man. It is here where we see the advantage of primary and primitive forms over the later and more complex ones.

That is why all the characteristic features of this third developmental stage of behavior, all the specificity distinguishing it from the previous two, all the connections linking the third with the first two stages, are found here in the most clear cut form. It is as if we had a "pure culture" of intellectual reactions, experimentally created for the purpose of studying the qualities of this stage in development in all its purity. This explains the great significance of these experiments, which are important not only for understanding the upward development of behavior from ape to man, but also for correctly understanding behavioral development from the bottom up, that is, from the instinct to the conditional reflexes of the mind.

Köhler's experiments basically involved three fundamental operations that an animal has to perform to solve a task. The first condition necessary for the solution of the task was that the animal had to find *a roundabout way* to reach the goal in situations where for some reason the direct solution was impossible; the second condition was linked to the need to *bypass or eliminate an obstacle* found on the path leading to the goal; and finally the third condition was the need to use, invent, or produce tools as a means for achieving an otherwise unachievable goal.

In the most complex experiments, two conditions, sometimes even all three, were combined together in one task. Sometimes these conditions appeared separately, but, in general, the experiments were all designed in such a way that the complexity increased so that the ability to solve a simpler task included in the previous experiment became a necessary prerequisite for each subsequent experiment.

KÖHLER'S EXPERIMENTS

Now we dwell briefly on some of Köhler's most important observations in order to delineate the characteristics of the third form of behavior. Even in the apes' play, Köhler had numerous occasions to observe their ability to use tools. The play of these animals gives us a rough picture of their behavior in the wild (in the forest).

In play, one very easily finds a connection with the animal's real-life experience. The animal quite easily carries over certain types and modes of behavior from play to nonplayful activities, and, vice versa—the animal immediately transfers to its play some new life experiences and some solved tasks.

According to Köhler (1921/1926): "If under the pressure of 'necessity,' in the special circumstances of an experimental test, some special method, say, of the use of tools, has been evolved—one can confidently expect to find this new knowledge shortly utilized in 'play,' where it can bring not the slightest immediate gain, but only an increased *'joie de vivre'* " (p. 71).

At Köhler's station, it was found that the apes' favorite toy, used for different aims, was the stick. While at the station, Sultan, the cleverest of the apes, invented the game of jumping from a stick; climbing as fast as possible up a stick set almost perpendicular to the floor, the animal jumped down to the ground or to some elevated spot once the stick started to fall, or even before. The other apes imitated this play and became surprisingly skillful at it.

This method, which first appeared in their play, was later used by the apes in those experiments where they had to get a hold of some fruit hung

FIG. 1.1 Chica on the jumping stick. Rana watching (Köhler, 1926, p. 72).

up high. Figure 1.1 (taken from Köhler, 1921[5]) the apes, taking part in such an experiment.

Still another ape holds a piece of straw in a stream of ants and, waiting for several of them to climb up, he then licks them off, passing the straw through his mouth. After the others adopted this trick, all the animals at the station "were to be seen squatting side by side along the ants' pathway, each armed with straw or twig like anglers on a river's bank" (Köhler, 1921/1926, p. 80).

Using a stick, an ape brushes off dirt, touches a lizard, an electric wire, or anything he does not want to touch with his hand. Most fascinating, perhaps, is that the chimpanzee digs grass roots out with a stick and, in general, likes to dig in the ground. In these cases the stick serves as a shovel that is guided and pressed down with both hand and leg. When the ape wants to lift the heavy lid of a water container, he thrusts strong sticks and iron rods in the crack under it and uses them as levers.

When playing, the animals like to tease each other suddenly shoving a comrade in the side. Sometimes when angry, in self defense or during an attack, they use the stick as a weapon. In Bühler's words:

---

[5]Wolfgang Köhler, (1921) *Intelligenzprüfungen an Menschenaffen.* All English translations of this text are taken from Köhler, (1921/1926) *The Mentality of Apes.* Figure was taken from the German original.

these various modes of using [the stick — J. K.], along with the fact that in play or out of necessity the chimpanzee snatches a stick all by himself and without any instruction and skillfully uses it, give us sufficient grounds to think that, as an animal living in a tree, he already knew about the stick and had used it in the wild. At least he must have been acquainted with the tree branch as both a bearer of fruit and a natural means of getting it.

The best example of the connection between an ape's behavior in experimental conditions and in natural forms of behavior in play is illustrated by the simplest task solved by all animals. In this experimental situation, the ape sits in a cage in front of which there is some fruit on a rope. Without any hesitation or any exploratory or random movements, all the apes tugged the fruit toward themselves by pulling the other end of the rope that was lying in the cage. In this way, they are able to use a rope as a tool for getting a hold of fruit. It is interesting to note that the same task cannot be solved by a dog.

In similar experiments with a dog, where meat was placed in front of the cage, the dog would howl looking at the meat and try to get a hold of it by thrusting his paw through the bars; he would rush about the cage, run along the bars, but would prove to be unable to use the rope stretching from the meat to the cage or to use the stick lying there. It is true that without any great effort, a dog may be taught to use a rope or a stick, but the dog's new reaction in this case would be only the result of learning or training. The dog by himself would not make use of a tool.

One more curious phenomenon was found in further rope experiments with the apes. Several ropes are extended from the place outside the cage where a piece of fruit is located; only one is attached to the fruit while the remaining ropes just fill the space between an animal and a banana. Usually, the apes pull the wrong rope, that is, one not attached to the fruit, but one which is shorter. Only upon seeing the futility of attempts to pull down the fruit in this way, they switch over to the correct solution of the task. Five such experiments with Sultan are presented schematically in Fig. 1.2 (taken from Köhler, 1921). The numbers show the order in which the animal pulled different ropes toward itself. In four out of five cases, he chose the rope covering the shortest distance between the goal and the bars. This illustrates the role that visual factors — the structure of the visual field, the optic contact between tool, and the goal — play for the ape in its solution of the task.

In another experiment without any rope, fruit is placed in front of the cage and a stick is placed inside (Fig. 1.3, taken from Köhler, 1921). The ape is able to guess that he can use the stick as a tool to bring the fruit nearer and then to snatch it with the hands. One interesting thing found in these experiments was that the task could be accomplished only when both the

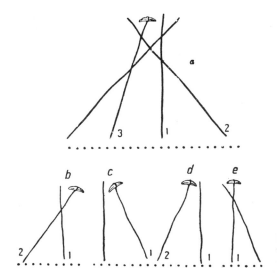

FIG. 1.2 Five experiments with Sultan and ropes (Köhler, 1926, p. 29).

fruit and the stick were so close to each other that they were in the same visual field and the animal saw them simultaneously. But whenever the stick was placed far enough away so that the ape could not take in at one glance both the tool and the goal, the solution of the task turned out to be either impossible or very difficult.

Here, the role of visual factors can be seen quite clearly. However, a small amount of training is enough for the ape to learn how to overcome this problem and use a stick located even outside the same visual field as the goal. In cases where there was no stick in the cage, the ape broke off a tree branch, used a handful of straw, broke off a board from a box, took out a wire from the grating, used a long piece of cloth to strike out at the banana, and so on.

Another more complex technique discovered by Sultan is an example of real invention and production of a special tool. Fruit is placed in front of the cage bars and inside there is a piece of reed too short to get the fruit. There is a second reed as short as the first one, but thicker and hollow at

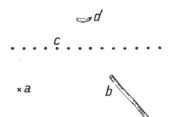

FIG. 1.3 a the position of the animal, b the stick, c the bars, d the fruit (Köhler, 1926, p. 6).

both ends. Under these circumstances the chimpanzee takes both reeds, attaching their ends one on top of another. Then he grasps the point of attachment using his hand like a buckle and tries with this elongated stick to get the fruit. The wrong position of the hand — holding this elongated stick not by the end but in the middle, at the point of sticks' connection — prevents the ape from achieving his goal. For hours on end, Sultan tried to get hold of the fruit in this way.

Finally, moving away from the bars, he took both reeds and sat down at a distance, twirling them until the end of one reed slid into the other and stuck there. Immediately Sultan came up with the elongated stick to the bars and brought the fruit nearer to himself. From then on Sultan always got out of similar situations easily. When it was necessary, he inserted three reeds one into another, sharpening the end with his teeth if it did not fit into the hole. In this way, he produced an elongated stick and used it quite correctly after that. Upon seeing this, the other animals imitated him (Fig. 1.4, taken from Köhler, 1921).

The animals faced somewhat similar tasks when fruit was hung up so high in the cage that it could not be reached either by standing on the ground or by jumping up. In this case, the smarter apes moved a box that was in the cage, put it under the hanging fruit, climbed on top, and in this way got hold of the target.

In their games, apes play with boxes just as eagerly as they do with sticks; they carry them, drag them, lug them, pile them on top of each other, and throw them, enjoying the noise the boxes produce when they hit the floor or the walls. In the experiment just mentioned, the ape climbs on top of a box, then jumps up from it, and in doing so, tears away the fruit. Sometimes, the

FIG. 1.4 Sultan making a double stick (Köhler, 1926, p. 132).

door opening into the cage serves the same purpose as the box. The chimpanzee opens the door, climbs up it, and throws down the fruit hanging from the ceiling.

When the fruit is hanging up too high, the ape carries over several boxes, piles them on top of each other, and in this way, using three or even four boxes, he constructs a tower or a staircase to climb up (Figs. 1.5 and 1.6, both taken from Köhler, 1921). Sometimes, the chimpanzee combines both means, the box and the stick, to obtain the fruit (Fig. 1.7, taken from Köhler, 1921). The experiments with boxes reveal one extremely interesting detail in the ape's behavior: the apes' constructions turn out to be utterly disordered and unstable, and the task of balancing the construction seems overwhelmingly difficult for them. According to Köhler (1921/1926), the ape lacks adequate understanding of the statics of its construction (p. 154).

Bühler stated:

> It seems to me that a comparison [of the ape's constructions] with a tree will help us to better see what is lacking in the ape's understanding. Limbs of a tree grow irregularly and any branch which reaches far out to the side, holds him quite safely. Clearly an animal living in a tree does not understand that it is quite a different matter with boxes piled on top of each other: the upper boxes cannot stick out to any great degree above the lower ones; they have to be adjoined by planes, not by edges or corners; the construction cannot be stable, if the open side of the upper box is thrust down on top of the lower one, etc.

FIG. 1.5 Grande achieves a 4-story structure (Köhler, 1921, p. 144).

FIG. 1.6 Grande on an inse-
cure construction (Köhler,
1921, p. 142).

That is why an ape sometimes tries to stick a box up against a flat wall. If it stayed up like this, the task would be solved. Something similar may be seen in the case of a ladder which is used simply as a pole for jumping or is attached in some technically unsound manner, for example, as if it were glued or attached to the wall only on one side, leaving the other without any support, etc.

Apes also easily cope with the experiments where indirect paths are required to achieve the goal. Here, in Bühler's view, the apes' behavior in general does not differ greatly from what we can observe in the behavior of a squirrel, cat, or dog. Köhler himself discovered that a dog can use very complex, roundabout ways to achieve a goal. According to Bühler, the root of the ape's ability to use indirect ways again lies in the ape's natural habitat. Köhler explained:

> Let us imagine that through the thick foliage an ape sees a piece of fruit which he cannot reach from the branch of the tree where he is sitting. Subsequently, in order to reach this goal he will take a roundabout way; for example, he will get down from one tree and climb another. This presupposes a certain ability to seize up the situation at a glance and choose the correct path.

Here we introduce still another related experiment. The fruit is now located on the floor of a box on top of which heavy stones have been

FIG. 1.7 Chica beating down her objective with a pole (Köhler, 1921, p. 146).

placed; a horizontal crevice has been made rather high up on a board on one side of the box; the vertical bars are located at the other end of the box. Nearby, there is a stick that is fastened to a rope in such a way that with the stick one can reach only as far as the crack. The animal must first insert the stick through the crack and push the fruit away from himself toward the bars [on the opposite end of the box—J. K.], and then, after going around the box, take hold of the banana by thrusting his hand through the bars. The smarter animals correctly solved this task (Fig. 1.8, taken from Köhler, 1921/1926).

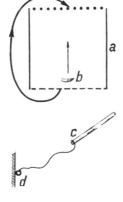

FIG. 1.8 *a* is the box with the bars (. . . . .) and the crack (= =), *b* is the fruit, *c* the stick, and *d* the tree. The arrow indicates the direction of the roundabout path (Köhler, 1926, p. 264).

A more difficult task requires passing [the fruit] around a board [i.e., one wall of a box]. Outside the bars [before which the ape is sitting] there is an open box (like a desk drawer) with the front board missing [i.e., the whole construction looks like a low three-sided drawer with one board missing — J. K.]; inside lies the fruit. The side with the missing board faces the opposite direction from the bars [and the ape — J. K.]. The animal, using a stick, must first move the fruit away from himself, rolling it out of the box, then to the side, and only after that can he easily get hold of the fruit with his hands. Only one, the smartest chimpanzee, solved this difficult task. For all the other apes, this roundabout course of solving the task turned out to be too difficult (Fig. 1.9, taken from Köhler, 1926).

Indeed, instead of using the stick to bring the fruit *towards himself,* as the ape had usually done in these experiments, now he was required to move the fruit *away from himself,* that is, to proceed in precisely the opposite direction.

The experiments with obstacles turned out to be even more difficult for the animals than those with roundabout paths. "An animal which scales," Bühler said, "would definitely go around any obstacle blocking his path in the woods, and would hardly ever have a cause to remove it," and therefore all the tasks with obstacles proved to be very complicated for the apes.

If the box needed by the ape for his construction contains heavy stones or sand so that the animal is unable to move it, then considerable effort is required for him to figure out that he must dump out the sand or the stones in order to free the box. If the box stands right up next to the bars, thus occupying the place from which it is possible to get the fruit, it takes many of the apes hours and hours laboring over the various other means to finally guess that they have to move the box aside. This dominance of the immediate visual situation over the ape's actions turns out to be of utmost importance for correctly understanding the overall behavior of the ape.

One of Köhler's experiments with boxes is extremely demonstrative in this respect. Here it is interesting to observe how an animal, who has already found the correct solution to a task in one situation, cannot for some reason, use it in another. In this case, it is very easy to discover the

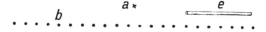

FIG. 1.9   *a* is the position of the animal, *b* the bars, *c* the box, *d* the fruit, and *e* the fruit (Köhler, 1926, p. 240).

circumstances that prevent the correct solution to the task. For example, in one experiment the [female] ape Chica tries her best to seize the banana suspended from the ceiling, but does not attempt to make use of the box standing in the middle of the room, even though on several occasions she has already used this very box as a stairway.

The ape exhausts herself by jumping up and trying to tear away the fruit. All the while she sees the box, even sits down on it more than once to have a rest, but does not make the slightest effort to drag it toward the goal. All this time another animal, Tercera, is lying on the box. When the latter incidentally gets up, Chica immediately seizes the box, drags it toward the target, and gets hold of it.

The box, on which Tercera lies, does not appear to the ape to be "an object from which to get fruit," but only "something upon which to lie" (cited in Koffka, 1925/1928, p. 215). Under these circumstances, the ape in no way links the box with the target; the box seems to be included in a different structure and therefore cannot be incorporated as a tool in the main experimental situation. According to Koffka (1925/1928): "To release a thing from one configuration, and transfer it by reconstruction into another configuration, would seem to be a relatively high-grade accomplishment" (p. 215).

Finally, the most difficult experiments are those that combine together two or three techniques [modes of action — J. K.]. A good example of this may be seen in the following experiment. A piece of fruit is located in front of the bars and a stick is located inside the cage. This stick is too short to reach the fruit, but beyond the bars there is another, longer one. By using the short stick, the ape must first move the long stick toward himself, and then, with the help of the longer one, get hold of the banana, as in Fig. 1.10. (taken from Köhler, 1921; cited in Köhler, 1921/1926, pp. 130–133).

Or take for example another experiment. A banana lies in front of the bars, a stick is suspended from the ceiling, and a box is in the cage. The ape must climb up onto the box, take down the stick and, with it, bring the banana closer. Experiments of this type including two or three goal-oriented operations also seem to be analogous to those experiments requiring a roundabout solution to the task. On the way to the final goal, an ape interjects some intermediate [goals — J. K.], like getting the stick. The

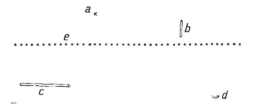

FIG. 1.10   a is the position of the animal, b the stick, c the long stick, d the fruit, e the bars (Köhler, 1926, p. 180).

majority of the apes proved to be able to cope with these tasks, usually solving them faultlessly.

THE LAW OF STRUCTURE AND APE BEHAVIOR

Everything the apes did in Köhler's experiments was closely connected with the perception of space. Finding roundabout paths, removing obstacles, and using tools — all turned out to be a function of the apes' field of vision. The ape perceived this visual field as a certain entity, a structure (configuration), and thanks to this, each individual element of this field (e.g., the stick) acquired the role of tool or functioned as a part of this structure.

As Köhler demonstrated, the reason the stick became a tool was that it belonged to the same structure as the fruit. However, once the stick was placed so far away from the fruit that the ape could not perceive in a single glance both the tool and the goal, then the correct solution became more difficult. Similarly, if the box, usually used as a stairway, is used by another animal as a resting place, that is, if this element is incorporated into another structure, then the ape finds himself in a difficult position; the box loses its previously established link with the operation of getting fruit.

Thus, Köhler came to the conclusion that, in general, the behavior of the apes during these experiments is defined by the *law of structure*. The essence of this law is the notion that all the processes of our behavior, including all our perceptions, are not simply an additive sum of individual elements. On the contrary, both our action and our perception together form a certain whole, the properties of which determine the function and meaning of each individual component.

Psychologists call a whole that determines the properties and meanings of its parts a structure. This is a very important notion for understanding the behavior of apes. Köhler's experiment with the child, the chimpanzee, and the household chicken presents the simplest example clarifying the meaning of a structure. The experiment consisted of the following.

A chicken was given some grain on two sheets of paper: light grey and dark grey. On the light grey paper lay loose grain for the chicken to peck at, however, the kernels of grain on the dark grey paper were glued in place. By trial and error, the chicken gradually developed a positive reaction to the light grey paper and a negative one to the dark grey paper. Unerringly, it would approach the light grey sheet of paper and peck at the grain. When this reaction was sufficiently established, Köhler moved on to a critical stage of the experiment and gave the chicken a new set of sheets: one was *the same light grey sheet,* to which the chicken had developed a positive reaction, whereas the other was a new white sheet. How will the chicken perform in this situation?

It would be natural to expect the chicken to unerringly approach the light grey sheet of paper, since it had been trained to peck the corn precisely from this paper. Or one might suppose by a stretch of the imagination that, due to the appearance of the new white sheet of paper, the results of the previous training would be annulled and the chicken, again by trial and error, would approach first one then the other piece of paper, with 50% probability for each. The results of the experiment proved quite the opposite.

It was *the new white sheet* of paper, seen for the first time, that the chicken usually approached, demonstrating a negative reaction *to the light grey sheet* of paper, the one that a stable, positive selection response had been established with over the course of much training. How can the chicken's behavior be explained in this case?

Köhler suggested the following explanation. The light grey sheet of paper from the previous set was replaced by the white one in the new combination. Here it fulfilled the same function as that of the lighter of two shades. The chicken was trained to discriminate not absolute darkness or lightness of the shade but *the relative* intensity of shades. It was the lighter shade to which the chicken reacted. What the chicken did was to transfer to this crucial experimental situation the relationship between the elements of the initial set. A brilliant support for this interpretation may be found in one more consequential experiment.

Immediately after the procedure just described, the same chicken was presented a new set of sheets: the dark grey one used at the first stage of experimental training and a new black one. It must be remembered that there was a negative response to *this very same dark grey piece* of paper in the first experiment. Now the chicken goes to *precisely this sheet* to peck the grain.

Clearly, the reason for this is again that the functional meaning of this sheet in the new set has changed. In the first set, this sheet functioned *as a darker shade,* whereas here it served *as the lighter one* (Fig. 1.11).[6]

All these experiments demonstrate with absolute and convincing clarity that the chicken reacts to the given situation as to an integral entity. The elements of this situation (the individual sheets of paper) can be changed — they may disappear, others may reappear, but the situation as a whole produces the same effect: the chicken reacts to the lighter shade.

One may say that the properties of the components of the chicken's visual perception are determined by its structure as an integral entity. This is indeed the most important characteristic of the structure: the meaning of

---

[6]Vygotsky most likely knew about these experiments from the Russian translation of Volkelt (1926/1930) and the German original (1926/1962). Fig. 1.11 was taken from the Geran version (Volkelt, 1962).

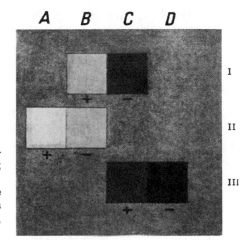

FIG. 1.11 I is the fundamental experiments (training); II—the first critical test, III—the second critical test, + the positive reaction, and — is the negative reaction (Volkelt, 1962, p. 207).

each individual element in this situation depends on the element's relation to the whole and on the structure of that whole, in which it is included as an element. *This very same* light grey or dark grey sheet may cause either a positive or a negative reaction, depending upon which whole it is included as a part. In this remarkable experiment, Köhler managed to reveal the importance and role of a structure in our behavior.

Certain psychologists also used this concept to explain the relations existing between an instinct and a reflex. Traditionally, a reflex is understood as the primary and simplest unit or element of behavior, whereas an instinct is considered to be a complex chain of reflexes constructed from these units, these elementary links. In fact, there is much proof that an instinct is the genetic predecessor of a reflex. Reflexes are nothing but residual, isolated elements of more or less differentiated instincts.

It is worth calling to mind, for example, the behavior of the simplest one-cell organisms. The reaction we see in such organisms is in essence *the holistic response of the entire organism*. This reaction fulfills a function analogous to that of our instinct. Only later on in the higher developmental stages of the organism are individual organs differentiated, each carrying out its own role in this overall differentiated reaction and thus acquiring a certain degree of independence.

Köhler's experiments with chimpanzees clearly demonstrated that the apes' use of tools is primarily the result of the above described structures of a visual field. Köhler found brilliant experimental proof of this. The apes always coped with tasks involving the necessity to perceive and use those relations, forms, situations, and structures that had already been given or established. However, as soon as Köhler shifted to tasks involving any *mechanical* connection or attachment of objects, immediately "no trace of the ape's insight seemed to be left."

Köhler placed the stick used for obtaining the fruit some distance from the bars. To the stick he tied a short rope that was fastened to a metal ring on a vertical nail. The animals could not cope with such a simple task (taking the ring off the nail). They would tug the stick, gnaw at the rope, break the stick, but only once was one of the apes able to solve this task.

When the ring was attached directly to the stick, the task proved easier. On their better days, several chimpanzees took the stick off the nail, but for the most part this task presented an insurmountable difficulty. To this end Köhler (1921/1926) said: "The ring over the bar (the stick) seems to represent to the chimpanzee an optical complex which may still be mastered completely, . . . if there is concentration of attention and so on but it has a strong tendency to be seen less clearly if the animal fails to make the proper effort on its part" (p. 260).

From this point of view, the first experiment in Köhler's research on the chimpanzee is very demonstrative. As shown in Fig. 1.12, (taken from Köhler, 1921/1926) a basket of fruit was suspended 2 meters above the ground in such a way that the cord holding it was passed through an iron ring; the end of the cord was fastened by a loose loop to the bough of a nearby tree. The animal, who sees the goal and wishes to seize it, stands under this hanging basket. In order to solve the task he has to take down the loop from the bough, causing the basket to fall to the ground.

This task turns out to be too difficult for the apes. Here is how Sultan, the cleverest of the apes, solves the problem. A few minutes after the experiment has begun, Sultan suddenly climbs up the tree to the very loop and for a moment remains still. Looking at the basket, he pulls the cord toward himself so that the basket comes right up to the ring, then he again loosens his grasp; he pulls it up a second time more strongly so that the basket flies upward, and one banana accidentally falls to the ground. Sultan comes down, seizes the fruit, again climbs up the tree, and pulls the cord so

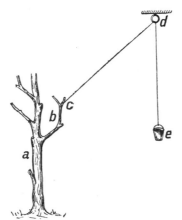

FIG. 1.12 *a* is the tree, *b* the bough, *c* the loop, *d* the ring, *e* the basket (Köhler, 1926, p. 8).

strongly that it breaks and the whole basket falls. The chimpanzee takes possession of the basket and goes off to eat the fruit (Köhler, 1921/1926, pp. 8–9; Koffka, 1925/1928, p. 201).

Three days later, this very same experiment was repeated under somewhat altered conditions. This time, the ape immediately chose the last mode of solving the problem, that is, breaking the cord.

Thus, the simplest mechanical connections proved extremely difficult and complicated for the apes, whereas in situations with tasks connected with visual structures, the animals cope with utmost ease.

In this respect, another observation by Köhler is of great interest to us: A certain animal, watching the actions of the others, can at the necessary moment sensibly intervene in the complex action of another. For example, Sultan sits some distance from the bars on the same side with the fruit and watches what the ape on the other side of the bars is doing to move the fruit toward itself. According to Köhler (1921/1926), the experiment was designed so that the subject ape was to find a substitution for the missing stick and use a stick that he must break off the lid of a box standing near the bars (p. 176).

Staying where he was, "Sultan watches the other animal's ill-adapted efforts quietly for a time. . . . Suddenly Sultan began to shuffle towards the bars, until he was quite close to them. He cast a few cautious glances at the observer, stretched his hand between the bars, and tore a loose board from the lid" and then put it into the hands of his comrade (Köhler, 1921/1926, pp. 176–177)

> It is clearly proved by the following instance that he really sees the task to be carried out, *from the standpoint of the other animal.* I was endeavouring to teach Chica the use of the double-stick. I stood outside the bars, Sultan squatted at my side, and gazed seriously, slowly scratching his head meanwhile. As Chica absolutely failed to realize what was required, I finally gave the two sticks to Sultan, in the hope that he would make things clear. He took the sticks, fitted one into the other, and did not himself appropriate the fruit, but pushed it, in a leisurely manner, towards Chica at the bars. (Köhler, 1921/1926, p. 177)

We see that both in play and in the experimental sessions, the apes pass on to one another some already acquired experience or mode of solving a task. Thus, at Köhler's station, the entire ape colony shared their experiences with each other. This was particularly obvious in the games where an invention or an innovation of one animal immediately became the general property (practice) of the entire group. Here the so-called "fashionable" games are especially noteworthy: the moment such a game was invented by one of the apes, it spread through the entire colony like the latest fashion in season. (Köhler, 1921/1926, pp. 171–178)

This, however, does not rule out the enormous individual differences so vividly revealed in Köhler's experiments. The apes differed greatly in mental abilities, deftness, and shrewdness. Those operations that the smartest was able to carry out proved absolutely beyond the scope of the "less clever."

Köhler believed that giftedness in anthropoid apes is no less variable than in man; at least, this is true of the intellect, a new, not yet established function. We know that, according to the famous biological law, new and not yet established features are characterized by the greatest variability, and that their diversity is the starting point for the development of a new form of adaptation in the process of natural selection.

INTELLECT AND THE NATURAL EXPERIENCE OF APES

With full justification, Bühler pointed out that Köhler's experiments showed the existence of a psychological connection between the apes' previous experience in the wild and their behavior at the station, a very important fact for understanding the experiments. He noted that in positively all of Köhler's experiments, the apes used in essence *only two general means of solving the task:* they always solved tasks either by proceeding from the spatial structures or by altering them. Simply put, they either moved themselves closer to the goal, using an indirect path, or they brought the goal closer to themselves.

Bühler went so far as to say that "the principle of using a roundabout path and the principle of obtaining fruit by lowering a branch, tearing it off, bringing it closer, are given to the animal like other instinctive mechanisms, some of which we cannot yet fully explain but whose existence we have to acknowledge as a fact."

Thus, according to Bühler, one must attribute very many of the apes' behaviors to instincts and natural training in the forest. Bühler tended to explain everything new and beyond instinct or training—that which was demonstrated in Köhler's experiments—as a special form of combinations of the apes' previous experiences or reactions.

It scarcely seems remarkable to us that the animal knows how to use branches for its ends, e.g., bending a branch to get at the fruit hanging on it, or breaking it off, striking with it, etc., as all this does not go beyond instinct and training. At any rate the correspondence between branch and fruit must be pretty well known to the tree-dweller. Now when he is sitting inside the experimental cage, with the branchless fruit outside and the fruitless branch inside, then from the psychological point of view, the main achievement is that he, as it were, brings them together perceptually or conceptually. The rest is self-evident. Similarly with the box: when the ape notices a fruit high up in the forest, nothing is more natural than that he should look about him for that tree trunk up which he has to climb to get at the fruit. In the cage there is a box in the field of vision instead of a tree and the psychic achievement consists in imagining this box placed at the proper spot. To wish and to do are then one, for the captive chimpanzee is always playing with boxes and dragging them about the place. (Bühler, 1930, p. 13)

Of utmost interest is Bühler's description of the way apes elongate a stick by inserting one piece of reed into another. In Bühler's view, the apes come across situations in their natural habitat where they have to connect two branches from different trees in order to move from one tree to another; for this they have to grasp the point of connection using the hand as a buckle, then move along this artificial bridge.

We may remember that this was precisely the way Sultan tried to make a long stick out of two short ones: that was how he clasped the point of connection with his hand. Thus, this detail in Köhler's experiments has, according to Bühler, its predecessor in the apes' natural forms of behavior.

Finding a link between the ape's reactions in the experiments and his previous experience provides us with the possibility of explaining with reasonable accuracy the third stage of development, which we call intellect. Just as the second stage of development (the conditional reflexes) is superimposed on top of the first and represents nothing more than a certain transformation, alteration or regrouping of inherent reactions, so too the third stage quite naturally develops from the second, and represents nothing more than a new and complex form of combinations of conditional reflexes.

Furthermore, in the same way that the development of the second stage from the first results in the appearance of an absolutely new quality and form of behavior and thus a new biological function, the third stage (the stage of intellectual reactions), developing from a complex combination of conditional reflexes, also brings to life a new form of behavior character-ized by its own specific biological function.

We shall briefly analyze the similar and different traits of the third and second stages, the links between the intellect and conditional reflexes, [in short] the features that characterize the intellect as a new and unique stage in behavioral development and, the stage that served as the starting point for development of all higher forms of human behavior.

Clearly, all the inventions the apes made in Köhler's experiments proved possible only because many of the situations in their previous wild life, as well as in the life of their ancestors, closely resembled the experimental situations artificially created by Köhler. This close bond between the apes' wild life and their performance in the experiments is most clearly seen, as was already mentioned, in play where the animals are by themselves and their "natural behavior" appears in its purest form.

Remember that in play the ape uses a stick for no special reason, as an object of play. As such, this stick begins to take on different functions: one time as a pole for climbing up, another time as a spoon to eat with, still another time as a weapon to attack or defend himself, then as a shovel to dig out roots. Lastly, in Köhler's (1921/1926) words, the stick is used simply as "a general tool" to touch things impossible to reach directly with the hand or things that for some reason [the animal] does not want to touch; for example, dirt on his body, a lizard, a mouse, an electric wire, and so on. (pp. 76–82).

Thus, the ape's ability to use a stick is not a sudden acquisition, but the result of all his previous experience in the wild. From this point of view, the ape's behavior in the experiment becomes clearer. The situation set up by Köhler does indeed resemble one in the forest.

In the forest, the ape often does see a piece of fruit at the end of a branch; he also sees the branch located between itself and the desired fruit and is able to use the branch for reaching its goal. When the fruit alone is placed on the other side of the bars and a branch without fruit is inside the cage, all the ape has to do is *to reestablish the former situation under new conditions,* that is, to reconnect the fruit and the branch. It goes without saying that constructing previous experience under new conditions plays an enormous role in the ape's behavior.

Consequently, an ape is capable of transferring an old structure to a new situation, a phenomenon that is absolutely analogous to the transference of structure in the experiments with the chicken. This type of transference can also be observed in Köhler's experiments. According to the law of structure, as we may recall, the individual elements of a situation may change, but the structure continues to act as an integral whole; and the structure as an integral whole determines all the features of every one of its elements. *The branch acquires this very structural meaning for an ape* and that is why the transference of the ape's previous experience to the new conditions becomes possible. According to Köhler (1921/1926):

> if we assert that the stick has now acquired a certain *functional or instru-mental value* in relation to the field of action under certain conditions, and that this value is extended to all other objects that resemble the stick, however remotely, in *outline* and *consistency*—whatever their other qualities may be— then we have formed the only assumption that will account for the observed and recorded behavior of these animals. Hats and shoes are certainly not visually identical with the stick and, therefore, interchangeable in the course of the test experiments; *only in certain circumstances are they functionally* sticks, after the function has once been invested in an object which resembles them in shape and consistency, namely a stick. (p. 37)

Remember that the ape who solved the task of getting the fruit with the help of a stick then substituted the stick with such things as a clump of straw, a rather long piece of cloth, and definitely any object that bore at least some slight resemblance to a stick. This demonstrates *the relative independence of a structure as a whole from the changes in its individual elements.* The type of transference performed here by the apes is, in essence, the reconstruction of the former structure in altered conditions.

This interpretation of Köhler's experiments allows us to understand, albeit in hypothetical terms, the inner processes occurring in the ape when it performs an experimental task. Let us remember again that in the most pure and simple case, the ape is able to solve the main task when two stimuli, both the stick and the fruit, act simultaneously [on the ape]. These two interconnected stimuli [the branch and the fruit — J. K.], although in a different combination, have already long influenced the ape during his wild life. Therefore, it comes as no surprise that both of these stimuli, now perceived independently of one another, reactivate those centers in the nervous system that had previously always acted together. The effect of this phenomenon is probably something like a short circuit of nervous current, that is, a connecting of two rather strongly excited centers.

One extremely important and significant circumstance may facilitate this process. This is the fact that the ape's reaction appears without fail in one condition: when instinctive and learned reactions fail the animal. In other words, the reaction appears when the ape finds itself in new conditions differing from those in which it has already grown accustomed to live and act or when it comes across a difficulty, a barrier, or an obstacle in the form of bars, of space separating him from the fruit, and so on.

Thus, the ape's intellectual reaction appears always in response to some obstacle, delay, difficulty, or barrier preventing its realization. The role that difficulties play in the process of acquiring new modes of action was made perfectly clear by Groos (1898/1907). He says,

> The moment repetition of a habitual reaction is interrupted, diverted, or delayed onto other paths, immediately consciousness rushes to the scene (if I may say so figuratively) in order to regain control over what it had before relegated to the domain of the unconscious processing of the nervous system.

> One question of particular interest for a psychologist concerns those most general *preexistent conditions* that primarily cause mental phenomena to appear. When the *set* (Einstellung) *for the realization of a habitual pattern does not find either immediately or ever the appropriate response* (the law of stoppage), then this conduces mental assessment in its, so to say, "natural form." Such a stoppage, activating the intellect although still not cognition itself, is connected either with a simple stumbling block when something unusual is confronted or when the expectation of something habitual [is thwarted — J. K.]. (Groos, 1898/1907)

Lipps (1907) described this phenomenon, formulating it as a fundamental psychological law that he called figuratively "the law of damning up."

According to this law, if, in the course of its realization a psychological process is delayed or hindered by some obstacle, then at this point there occurs an increase in power and energy of the process itself. In response to this damning up, the process tries with increased force either to overcome the obstacle or to get around it.

Lipps believed that this "law of damning up" explains the origins of any thought activity. "This law," according to Bühler, "is a type of biologically foreseen condition for the intervention of higher levels of our nervous system and spiritual life in the activity of lower levels."

Pavlov (1951) stressed the obstacle's stimulation of a goal-oriented reflex, which, from this viewpoint, is the main form of life's energy for any of us:

> All life, it's advancement, its culture, is created by the goal-oriented reflex, i.e., only by people striving towards this or that goal which they have set for themselves. An Anglo-Saxon, is the best embodiment of such a reflex and is well aware of it; for this reason when questioned about the main condition for achieving a goal, his response would seem startling and inconceivable to the Russian ear: the presence of obstacles. [To put in other words], he seems to be saying, 'Let my goal-oriented reflex exert itself in response to obstacles, then I will indeed reach the goal, however difficult it may be.' It is interesting that this answer completely ignores the impossibility of reaching the goal. (pp. 310–311)

Finally, let us remember that *all* our thinking develops from such difficulties. As Dewey demonstrated in his brilliant analysis of thought, any thinking develops from a difficulty. In theoretical thought, the difficulty from which we start is usually called a problem. Whenever everything is clear, whenever nothing is difficult for us, whenever there is no problem, then the thought process cannot even begin.

Coming back to the apes, we see that in the experiments, the most characteristic of their behavior was a delayed reaction to an obstacle. It is easy to see that even in the simplest experiments, any delay or obstacle impeding the animals' habitual course of action causes an increase in and overproduction of movements. The organism compensates for the confrontation with a difficulty.

Imagine a chicken accustomed to going every day after food through holes in the garden fence. Once, upon coming to the fence, she finds the holes so narrow that she cannot get through. How does she behave then?

She tries to crawl through too narrow a hole. Failure makes her try again and again, to go through the second, third, and fourth holes. A second failure produces great excitement in the chicken and results in so-called hyperkinesis, that is, overproduction of movements. Cackling, the chicken dashes about and runs along the fence, bustling helter-skelter through all the holes. The delay brings on a violent increase in all her activity. Thanks to these chaotic aimless attempts, thanks to the overproduction of movements, the chicken occasionally comes across a hole still wide enough for her to get through.

According to Bühler:

> The second, third, fifth time the hen behaves no differently, but when the same process is repeated a few dozen times, she gradually reaches the goal more quickly and eventually avoids useless routes altogether, by making straight for the hole. Frequent success has given this particular mode of behavior an advantage, failure has suppressed the others: a clear, unequivocal and sufficiently definite connection between the certain sense-impressions, and the successful mode of behavior has now been established. (1927/1930, p. 6)

An ant would behave in exactly the same way. If one puts an obstacle in its way, the ant starts running inconsistently in all directions, as if at a loss, but this reaction of confusion is of great biological significance. In response to difficulty, an animal does everything within its power [to overcome it — J. K.]. It makes many attempts, it rushes about, searching, and as a result, it increases its chances for finding the correct roundabout path.

This is also how a hungry dog behaves when, encaged like an ape, he sees a piece of meat outside the bars. Barking, he rushes to the meat. Again and again he tries to thrust a paw or muzzle through the bars; he runs along the bars, demonstrating great nervous excitement.

All these data suggest the indisputable conclusion that by itself an obstacle or delay in instinctive or habitual action augments nervous excitement and produces an increase in activity. Let us remember only that in the experiment, an ape can sit for hours, looking at fruit that is out of reach, or twiddle endlessly with sticks that prove to be of no use to him.

We see that the nervous excitement produced in the ape by the banana alone would never be able to sustain such a degree of attention, concentration, and constancy, if the stimulus were not combined with the augmenting influence of a delay, which in this case assumes the role of "teasing the instinct," to use the words of one psychologist. Indeed, if an ape were shown a banana that was then taken away, he would hardly concentrate his attention and efforts for hours on end trying to get hold of the fruit.

Thus, we must now incorporate the augmenting influence of a delay into our previous description of the processes taking place in the ape. We may assume that, due to this phenomenon, a "short circuit" is brought about between the excited centers in the ape's brain. In any event, the ape's external behavior gives us absolute grounds for such a supposition.

What in fact does distinguish the ape's behavior from that of an ant, chicken, or dog—all of which react with greatly increased movements in response to a delay or an obstacle? We could say that the more developed brain of the ape allows for the possibility of other forms and ways of rechanneling that nervous excitement that results from the "law of damning up." It is true that an ape in this case also behaves like the lower animals; sometimes he rushes about endlessly, trying to get the fruit, although even the first attempt may convince him it is impossible to do this directly.

However, quite soon a sudden and crucial change in the ape's behavior usually occurs. Instead of producing redundant movements, the ape usually stops his external reactions altogether; he remains seemingly immobile, his eyes fixed on the goal. A general delay or suspension of actions takes place.

(Here) amplified nervous excitement is not wasted on external chaotic movements, but is transformed into some complex, inner process. Along with Bühler, we might suggest that the ape shifts from external efforts to a type of inner probings, that is, we could say that the ape's excited nervous centers enter into some complex interaction or interrelation and that this results in the "short circuit" that could presumably explain [the mechanism of—J. K.] the ape's guess work.

We are still very far from a real psychological explanation of intellectual reaction. To this end, we can only construct schematic and more or less plausible assumptions. But we do have grounds to admit that this reaction is based on a complex interaction between present stimuli and previous conditional connections.

INTELLECT AS THE THIRD STAGE
IN THE DEVELOPMENT OF BEHAVIOR

We now dwell briefly on those new and specific features that the apes demonstrate in Köhler's experiments and that profoundly distinguish the third developmental stage from the second, that is, from conditional and trained responses. We can name several such features constituting this specificity.

The first and most significant feature differentiating these responses from a conditional reflex in the ape is the way in which they originate and emerge.

Let us examine the way a conditional reflex arises, that is, the way a response is established as a result of instruction or training. This is a slow and gradual process. Imagine that you are memorizing some poem. Every time you recite it, the number of mistakes [lapses of memory or omissions—J. K.] will be assessed: after the first time, there will probably be very many gaps—about 100%; after the second time, their number will slightly decrease; after the fifth or tenth time, it will decrease even more, so that after a certain number of repetitions, slowly and gradually the amount of mistakes will reach zero. If this process of learning—the decrease in mistakes after every repetition—is depicted with a curve, we will see a gently sloping line. The conditional reflex is usually established gradually and slowly.

The ape's reactions develop quite differently. If we drew a similar diagram for an ape as he solved this or that task, we would notice that in this case the mistake curve would drop vertically. When solving a task, the ape either makes 100% mistakes, that is, he cannot solve the task at all, or, once the correct solution is found, it solves the problem under any circumstances without memorization, repetition, or training—the number of mistakes immediately falls to zero.

A striking phenomenon found in Köhler's experiments is this remembering "once and for all" observed in apes. Bühler (1930) compares this with the well known facts about human memory (p. 14).

Everyone knows, Bühler (1919/1930) stated, that:

> a mathematical proof, for example, is not learnt by continued repetition, like a poem or vocabulary [of a foreign language—J. K.]. I was able to find this astonishing capability to remember in all those cases where the subject finds or 'discovers' the relation itself, and I think this is the main principle not only of so called logical memory but, if understood correctly, of all mnemotechnical systems which mnemonists used to astonish the world since ancient Greece]. (p. 14)[7]

Köhler's experiments proved that the chimpanzee's reactions were of absolutely the same type. Most often when some technique met success at least once, the animal was able to apply this new mode under greatly altered perceptible conditions.

Some psychologists find the grounds to explain this phenomenon of remembering "once and for all" in the law of structure.[8] The ape discovers the structure organizing a given situation and, having discovered this structure, it will from then on correctly determine the place and the meaning of each separate part in similar situations, even in altered conditions. From our personal experience, we all know that there are some things that must be remembered by many repetitions, whereas there are others that need to be understood only once for their structure to be preserved for a long time.

Furthermore, we can suggest that this type of remembering is directly connected with the difficulty and effort accompanying the ape's intellectual

---

[7]Within the brackets is the translation from the Russian text, the Bühler's English text seems to be a shortened version; there are many editions of Bühler's work, so the inconsistency is understandable.

[8]Law of structure is from the German term *Gestalt Theorie* and is also sometimes translated as the law of form or law of configuration.

reaction. As is well known, functions of memory are based on the development of nerve paths, and it is easily understood that in cases when activation is relatively weak, development of such a nerve path, that is, leaving a "trace," requires long and multiple nervous activation of the same route. [We could compare this with] how a wheel slowly and gradually makes a rut in the road. When a new nerve route is being established, strong nervous activation accompanying a delay may act like a short circuit, like an explosion used to make mountain tunnels.

In any event, many psychologists have experimentally proved that any great effort that we exert in the act of remembering may in and of itself serve as a stimulus for a faster and more permanent remembering. However paradoxical this may sound, we remember better what is difficult than what is easy; in certain circumstances we remember better those things that require mental efforts than those that pass easily before our eyes and ears, calling for no effort.

The second new feature that elevates intellect above conditional reflexes and distinguishes it from all other reactions is its biological function. In Köhler's experiments, the ape makes discoveries; he invents. Bühler explained:

> Invention in the real sense of the word is the biological function of intellect. Man creates tools for himself and uses them, while animals do not. However, this ancient thesis founded on obvious facts is, as we learned in 1917, not without exception, since anthropoid apes do use and, when the need arises, create tools themselves.[9]

In Köhler's experiments, the ape finds himself in a new situation every time. No one shows or instructs him how to act in order to get out of some difficulty. The ape's behavior is that of adapting to new circumstances and

---

[9]In *Mental Development of the Child*, Bühler (1919/1930) said that the ape:

> is able to do justice to new, unusual situations suddenly. . . . not by trying, nor by acquiring rapidity and precision with practice, but by an inner (psychic) process. This psychic process is equivalent, as far as its results go, to those processes which in ourselves we call *reflection;* quite possibly in simpler cases it is no more than a kind of inner groping, as it were, a (relatively) lively mechanism of imaginal processes to which chance finds the key. Many an invention and discovery of man takes place in the same way. (p. 14)

This psychic inner process seems to correspond to what Vygotsky refers to as a "short circuiting" that occurs when some new path or channel is suddenly taken or discovered. This "psychic" energy or inner activity that occurs in face of a difficult situation seems for both Bühler and Vygotsky to be the biological basis for the "intellect" or reflection, providing the ability "to discover and invent," which "is precisely the specific achievement of this third stage in mental development." (Bühler, 1919/1930, p. 14).

new conditions where instinctive and trained movements are no longer of use.

Thus, the work of the intellect begins at the point where the activity of instinct and conditional reflexes stops or is blocked. Adapting to altered conditions, new circumstances, and new situations is what characterizes the behavior of apes. The animals in Köhler's experiments adapt to these new circumstances not the way the chicken does before the garden fence, that is, not by trial and error, but by delaying external movements and by "probing internally."

Bühler stated:

> I would introduce the word 'invention' as a technical term for such actions by the ape. The reason here is that in essence the apes *overcome* the new situational difficulty not by external techniques or various effects and attempts, but evidently by an inner (psychophysical) process, subsequently the decision seems to appear suddenly as a ready made response, i.e., the observable action is immediately performed quite smoothly as if a well learned habit.

Köhler supplied interesting descriptions of the animals' appearance and expressive gestures in mid-stream of solving a particular task:

> One has to really see how incredibly foolish a chimpanzee looks, when he cannot find a solution; how, in a man-like fashion, he scratches his head, when he falls into thought; how a sudden change occurs in the animal's behavior, how ideas, distracted glances and chaotic motions cease; how at this moment the animal's entire facial expression and movements are filled with lucidity and how he then solves the task within seconds, though previously he had behaved for hours on end nonsensically, incoherently and stupidly.

Bühler (1919/1930) compared this sudden change in the apes with a similar phenomenon that he observed in experimental situations with people whom he had given difficult mental tasks. "Very often the solution dawns upon us suddenly." He continues:

> The only account that they could give was that their decision had come to them with a sudden 'inner exclamation—AHA!' and therefore I am of the opinion that language has created a special interjection for this sudden 'inner illumination'—AHA' exclusively for the purpose of reporting these and similar experiences. Köhler's chimpanzees have experienced this 'AHA!' or something analogous to it (p. 14).

The apes' discoveries pose still a third distinctive property. This is the definite independence of the invented behavioral mode from the concrete situation in which it was discovered. Having found the true solution, the ape immediately acquires the ability to transfer it widely to other situations.

As we have already indicated, for the ape a tool acquires a "functional meaning" that subsequently may be transferred to any other object — a piece of cloth, a clump of hay, a shoe, a brim of a straw hat, and so on. Thus, the ape [solving the task — J. K.] deciphers the structure, instead of developing the habit of reacting to the constituent parts, and therefore his solution proves to be largely independent of the concrete elements. (See Koffka, 1925/1928, p. 210.)

If the ability to use tools was developed in the ape as a result of instruction and training, then this ability would be tied to the objects used for training. Had the ape, for example, been trained to get fruit with a stick, he would in no way use a piece of cloth or hat brims for the same purpose. It is this transference of structure from some objects to others that also sharply distinguishes the apes' intellectual reaction from conditional reflexes.

According to Edinger:

> study of the animal kingdom has shown that the whole of the mechanism, from the end of the spinal cord to the olfactory nerves, including the paleencephalon [primary brain], is in principle similarly arranged in all higher and lower vertebrates, that is to say, the basis of the simplest functions is the same right through the series, in man as well as in fish. (cited in Bühler, 1919/1930, p. 17)

Edinger believed that each new psychological ability or form of behavior appearing in phylogenetic development is also accompanied, as we may observe, by a new brain formation that gives rise to this ability. "But the neencephalan superimposes itself on the palaencephalon as a new apparatus, beginning with the reptiles and growing rapidly, until in man it spreads like a large cloak over the whole of it" (cited in Bühler, 1919/1930, p. 17). Edinger found this to be the basis of the animal's increasing capacity to be trained. Moreover, Pavlov's research has shown that the brain cortex is the organ circuiting conditional reflexes, that is, the organic basis of the second stage in behavioral development.

According to Bühler (1919/1930): "There seem also be be anatomical facts in support of the assumption of a third level in the structure of the human brain. In the anthropoid apes, and far more so in man, one finds a new increase in the relative weight of the brain, which takes place chiefly in the cortex. New fields with rich fibre connections in all directions are developed in the cortex and pushed in between the old ones, in man above all the infinitely important centres for speech" (p. 18).

Just as the new brain is superimposed on top of the old one, so too any new step in behavioral development associated with the new brain formation appears on top of the previous stage. In his description of the ape's behavior, Bühler (1919/1930) said: "We can see no break with the past. This new great step forward [perhaps all that places a chimpanzee above a dog] was perhaps introduced merely by a small advance on conceptualization or a somewhat freer play of associations. The point is *that proper use had to be made of it*" (p. 19).

Thus, we see that in the ape's behavior a new form — the intellect — begins to emerge quite distinctly; it is the basic prerequisite for the development of labor activity and also serves as the link between the behavior of ape and of man. The most important thing, according to Köhler, is that the anthropoid ape in many respects is closer to man than to other breeds of apes: "Especially the somatic chemism, revealed in the characteristics of the blood, and the structure of the highest organ — the major brain — turned out to be more akin to man's than to the lower apes."

No less important than the experimental data are Köhler's observations of ape behavior in play that were mentioned earlier, which have great significance for his research. Here, as we saw, apes on their own widely used tools and then transferred this activity along with the means of the solution to experimental tasks, and, vice versa, they quite eagerly used in play those achievements that they recently managed to attain in an experiment.

The fact that in play apes manipulate things undoubtedly suggests that their use of tools is not accidental, but highly consequential from a psychological point of view. As we have already mentioned, a very special role in these games belongs to the stick. Köhler (1921/1926) explained: "The stick is a sort of general tool in the chimpanzee's hands; it can be turned to account in almost any circumstances, when its use has become knowledge and property; its functions extend and vary from month to month" (p. 76).

It has already been shown that the apes use the stick as a lever, a spoon, a shovel, and a weapon. Köhler described all these cases in the apes' play with great detail.

The apes reveal a similar "handling of things," a similar use of objects, when decorating themselves. In their games, we see the apes decorating themselves with various odds and ends. As Köhler describes, the apes eagerly put on a large number of the most different objects. Almost daily, one can see some animal with a cord, a cabbage leaf, a twig, or a scrap of wool over his shoulders. When Tschego [a female ape] was given a metal chain, it immediately ended up on her body. Countless numbers of reeds are often strewn over the back and a cord or scrap of wool is usually draped across the neck, hanging down from both shoulders to the ground.

Tercera hangs a rope around her neck and over her ears so that it frames both sides of her face. Whenever these things fall down, the ape holds them with her teeth. Once Sultan got the idea to decorate himself with empty tins, holding them between his teeth. Chica sometimes derived pleasure from decorating her back with heavy stones; upon finding heavy pieces of lava, she started with four and eventually reached nine German pounds (Köhler, 1921/1926, p. 95).

The essence of all these decorations, as Köhler (1926) showed, is not the production of a visual effect, but "the extraordinary *heightened bodily consciousness*" — a feeling of self (p. 97). The basis for this increase is that when some other object moves together with the body, it enriches and magnifies the sensation derived from movement.

Summing up his studies, Köhler (1921/1926) concluded:

> The chimpanzees manifest intelligent behavior of the general kind familiar in human beings. Not all their intelligent acts are externally similar to human acts, but under well-chosen experimental conditions, the type of intelligent conduct can always be traced. This applies, in spite of every important difference between one animal and another, even to the least gifted specimens of the species that have been observed here, and, therefore, must hold good of every member of the species, as long as it is not mentally deficient, in the pathological sense of the words. . . .

> At any rate, this remains true: Chimpanzees not only stand out against the rest of the animal world by several morphological and, in its narrower sense, physiological, characteristics, but they also behave in a way which counts as specifically human. As yet we know little of their neighbours on the other side, but according to the little we do know, with the results of this report, it is not impossible that, in this region of experimental research, the anthropoid is nearer to man *in intelligence too,* than to many of the lower ape-species. So far, observations agree well with the theories of evolution; in particular, the correlation between intelligence, and the development of the brain, is confirmed. (pp. 275–276)

USE OF THE TOOL AS A PSYCHOLOGICAL PREREQUISITE FOR LABOR

There are, however, extremely important characteristics that allow us to delineate the apes' behavior from that of man and to present in a true light man's behavior, in the proper sense of the word. All researchers agree in their portrayal of these characteristics. We explain them with a simple example taken from Köhler.

At one point, lumps of white clay were brought to the apes' play area. Without any outside instigation, the apes, while playing with the clay, "discovered" painting. The next time the apes got the clay, the same thing immediately began again. Köhler (1921/1926) explained:

At first the chimpanzees licked the unknown stuff; very likely they wanted to see how it tasted. The result being unsatisfactory, as usual in similar cases they wiped their protruding lips on the nearest object they could find, and, of course, made it white. But, after a while, the painting of beams, iron bars, and walls grew to be quite a game on its own; the animals would seize the clay with lips, sometimes crush it into paste in their mouths, moistening it, and would then apply the mixture, make fresh paint, and daub again, and so on. *The point is the painting, not the chewing of the clay;* for the painter himself, and the rest of them, when not too much occupied with their own affairs, are most interested in the result.

Soon, as is to be expected, the chimpanzees stop using their lips as paint-brushes and, taking the lumps of clay in their hands whitewash their objects much more quickly and firmly. Of course, they have not yet achieved more than big white blobs, or, when particularly energetic, getting a whole beam-surface whitened. Later on the animals were given other colours. (pp. 100–101)

Precisely the absence of at least the beginnings of speech in the widest sense of the word—the lack of ability to make a sign, or introduce some auxiliary psychological means that everywhere marks man's behavior and man's culture—draws the line between the ape and the most primitive human being. Apropos of this, Bühler recalls Goethe's thesis on colors, which says that "mixing, smearing and dabbling with paints are inherent in man."

"According to Köhler's observations," Bühler said, "it turns out that mixing, soiling and smearing paints are inborn tendencies for the ape as well, but, in as much as we know, it is highly unlikely that at some time the chimpanzee saw a pictorial sign in a stain left by a crushed berry."

Köhler himself attempted to set the scientific boundaries for an accurate evaluation of the results from his experiments. In connection with this, Köhler noted that all the apes' actions in his experiments related to *"a given actual situation,"* and therefore, it is impossible to judge how far back and forward the time in which the apes lived stretches.

A great deal of time spent with chimpanzees leads me to venture the opinion that, beside the lack of speech, it is in extremely narrow limits in *this* direction that the chief difference is to be found between anthropoids and even the most primitive human beings. The lack of an invaluable technical aid (speech) and a great limitation to those very important components of thought, so-called 'images', would thus constitute the causes that prevent the chimpanzee from attaining even the smallest beginnings of cultural development. (Köhler, 1926, p. 277)

Of utmost importance for the history of thought development is the fact that thinking in a chimpanzee is absolutely independent of speech. We see the chimpanzee in a purely biological form of nonverbal thought that convinces us of the view that the genetic roots of thought and speech are different in the animal world. All the factors separating the behavior of ape and man could be summed up and expressed in one general statement to this effect: in spite of the fact that the ape displays an ability to invent and use tools — the prerequisite for all human cultural development — the activity of labor, founded on this ability, has still not even minimally developed in the ape. *Use of tools in the absence of labor* is what draws the behavior of man and ape closer and at the same time separates them.

This position finds indisputable confirmation in the biological role that the use of tools plays for apes. In general, this form of behavior does not constitute the main form of adaptation for them. We cannot say that the ape adapts itself to its environment with the help of tools.

Darwin's rejection of the opinion that only man uses tools is well known. He demonstrated that in rudimentary form, the use of tools is peculiar to other animals, particularly in apes. Addressing this issue, Plekhanov said: "Darwin is most probably right from his own point of view, i.e., in the sense that in the notorious 'nature of man' we cannot find a single feature not seen first in some species of animal, and that for this reason, we have absolutely no grounds for designating man as some kind of unique creature, or, in other words, for placing him in a special 'kingdom.' "

However, we must not forget that *quantitative differences may transform into qualitative ones.* What may exist as *a rudimentary form* in one animal may become *outstanding signs* (in other species). We have to say that this is particularly true when it comes to the use of tools. An elephant breaks branches and uses them to swish away flies. This is interesting and instructive. But using branches to battle flies probably played no substantial role in the history of the development of "the elephant" species. Elephants did not become elephants for the reason that their more or less elephant-like ancestors swatted flies with branches.

This is not the case with man. The entire existence of an Australian aborigine depends on his boomerang, just as the entire existence of modern England depends upon her machines. Take the boomerang away from the aborigines make him a farmer, then out of necessity he will have to completely change his life style, his habits, his entire style of thinking, his entire nature.

We see something similar with respect to the apes. True, the use of tools is incomparably more developed in apes than in elephants. In the ape's stick, we already see the prototype not only of a tool in general, but of a whole series of differentiated tools: shovels, spears, and so on. But even in the case of the apes, at the highest point of development of tool use in the animal world, these tools still do not play a decisive role in the struggle for survival. In the history of ape development, there has still not been that jump forward that constitutes the process of transforming ape into man, and that, from the point of view of our interest, is concluded in the fact that tools of labor become the basis of adaptation to nature. In the process of ape development, this jump forward is begun but not completed. In order for it to be completed, a new special form of adaptation to nature, foreign to apes, must be developed — namely labor.

Labor, as Engels (1960) showed, is the main factor in the process of transition from ape into man. "It is the primary basic condition of human existence, and this to such a degree that, in a sense, we have to say that labor created man himself" (p. 279).

Engels pointed out the following path of the evolutionary process from ape to man. He considered the first decisive stope in this transformation to be the separation of the functions of the hands and feet, a separation that developed as a result of the forest life, the emancipation of the hands from movement across the ground, and the beginning of learning to walk standing upright. Precisely this differentiation in the roles of the hands feet led to completely new functions that the hands began to take on.

With its hands, the ape seizes a club or stones, or builds a nest or a blind. "But it is just here that one sees how great is the gulf between the undeveloped hand of even the most anthropoid of apes and the human hand that has been highly perfected by the labour of hundreds of thousands of years. The number and general arrangement of the bones and muscles are the same in both; but the hand of the lowest savage can perform hundreds of operations that no monkey's hand can imitate" (Engels, 1960, p. 281). Thus, in one sense, freeing the hand becomes a prerequisite for labor. In another sense, it becomes the consequence of its process. Engels (1960) stated: "The hand is not only the organ of labor, *it is also the product of labour*" (p. 282).

The development of the whole unusually complex organism of man's ancestors occurred simultaneously with the development of the hand and its transformation into an organ of labor. Engels (1960) said: "The mastery over nature, which begins with the development of the hand, with labour, widened man's horizon at every new advance," Labor served to more closely unite society. Joint activity, mutual support become the basic factors of activity (p. 282).

"In short, men in the making arrived at the point where *they had something to say* to one another" (Engels, 1960, p. 283). Labor, strictly speaking, played no role whatsoever for that race of apes from which man evolved.

"The labour process begins with the making of tools. . . . They are hunting and fishing implements, the former at the same time serve as weapons" (Engels, 1960, pp. 286–287). But, as we well know, similar forms of adaptation still play no role whatsoever for the ape. "By the co-operation of hands, organs of speech, and brain, not only in each individual, but also in society, human beings became capable of executing more and more complicated operations, and of setting themselves, and achieving, higher and higher aims" (Engels, 1960, p. 288).

Engels saw the existence of a difference between the behavior of animals and the behavior of man *not in the fact* that animals lack the ability to plan actions:

> On the contrary, a planned mode of action exists in embryo wherever protoplasm, living protein, exists and reacts, *i.e.* carries out definite, even if extremely simple, movements as a result of definite external stimuli.

> But all the planned action of all animals has never resulted in impressing the stamp of their will upon nature. For that, man was required. In short, the animal merely *uses* external nature, and brings about changes in it simply by his presence; man by his changes makes it serve his ends, *masters it*. This is the final, essential distinction between man and other animals, and once again it is labour that brings about this distinction. (pp. 290–291)

Something similar occurs also in the realm of man's psychological development. Here we may say that the animal is totally bound up in his own nature, whereas man rules nature and forces it to serve his goals. Here again he is obliged to labor. The process of labor demands that man has a certain degree of control over his own behavior. This control over himself, in essence, is based on the same principle as is our control over nature.

> Thus, at every step we are reminded that we by no means rule over nature like a conqueror over a foreign people, like someone standing outside nature — but that we, with flesh, blood, and brain, belong to nature, and exist in its midst, and that all our mastery of it consists in the fact that we have the advantage over all other beings of being able to know and correctly apply its laws. (Engels, 1960, p. 292)

An active intervention in nature's course is based precisely on this understanding of its laws. Engels (1960) continued: "But the more this happens, the more will men not only feel, but also know, their unity with nature, and thus the more impossible will become the senseless and anti-natural idea of a contradiction between mind and matter, man and nature, soul and body, such as arose in Europe after the decline of classic antiquity and which obtained its highest elaboration in Christianity" (p. 293).

Thus, in the sphere of adaptation to nature, the absence of labor and, connected with it, control over nature distinguishes ape from man. In the ape, the process of adapting can be generally characterized as a manipulation of external natural conditions and passive adaptation to them. In the psychological sphere, it is again characteristic for the ape to lack self-control over behavior or, in other words, to be unable to control behavior with the help of artificial signs. This constitutes the essence of the cultural development of man's behavior.

"The use and creation of means of labor," wrote Marx, "even if in embryos for certain animal species, makes up the specific feature characteristic for the human process of labor, and therefore Franklin defines man as a tool creating animal."

Plekhanov stated:

In tools, man seemingly acquired new organs, changing his anatomical structure. Since that time, when he rose to the use of tools, he has given an absolutely new form to the history of his development: formally, as in the case of all other animals, this led to a modification of his natural organs; now it first and foremost becomes *the history of perfecting his artificial organs, of the growth of his productive forces.*

Marx saw the essence of the labor process in the fact that: "an object given by nature itself becomes an organ of his (man's) activity, an organ which he annexes to the organs of his body, in the way extending, in spite of the bible, the natural dimensions of the latter."

Therefore, from the moment of his transition to labor as the basic form of adaption, man's development consists of the history of perfecting his artificial organs and advances "in spite of the bible," that is, not along the line of perfecting his natural organs, but along the line of perfecting artificial tools.

In the same way, in the area of man's psychological development from the moment of the acquisition and use of signs, which allow man to gain control over his own processes of behavior, the history of behavioral development, to a significant degree, transforms into the history of the development of artificial, auxiliary "means of behavior"—into the history of man's mastering his own behavior.

In this light, Engels explained the concept of free will, saying that:

freedom stems from [man's] dominance *over himself and over surrounding nature,* a dominance which is based on an understanding of the laws of nature, and therefore it necessarily is a product of historical development. The first human beings to emerge from the animal kingdom were in all respects just as unfree as the animals themselves; however, each step in the progress of culture led forward to freedom.

Thus, we see that in the sphere of psychological development a sudden change occurs at the very moment that tools are introduced into use—the same time at which it occurs in the sphere of biological adaptation. This view, best expressed by Bacon, we have introduced here in the form of an epigraph that says the following: "The bare hand and the intellect left to its own disposal is not worth very much: everything is accomplished with the help of tools and auxiliary means."

This, of course, does not mean that the development of the hand, of this fundamental organ, and of the intellect, when at its own disposal, ceases the moment man's historical development begins. On the contrary, the hand and the brain as natural organs probably never developed as fast or with such a giant tempo as in the period of historical development.

The development of man's behavior, however, is always development conditioned primarily not by the laws of biological evolution, but by the laws of the historical development of society. Perfecting the "means of labor" and the "means of behavior" in the form of language and other sign systems, that is, auxiliary tools in the process of mastering behavior, occupies first place, superseding the development of "the bare hand and the intellect on its own."

If we look at this whole stage through which the ape passes in the development of behavior, we have to say that the embryo of labor activity — the necessary prerequisite for its origin — exists in the ape in the form of the development of the hand and the intellect that, when taken together, lead to the use of tools. However, we will not find in the ape prerequisites for self-control or for the use of signs, however primitive. These appear only in the historical period of the development of human behavior and makes up the main content of the entire history of cultural development. In this sense, "labor created man himself" (Engels, 1960, p. 279).

2 Primitive And His Behavior

THREE LINES OF PSYCHOLOGICAL BEHAVIOR

In the science of psychology, one thought has taken deep roots, namely that all man's psychological functions must be examined as a product of development. "The behavior of man," Blonskii[1] says, "must be understood exclusively as the history of behavior."

Up to now, two lines of psychological development have been studied very extensively. Psychology has analyzed the behavior of man as the result of prolonged biological evolution, finding embryos of the most complicated forms of human activity in the simplest one-celled organisms. Psychology has taken primitive reactions, "movements *from something to something,*" as the starting point for an understanding of the highest forms of thought and will in modern man.

Psychology sees in animal instincts the prototype of emotions; it finds in human fear and anger traces of the predatory animal's flight and attack instincts. Psychology sees initial conditional reflexes, being studied in the laboratories, as the basis for the development of all human complex activity, a product of the cortex. It attempts to incorporate within a single law the movement of plants stretching toward the sun and Newton's

---

[1]Pavel Petrovich Blonskii (1884–1941), an older colleague in Soviet psychology, had already adopted a developmental approach prior to Vygotsky's work. Vygotsky does not give a reference for this quotation. For a list of Blonskii's works, see volume 4 of Vygotsky's (1984) *Sobranie Sochinenii,* (p. 426). Blonskii was first and foremost a pedologist, and it was that side of his work that Vygotsky borrowed from extensively.

calculations for the law of universal gravity "as individual links," to use Pavlov's words, "in a single chain of biological adaptation of organisms."

Finally, with the recent discoveries of Köhler, the subject of the preceding chapter, psychology has gained the missing link that unites the behavior of man with the behavior of his nearest relative in the biological evolutionary line—the anthropoid apes. The complete triumph of Darwinism in psychology was made possible only thanks to the discovery that revealed that the essential trait of human intellect—the invention and use of tools—goes back in its development to the behavior of apes who, in certain conditions, are also able to invent and use the simplest tools.

Thus, in the animal world we have succeeded in discovering the roots of even that specific form of human active adaptation to the environment that distinguished man from the all the rest of the animal kingdom and brought him along the path of historical development. The role of labor in the transformation of ape to man, [first—J. K.] pointed out by Engels, was confirmed in this case by scientific experiment.

All of this taken together has firmly and inseparably linked the psychology of man with a biological evolutionary psychology and has taught investigators to see that, to a significant degree, the behavior of man is up to now the behavior of an animal that has raised itself up on its hind legs and speaks, to use Blonskii's expression.

Another line of development has been studied just as extensively. Human adult behavior, as psychologists long ago established, is not formed immediately, but arises gradually and develops from child behavior. Albeit, psychologists and philosophers previously were eager to admit that man's ideas and thoughts constitute the innate core of his human soul and do not undergo development when the body of the child develops.

They were inclined to assert that the loftiest of man's ideas are present in the child at the moment of birth or even earlier. "I do not contend," wrote Descarte on this subject, "that the spirit of an infant in his mother's womb meditates about metaphysical questions, but he does have ideas about God, himself and all other truths which are known in and of themselves, just as they exist for adults, even when the latter don't think about these truths."

Conclusions drawn on the basis of such an assertion were formulated by Malebranche,[2] who maintained that abstract, logical, metaphysical, and mathematical knowledge is most accessible to children. If ideas innately exist in children, then it is necessary to communicate eternal truths to them as early as possible. The closer to the innate source, then the purer and truer the idea itself will be. The child's later sensory experience, grounded on incidental facts, will cloud the initial purity of an innate idea.

---

[2]Nicolas de Malebranche (1638–1715), a French Cartesian philosopher and physicist who attempted to extend Descarte's philosophy with respect to body–mind interaction.

The science of psychology long ago formulated these positions and adopted the principle that adult thinking and behavior must be analyzed as the product of a very prolonged and complicated process of child development. Psychology has tried to establish as carefully as possible all the quantitative transformations from one form of behavior to another, that is, all the quantitative changes, which when taken together make up the basis of child development.

Psychology has traced how, little by little, individual flashes of human speech arise from the cry of a newborn and the babble of an infant and how the process of speech acquisition basically comes to an end only by the age of sexual maturation, because only at this time does speech become an instrument for forming abstract concepts — a means of abstract thought — for the child.

It [psychology] then traces how play reveals, develops, and shapes a child's future leanings, abilities, and talents; how in children's inventions, elements of creative imagination ripen and are given practice and how this will facilitate his future artistic and scientific activity.

Both of the just-mentioned approaches to development have taken sufficient hold in psychology. There is, however, also a third line of development, which has made far less headway in the consciousness of psychologists and that is uniquely different when compared with the other two types of behavior — this is historical development.

The behavior of modern, cultural man is not only the product of biological evolution or the result of childhood development, but also the product of historical development. In the process of mankind's historical development, change and development occurred not only in the external relations between people and in man's relationship with nature; man himself, his very nature, changed and developed.

As a result of these changes occurring over a long period of time, a psychological type of modern cultural man, the European or American, was formed. We can only understand the features of this type if we also add the genetic point of view to their explanation — if we ask from where and how they originated.

The historical development of man's behavior has been less adequately studied than the other two lines of development because science has had at its disposal much less material relating to the historical changes in human nature than that relating to child development or biological development. The vast and varied animal world, which came to a stand still at different stages of the "origin of the species," gives us a type of live panorama of biological evolution and allows us to add statistics of comparative psychology to the data of comparative anatomy and physiology.

Child development is a process that takes place over and over again before our very eyes. It offers us the most varied types of research. The process of historical change in human psychology, however, is placed in far less favorable conditions for research. Vanished historical epochs have left documents and traces of the past.

A superficial history of the human species can be rather easily reconstructed on the basis of these documents and remnants. At the same time, psychological mechanisms of behavior did not leave traces in any objective or complete form. Therefore, *historical psychology* has considerably less material at its disposal.

Therefore, investigation of so-called primitive peoples is one of the richest sources for psychology. Certain peoples of the uncivilized world, being on the lowest rungs of cultural development, are usually called primitive or primal people in, of course, the relative sense of the word. These people cannot by full right be called primitive, because they all seem to possess a greater or lesser degree of civilization. They all come from the prehistoric period of man's existence. Many of them possess very ancient traditions. A few have experienced for themselves the influence of distant and powerful cultures. Others regressed to a lower level of development.

In the strict sense of the word, primitive man now exists nowhere, and the human type, as he is represented among primeval [the earliest] peoples may be called primitive only relatively speaking. Primitiveness in this sense is the lowest stage and starting point of man's historical development. Data about prehistoric man, about peoples at the lowest rung of cultural development, about comparative psychology of peoples of a different culture, serve as material for the psychology of primitive man.

The psychology of primitive man has not yet been established. Now psychological materials are being accumulated in this area, methods of working with them are being developed, and, according to Thurnwald,[3] a psychological view is permeating ethnographic material.

THREE THEORIES OF CULTURAL HISTORICAL DEVELOPMENT

The first task that arises when facing the question of man's historical development is defining the specificity of that developmental process encountered in this case. Psychology has advanced, one right after another,

---

[3]Richard Thurnwald (1869–1954), a psychological anthropologist and socialist who departed from the views of Wundt and Lévy-Bruhl, believing that the comparison of different social institutions of different societies could establish sequences of historical development and differences in *functional* social structures that foster higher mental processes. His book, *Black and White in East Africa* (Thurnwald, 1935) is devoted to his study of primitive communities and drew Vygotsky's interest here.

three viewpoints and three principles that characterize man's historical development.

The first point of view advanced in their day by Tylor[4] and Spencer[5] guided the first ethnographists and ethnologists, who collected a vast amount of factual material on the questions of the morals, beliefs, habits, institutions, and language of primitive peoples.

In psychology, these authors stood for the view point of so-called associationism.[6] They proposed that the basic law of psychology is the law of association, that is, the connection established between elements of our experience on the basis of their contiguity and likeness. Laws of the human spirit, as these authors suggested, are always one and the same at all times throughout the entire global sphere.

The mechanism of mental activity, the structure itself of the processes of thought and behavior, do not differ in a primitive man and an en-culturated man, and the entire specificity of a primitive man's behavior and thought in comparison with that of an en-culturated man may, according to this theory, be understood and explained *from those conditions* in which the savage lives and thinks.

If we, as enculturated people, on one fine day, were to be deprived of all the enormous experience accumulated by man and were placed in the conditions of life in which the primitive man lived, we would think and act,

---

[4]Sir Edward Burnett Tylor (1832-1917), an English anthropologist who investigated mythology, magic, and primitive mentality from a Darwinian point of view (cf. Tylor, 1874, 1877). Although Vygotsky does not indicate here which study he may have in mind, he no doubt is referring to Lévy-Bruhl's (1910/1926) *How Natives Think,* where the latter writes "At the time *Primitive Culture* appeared and for some years after, the philosophy of associationism seemed to have a definite sway" (p. 26).

[5]Herbert Spencer (1820-1903) advanced the theory of evolutionary associationism. He, along with Alexander Bain, was the last in the line of British associationists. His most important work was *Principles of Psychology* (1871). According to Corsini (1984):

Spencer applied J. B. P. Lamarck's evolutionary theory of inheritance of acquired characteristics to his own theory. He believed that when the same associations occurred over and over again in an individual, they could be passed onto that person's offspring. After many generations, these eventually would take the form of instincts (Vol. 3, p. 357).

Later, Pavlov in Russia and Thorndike in the United States put these principles to experimental tests. According to Lévy-Bruhl (1910/1926): "the evolutionism of Herbert Spencer, then greatly in repute, exercised considerable fascination over many minds" (p. 3). In all likelihood, Vygotsky himself shares the same view.

[6]The theory of evolutionary associationism was advanced, above all, by the British associationists, particularly Herbert Spencer (1820-1903) and Alexander Bain who proposed two basic laws of association: similarity and contiguity. Accordingly, "sensations and feelings come together in close succession in such a way that when one of them is brought to mind, the other is most likely" to follow. (See Corsini, 1984, Vol. 2, p. 419.)

Tylor and Spencer said, the same way that a primitive man thinks and acts. Consequently, this is not a question of the apparatus of thought and behavior and its special mechanisms, which distinguish a cultural [enculturated — J. K.] mind from one not exposed to culture — this is only a question of *the quantity of experience* that both have acquired.

Hence, from this position, animism or the theory of universal animation of all natural phenomena and objects is considered by these authors to be the central phenomena which lies at the heart of the cultural development of primitive man.

The law of the association of ideas and the naive application of the principle of causality is, for Tylor and Spencer, an explanation for the rise of animism (this natural philosophy of primitive man), which grows out of the natural laws of the human spirit. The sameness of the human spirit throughout the entire globe is accepted as an axiom by these two authors. In particular, the concurrence of individual religions, morals, and institutions, observed among peoples living in the most remote parts of the earth, speaks in favor of the correctness of this view.

Thus, the fundamental psychological mechanism of behavior — the law of association of ideas, and the basic principle of logical thought (the principle of causality) represent the common property of both primitive and cultural man. However, these two mechanisms — psychological association and logical thinking — have been put to extensive use only in cultural man, whereas the experience of primitive man is limited and the material is not large. This gives rise to the difference between the psychology of the former [cultural man] and the latter [primitive man].

It is easy to see that, when put this way, the very question of man's psychological development throughout the course of history is dismissed. As such, development is not possible when, at the very beginning of the path, we have absolutely the same phenomena as at the end. What is meant here is not development in the strict sense of the word, but sooner accumulation of experience. The very mechanism for accumulating and processing this experience in principle in no way differs at the initial and final stages. It [the mechanism — J. K.] alone remains unchanged in the course of universal historical change.

Psychology has long since abandoned this naive point of view. There is nothing more naive than picturing primitive man as a natural philosopher and explaining all his thought and behavior according to the particularities of his philosophy. Not theoretical and ideal interests, but material needs motivate the development of human thought and behavior: Primitive man acts more under the influence of practical rather than theoretical motives, and in his own mind [psychology], logical thought is subordinated to instinctive and emotional reactions.

M. Pokrovsky[7] wrote:

There is no greater fallacy than picturing the world view of a savage as the source of his religion; on the contrary, a world view is formed on the basis of certain already existing religious emotions. At the root of this primitive religion lies not some explanation, but precisely the absence of an explanation. Not some idea or logical thought, but affect — the point of departure for any conscious process in general — is the basis for religious thinking in a savage.

Subsequent research has shown that the psychological mechanism for the thought and behavior of primitive man is also *a historically inconstant quantity* [value — J. K.]. The law of associations of ideas and the principle of casual thought in no way encompass all sides of human thought. Lévy-Bruhl was the first to try to show that the psychological mechanism of thought in a primitive man does not correspond with that in a cultural man.

He attempted even to determine the difference between the former and the latter, and to establish the most universal laws that control the activity of the psychological mechanism in primitive man. His point of departure is directly opposed to Tylor's position.

He proceeded from two fundamental positions. The first is contained in the view that on the basis of the laws of an individual psychology, as, for example, the laws of the association of ideas, it is impossible to explain the beliefs and collective ideas that have sprung up as social phenomena in a community or people. These collective ideas arise as a result of the social life of a given people and are common to all members of a given group. In this case, they are conveyed from one generation to another. They are transmitted to an individual often in ready-made form and are often not further developed by that individual. They precede and outlive this person, just as language has a similar social existence, independent of any separate individual.

Thus, the main point of view on this question changes. To use the words of Comte,[8] Lévy-Bruhl tried to describe not "humanity. . . . through man, but, on the contrary, man through humanity" (cited in Lévy-Bruhl, 1910/1926, p. 15). He did not believe one can derive the traits of primitive peoples on the basis of the psychological laws of individual life, but, vice versa; he tried to base his explanation of the psychology of an individual on the character of collective notions that emerge in these groups, as well as on the type and structure of that society in which these people live.

---

[7]Mikail Nikolaevich Pokrovskii (1868–1932), a Soviet historian.
[8]August Comte (1798–1857), a French philosopher who advanced a theory of the three stages of mankind's intellectual development: theological, metaphysical, and positivist or scientific.

The second initial research position assumes the following: Various types of individual psychologies correspond to various types of societies. These psychologies differ from one another in the same way that the psychologies of vertebrates and nonvertebrates differ.

Of course, as with different animals, so too with various social structures there are universal traits inherent in every type of human society—language, traditions, institutions. But along with these universal properties, Lévy-Bruhl said human societies, like organisms, can present profoundly differing structures, and, consequently, corresponding differences in the higher psychological functions. Therefore, it is necessary to renounce the idea of reducing from the very onset all psychological operations to a single type independently of the structure of a society, and explain all collective ideas by a psychological and logical mechanism that always remains one and the same.

Lévy-Bruhl set himself the task of comparing two psychological types that are at a maximum distance from each other: thinking in a primitive man and in a cultural man. The basic conclusions to which he came in his experiments is that higher psychological functions in a primitive man differ profoundly from those functions in a cultural man, that consequently *the very type* of thought process and behavior represents a historically changing quantity, and that the psychological nature of man also changes in the process of historical development, just as does his social nature.

We have already said that Lévy-Bruhl believed that the type of psychological functions directly depend on the social structure of that group to which the individual belongs. Wishing to give an overall characterization of this special type of primitive mentality, Lévy-Bruhl (1910/1926, p. 78) termed it prelogical or mystical thought.

With this definition, he did not intend to say that thinking is antilogical, that is, contrary to logical thought, or alogical, that is, having nothing in common with logical forms and lying outside or on the periphery of logic. Lévy-Bruhl's intention was to illustrate more than the idea that this thinking is prelogical, that is, not yet developed to the point of logical thought.[9] Insensitivity to contradictions characterizes this type of thinking. Its main feature is the *participation law,* which means that according to a primitive man's notion, one and the same thing may participate in several absolutely different forms of existence. This participation law led primitive man to

---

[9]Lévy-Bruhl (1910/1926) defined these terms as follows:

> At any rate, the mentality of these undeveloped peoples which, for want of a better term, I call *prelogical,* does not partake of that nature. It is not *antilogical;* it is not *alogical* either. By designating it "prelogical" I merely wish to state that it does not bind itself down, as our thought does, to avoiding contradiction. It obeys the law of participation first and foremost. (pp. 9, 78)

establish in his mind those connections that provided Lévy-Bruhl the basis for ascribing a mystical character to all primitive thought.

Many researchers have noted the inaccuracy of this interpretation. If behavior and thought of cultural man are superficially analyzed from this point of view, they seem to be alogical and mystical. "Primitive thought," Thurnwald says, "really only seems alogical." In actuality, it is completely logical from the viewpoint of primitive man himself. Thurnwald illustrates this with a simple example.

When suffering from some attack or disease, primitive men assumed that some evil spirit had taken hold of them. In order to cure the sick man, they try to exorcise this spirit. For this they use those methods that are seemingly supposed to drive away an actual person: they give the spirit a name, demand that it leave, or frighten it with noise.

Such circumstances seem to us ridiculous because we understand an epileptic fit or illness in the terms of modern science. However, from the point of view of a primitive man, who imagines all these changes occurring in man to be the product or effect of some external forces, benevolent or malevolent, it is absolutely logical for him to try to exert an influence on these powers in the way that has been described for us in our example.

Not only Thurnwald's position, but also objective psychology has raised substantial objection to Lévy-Bruhl's theory. Thurnwald correctly noted that from the subjective point of view of primitive man himself, his magical ceremonies to exorcise the spirit and heal a sick man are absolutely logical.

It is easy to show, however, that this very same man also exhibits, objectively speaking, logical thinking in all those circumstances where activity is oriented toward direct adaptation to nature. Invention and use of tools, hunting, cattle-raising and farming, and waging war all demand from him real, not just apparent, thought. With complete justification, one critic observed that primitive man would assumably perish the next day, if he did not actually think in the sense that Lévy-Bruhl intended.

Obviously, in the arena of practical activity, along the type of thought described by Lévy-Bruhl, primitive man also possesses logical thought in the strict sense of this word, although it is not sufficiently developed.

However, in spite of all this, Lévy-Bruhl has performed an indisputable service in that he was the first to advance the problem of historical development of thought. He demonstrated that the type of thought in and of itself is not a constant quantity, but historically changes and develops. Researchers who have gone this route attempted to more precisely formulate what distinguishes the historical types of thinking in cultural and primitive man, or, what constitutes the specificity of the historical development of the psychology of man. With this, a third viewpoint on human cultural development has been established.

PRIMITIVE MAN AS A BIOLOGICAL TYPE

Primitive man differs from cultural man in the entire cast of his personality mould and all his behavior. In order to explain the difference that primarily determines the first and final points in the historical development of man's behavior, let us begin with the differences that immediately strike the eye.

The distinctive features of primitive man and his behavior, apparent from first glance, fall very easily into two different categories. On the one hand, what first strikes the observer who encounters primitive man, especially in his natural circumstances — in his country — is a *superiority* over cultural man. This superiority is described by all travelers, some of whom even go to extremes in their convictions, believing that the primitive man is in all respects better armed by nature than cultural man.

Observers and travelers glorify his unusually acute senses of sight, hearing, and smell, his enormous endurance, his instinctive adroitness, his ability to orient himself, his knowledge of his surroundings — the forest, the desert, and the sea. Several authors idealized his ethical principles, seeing in his moral behavior traces of instinctive morality, endowed to him by nature itself. Finally, all in unison praise (even scientific research works) wholly support the so-called "path finding ability" of primitive man, that is, his ability to recreate by the slightest tracks very complicated pictures of events, circumstances, and so forth.

Arsenev told about a Gold,[10] with whom he travelled through the thickets of the Ussuriiskii territory. "The Gold was able to effectively read tracks like a book, and in strict order to reconstruct all events." This ability to recreate complicated pictures of past events by the faintest signs that are imperceptible to the eye of a cultural man constitutes an enormous superiority of the primitive man over the cultural man and an enormous dependence of the latter upon the former in those circumstances in which travellers find themselves.

And thus the first group of differences relates to primitive man's superiority, which in turn gave rise to his glorification, as if he were a perfect model of nature, and to the conviction that he is distinguished by such a sum of positive qualities in comparison with the cultural man, that

---

[10]V. K. Arsenev (1872–1930) conducted expeditions and ethnographic research in the Far East where he studied the customs, habits, religious rites, and folklore of the local inhabitants such as the Golds *(Goldy)*. This was the archaic name of primitive people living on the shores and tributaries of the Amur and the Ussur in the Far Eastern part of the former Soviet Union. The Golds, now known as the Nanains *(nanaitsy),* live in the Khabarovsk territory. The Nanain language belongs to the Tungusmanchurian family of languages; it uses primarily the Russian alphabet for its written texts. For Arsenev's major works, see *Dersu Uzala* (1936), and *Selections* (1986). The famous Japanese filmmaker, Akira Kurosawa, based his now famous film *Dersu Urzala* on Arsenev's memoires of his expedition guide.

he surpasses the latter in the development of natural psychological functions.

The other group of distinctions presents the directly opposite picture of the primitive man: helplessness, backwardness, an inability to perform even a slightly complicated operation demanding calculation, reflection, or recall, and an entire series of minuses, that is, inferior deviations [from modern man — J. K.], that also strike a cultural man at first glance when he encounters a primitive man. All this long ago forced observers to equate the primitive man with a child and an animal, and to take notice of all his inferiority with respect to cultural man.

Thus, the result is a rather complex picture: On the one hand, primitive man *surpasses* cultural man in a series of aspects; on the other hand, he is inferior. Such is the picture from first glance. We shall now try to make sense of it.

The first question before the investigator is what biological type does primitive man represent? In the biological sense is he simply a being developed more or less differently than cultural man, and, consequently, can we attribute all these *twofold differences* between cultural and primitive man simply to a biological difference — in the same way that we do whenever we compare man with some animal?

Unfortunately, up to the present day we still do not have precise and definitive results from the biological research on primitive man in spite of the enormous number of works written in this area. Besides a few insignificant, dubiously established differences in the sphere of physiology (as, for example, a faster healing of the wounds of primitive peoples, a relative immunity to contamination and infection, a lesser susceptibility to malaria, and so forth) we do not know of any indisputably established, essential traits. It is true that an entire series of other factors have been established by certain investigators in direct connection with the cultural backwardness of primitive man.

If this assumption were true, if primitive man was indeed different from cultural man in his biological type, if it turned out that his very organism functioned essentially in a different way than the organism of a cultural man, then an explanation of the difference between the behavior of an primitive man and a cultural man could be found with unquestionable certainty. This is because it has been scientifically established with absolute precision that the behavior of any animal is a function of the constitution of its organism. Organisms with different constitutions also possess different forms of behavior.

The assertion that the cranial seams grow together in primitive peoples already by the age of puberty, that is, considerably earlier than in cultural people, represents one of those facts that could substantiate the opinion that biological differences exist between primitive man and cultural man.

With respect to the development of the brain, the direct organic base for behavior, it has been pointed out that primitive man possesses a smaller development of grey matter in the cerebrum, a relative simplicity of brain gyruses, and an early halt in brain development. The overall physiological development of a primitive man occurs at a different tempo and rhythm than for cultural man. It has been observed that the time span of overall development in primitive man is less than that of cultural man, that it ceases with the onset of puberty or shortly thereafter.

However, all these data do not give us the slightest reason to embrace a different organic type for primitive man. The early closure of skull sutures, as Thurnwald noted, does not indicate any essential limitation to brain development. Similarly a macroscopic brain structure does not mean a straight forward, direct reflection of either complex or primitive behavior. One should bear in mind the more complicated considerations that Thurnwald has pointed out.

"Much of what superficial observation ascribes to physiological organization," he said, "is caused by severe cultural backwardness." In this case the cause, therefore, may be confused with the effect and vice versa. It is not so much the case that underdevelopment may be blamed for primitive behavior as it is that primitive behavior results in an early halt in development.

According to [this] accurate commentary by Thurnwald, contemporary anthropology finds itself in the same stage of development as that of botany in the times of Linnaeus.[11] Current anthropological investigations began to compare the constitution of a primitive with that of the cultural man only very recently in connection with a study of the activity of the endocrinal system. In order to clarify the degree to which the physiological traits of the primitive man may be responsible for those observed differences between him and the adult cultural man, we must dwell on a question that up until now has been given the greatest significance and that is directly related to behavior, namely to the activity of the organs of perception.

Investigations demonstrated that the tales of travellers about the unusual keenness of sight, hearing, and smell of primitive man is in fact absolutely unjustified. In any comparison with the cultural European city-dweller, we could really only expect to be able to discover a superiority of sight and hearing in primitive man, because the conditions of a cultural life often lead to a decrease in sight and to nearsightedness. However, even here the investigator cautions us not to come to hasty conclusions.

"The acuity of the primitive man's senses," Thurnwald says, "is often the

---

[11]Carolus Linnaeus (1707–1778), latinized form of Carl von Linne, the first botanist to explore the principles for defining genera and species of organism.

result of practice; the city-dweller's deficit in these areas is very often the consequence of lack of use due to his lifestyle in confined quarters."

Connected with this is also the fact that the behavior of primitive people is often based not on the direct response of the sense organs, but on a given interpretation of certain signs or phenomena. For example, a certain ripple in calm water tells the experienced fisherman about a swimming shoal of fish; a dust cloud of certain height or form tells the hunter about a herd of animals of a certain breed and number. In these circumstances we are dealing not with the keenness of this or that sense organ, but with an experienced and trained ability to interpret signs.

During experimental research, it was found that the keenness of the senses — and in particular, sight — in primitive peoples does not essentially differ from ours. It is true that one may consider it an established fact that the nearsightedness of a European is undoubtedly the product of culture. Still, it turns out that this is not the only reason for the superiority of the primitive man's sight: The European needs greater clarity in a picture for him to form a judgement about it, whereas at the same time the primitive man became accustomed to deciphering and guessing even unclear visible images. In this respect, a decisive role is played by Rivers'[12] research on sight, Myer's[13] work on hearing, smell, and taste, McDougall's[14] work on skin, muscle sensations, and blood pressure, and Myer's work on speed of reactions.

All of this research shows that from the point of view of the elementary physiological activity at the base of our perceptions and our movements, that is, all the components of the simplest reactions forming our behavior, no substantial difference exists between primitive man and cultural man. Even with respect to color perception, it is impossible to establish any significant difference. In his research, Rivers found that in one group of Papuans there was a very large percentage of Daltonism,[15] whereas in another group, not one person having this problem could be found.

However, one has yet to discover a primitive race with overall color

---

[12]W. H. R. Rivers, "Primitive color vision" (1901). Vygotsky does not cite this work in this manuscript. However, Luria (1974) gave direct reference to it in the published results of his 1931–1932 investigations of primitive people in Uzbekistan.

[13]Charles Samuel Myers (1873–1946) accompanied Rivers and McDougall on 1898 anthropological expeditions to the Torres Straits. Here Vygotsky is most likely referring to Haddon's reports of these anthropological expeditions, cited in Lévy-Bruhl (1910/1926).

[14]Meyers' (Meyers & McDougall, 1903) contribution to William McDougall (1871–1938), an English-American psychologist who studied vision, attention, memory, fatigues, among other things. Important for Vygotsky is McDougall's (Meyers & McDougall, 1903) contribution to Haddon's reports of expeditions to Torres Straits, cited in Lévy-Bruhl (1910/1926).

[15]A disorder of color vision studied by and named after J. Dalton (1766–1844), an English chemist and physicist. Those having Daltonism most often confuse green and red.

blindness; even in apes, no one has succeeded in establishing this color blindness with any reliability. "It is necessary to admit," Thurnwald said later on, "that the development of color perception was perfected long before the emergence of man as such."

Somewhat similarly, the hearing of primitive people is considered superior to ours. However, the research of Myers and Bruner, has shown that hearing among Caucasians is, on the average, more acute than in primitive man. Again, the sense of smell in primitive people has been just as overrated. "Research on Negroes and Papuans," Thurnwald said, "has brought us to the same already established results with respect to sight and hearing." Some contradictory data has been obtained from research on tactile sensations. McDougall's experiment revealed a somewhat greater subtlety in distinguishing [tactile sensations — J. K.] However, no other studies of primitive people have successfully established any significant deviation from the level of development of this very same function in cultural man.

Moreover, the somewhat greater tolerance of pain revealed by research similarly does not directly point to a psychological basis for this phenomenon. Even right-handedness, which is not found in the higher apes, stands out as a general symptom of human nature and can be seen in primitive man to the same degree as in cultural man.

If one attempts to sum up the results of these experiments concerning the physiological difference of primitive man, it is possible to come to the conclusion that scientific research does not have available at the present time any positive material that would indicate that a special biological type might be the primary cause giving rise to the entire specificity of primitive man's behavior. On the contrary, the differences established by research on the one hand, turn out to be very insignificant. On the other hand, these differences are highly dependent on practice or lack of it — that is, to a large degree, the differences themselves turn out to be connected with cultural development. All this forces us to propose an inverse ratio between the cultural and biological differences of primitive man. These differences force us to attribute that backwardness, observable in the area of a primitive's psychological functions, sooner to cultural underdevelopment.

"The full title of man must be conferred upon primitive man," said Thurnwald. Apparently, man's development as a biological species was basically completed at the moment the history of man began. This, of course, does not mean that human biology stood still from that moment when the historical development of human society began. Of course not.

The plasticity of human nature has continued to change. However, this biological change in human nature has already become a value that is dependent on and subordinated to the historical development of human society. Like Thurnwald, present-day investigators ascertain that technology and social organization, which stem from a definite stage in the development of this technology, are the basic factors in the development of the psychology of primitive man.

Man's development, as we find it even among the most primitive peoples, is social development. Therefore, we must expect in advance that we will be able to discover here an extremely distinctive process of development that is profoundly different from that which we observe in the evolution from ape to man.

Let us say beforehand that the process of transformation of primitive man into cultural man and the process of his biological evolution do not coincide. The former does not represent a continuation of the latter; instead, each of the two processes is subjected to its own particular laws.

MEMORY IN PRIMITIVE MAN

Now we turn directly to concrete research material and attempt to explain what constitutes the specific nature of the historical development of man's behavior. For this we do not touch upon every last aspect and area of a primitive man's behavior. We dwell only on three of the most important areas that are of immediate interest to us and that allow us to come to several general conclusions about behavior as a whole. We first examine memory, then thought and speech, and finally the numerical operations of primitive man; we try to establish what direction these three functions develop in.

Let us begin with memory. All observers and travellers unanimously praise the unusual memory of the primitive man. Lévy-Bruhl pointed out with utmost justification that in primitive man's mind and behavior, memory plays a much more significant role than in our mental life because certain functions that memory fulfilled at some time in our behavior have isolated themselves from memory and changed.

Our experience is reduced to concepts, and we, therefore, are free of the necessity of storing an enormous mass of concrete impressions. For primitive man, almost all of experience is sustained by memory. However, primitive man's memory differs from ours not only quantitatively; according to Lévy-Bruhl (1910/1926), it possesses a particular tonality distinguishing it from ours (p. 119).

Constant use of logical mechanisms and abstract concepts profoundly changes the work of our memory. Primitive memory is both very accurate and highly emotional. It preserves representations with a wealth of detail and always in the same order of their connection in reality. In many cases, Lévy-Bruhl noted, mechanisms of memory replace logical mechanisms for primitive man: If one representation is evoked as the result of another, the latter has the quality of a conclusion. Therefore, a sign almost always is taken to be a cause (Lévy-Bruhl, 1910/1926, p. 119).

In light of all this, Lévy-Bruhl (1910/1926) said, "We must therefore expect to find the memory extremely well developed in primitives." He explains the surprise of travellers who give accounts about the unusual properties of memory in primitive peoples in the following way: these observers "unreflectingly assume that memory with these primitives has just the same functions as with us. . . . It seems to them that it is accomplishing marvelous feats, while it is merely being exercised in a normal way" (p. 119) What seems to be a production of miracles is at the same time the absolutely normal functioning (of memory).

Spencer and Gillen[16] said of the Australian aborigines:

> In many respects, their memory is phenomenal. Not only does a native know the track of every beast and bird, but after examining any burrow, he will at once, from the direction in which the last track runs, tell you whether the animal is at home or not. . . . Strange as it may sound . . . the native will recognize the footprint of every individual of his acquaintances. (cited in Lévy-Bruhl, 1910/1926, pp. 110–111)

Roth[17] similarly observed the exceptional memorizing powers of the North Queensland aborigines. He heard them reciting a song, the delivery of which takes upwards of five nights for its completion. These songs were produced with surprising accuracy. Most surprising in this respect is the fact that they are performed by tribes who speak in different languages, and different dialects, living at distances upwards of one hundred miles apart (cited in Lévy-Bruhl, 1910/1926, p. 111).

Livingstone[18] noted the outstanding memory of natives of Africa. He observed it in the chieftain's messengers who:

> carry messages of considerable length great distances, and deliver them almost word for word. Two or three usually go together, and when on the way the message is rehearsed every night, in order that the exact words may be kept to. One of the native objections to learning to write is that these men answer the

---

[16]Walter Baldwin Spencer (1860–1929), an English biologist and anthropologist, worked together with Gillen and studied the primitive aborigines of Australia. His work is frequently cited by Lévy-Bruhl. Most likely, Vygotsky's knowledge of Spencer and Gillen is at least in part based on his reading of Lévy-Bruhl.

[17]W. E. Roth (1897) is known for etnographical studies among the Northwest Central Queensland aborigines and is often cited by Lévy-Bruhl.

[18]David Livingstone (1813–1873), a Scottish missionary and explorer who travelled to Africa. His various works had a strong influence on Western attitudes toward Africa (cf. *Narrative of an Expedition to the Zambesi and Its Tributaries* Livingstone, 1865).

purpose of transmitting intelligence to a distance as well as a letter would. (cited in Lévy-Bruhl, 1910/1926, p. 112)

The most often-observed form of outstanding memory in a primitive man is the so-called topographic memory, that is, memory of the surroundings. It [this memory—J. K.] stores the images of surroundings in the minutest details thus providing the primitive man with the ability to find his way with a confidence that amazes the European.

According to one author, this sort of memory borders on a miracle. It is enough for North Americans to appear only once in certain surroundings to get an absolutely exact indelible image of it. However, large and wild as the forest may be, they will make their way through it without hesitation once they get their bearings. They are just as well-oriented at sea.

Charlevoix was inclined to attribute this to an inborn ability. He stated: "This gift is inborn; it is not the result of their observations, nor a matter of habit; children who have scarcely ever left their village go about with as much confidence as those who have travelled the country" (cited in Lévy-Bruhl, 1910/1926, p. 112). Recalling travellers' stories about an outstanding, seemingly miraculous topographic memory, Lévy-Bruhl noted that there is no miracle to it all, but a well-developed local memory. Von den Steinen described a primitive man whom he observed as follows:

> this primitive man saw, heard everything; he stored in his memory the most insignificant details, so that the author could hardly believe that anybody might remember so much without the use of written signs. This man had a map in his head; or, to express it more accurately, he had retained in their right order a number of apparently unimportant facts. (cited in Lévy-Bruhl, 1910/1926, pp. 114–115)[19]

According to Lévy-Bruhl, the same unusual development of the primitive man's concrete memory—so striking because it reproduces the smallest details of previously perceived phenomena exactly in the original order—can also be seen in the primitive man's wealth of vocabulary and complex grammar.

It is curious that the same people who speak these languages and who possess such an outstanding memory. For example, those living in Australia or Northern Brazil, cannot count above two or three. The slightest abstract

---

[19]Karl Von den Steinen (1855–1929). See *Unter den Naturvölkern Zentralbräsiliens* (1897) and *Die Marquesaner und ihre Kunst, Studien über die Entwicklung primitiver Südseeornamentik* (1969). Vygotsky does not give a direct citation from von den Steinen and most likely knew of his work through a reading of Lévy-Bruhl, who refers to von den Steinen's anthropological work.

reflection scares them so much that they immediately declare themselves tired and refuse to continue (Lévy-Bruhl, 1910/1926).

Lévy-Bruhl (1910/1926) explained:

> With us, in everything that relates to intellectual functions, memory is confined to the subordinate role of registering the results which have been acquired by a logical elaboration of concepts. . . . The amanuensis of the eleventh century who laboriously reproduced page by page the manuscript which was the object of his pious endeavour, is no further removed from the rotary machine of the great newspaper office which prints off hundreds of thousands of copies in a few hours, than is prelogical mentality, in which the connections between the representations are performed, and which makes use of memory almost entirely, from logical thought, with its marvelous stock of abstract concepts. (pp. 115–116)

Such a characterization of primitive man's memory is extremely one-sided; however, on the whole and in essence, it is undoubtedly true. We shall attempt to show how we may scientifically explain this superiority of primitive memory. Yet, at the same time, in order to obtain an accurate understanding of this memory, we must also point out that in many respects, primitive man's memory is profoundly inferior to that of cultural man.

An Australian child who has never been beyond the boundaries of his village amazes the cultural European with his ability to orient himself in a country where he has never been. However, a European school child, who has completed just one class in geography, can assimilate more than any adult primitive man can ever assimilate in his entire lifetime.

Along with the superior development of *innate or natural memory,* which seems to engrave external impressions with photographic accuracy, primitive memory also stands out for the qualitative uniqueness of its functions. When compared to the superiority of natural memory, this second aspect sheds certain light on the nature of primitive man's memory.

Leroy, with full justification, reduced all the peculiarities of primitive memory to its *function.* A primitive man must rely only on his direct memory—he has no written language. Therefore, we frequently find a similar form of primitive memory in illiterate people. The ability, then, of primitive man to orient himself or to reconstruct complicated events by tracks, in the opinion of this author, must find its explanation not in the superiority of direct memory, but in something else. The majority of dark-skinned people, as one observer testifies, do not find a road without some kind of external sign. Orientation, Leroy believed, has nothing in common with memory. Similarly, when a primitive man reconstructs some event according to tracks, he makes use of his memory to no greater extent, than when a judge who reconstructs a crime by traces left. Here, the power of observation and deduction play the dominant role, not memory. The organs of perception are more developed in the primitive man because of greater use, which accounts for his difference from us in this area. But this ability to decipher tracks is not the product of instinct, but the result of training. Parents teach their children to distinguish tracks. Adults imitate the tracks of an animal, and the children reproduce them.

Most recently, experimental psychology has discovered a particular, exceedingly interesting form of memory, which many psychologists compare with the amazing memory of primitive man. Although experimental research on primitive man in this area is only now taking place and is still not concluded, nevertheless, facts, on the one hand, gathered by psychologists in their laboratories and, on the other, reported by investigators and travellers about primitive man coincide so closely with each other that they allow us to assume with great probability that precisely this form of memory accounts for the main distinction between primitive man and cultural man.

According to Jaensch (1925/1930),[20] the essence of this form of memory is a person's ability to literally reproduce visually a previously preconceived object or picture immediately after seeing it, or even after a long interval of time. Such people are called eidetics and this form of memory is called eidetism. This phenomenon was discovered by Urbanchich in 1907 and has been investigated and analyzed by the Jaensch school only in the last decade.[21]

In chapter 3, on child psychology, we dwell in more depth on the results of research on eidetism. Now let us say that the research is usually conducted as follows. The child eidetic is usually shown some complicated picture with an enormous number of details for a short interval of time (about 10–30 seconds). Then the picture is taken away, and before the child the experimenter places a grey screen on which the child continues to see the absent picture with all the details, and begins to relate in detail what he finds before him, reading the inscriptions and so forth.

As an example that elucidates the character and specific nature of eidetic memory, we introduce Fig. 2.1, a picture that was presented to eidetic children in the experiments of Veresotskaia. After a short viewing of the picture (30 seconds), the child continues to see its image on the screen — a

---

[20]No reference is given, but it is clear from other texts that Vygotsky is refering to Jaensch (1925/1930), *Eidetic Imagery*. Vygotsky (1984) cites the German original (*Über Eidetick und die typologische Forschungsmethode, Zeitschrift der Psychologie,* 1911/1927) in volume 4 of his collected works on page 430.

[21]Erich Jaensch and others in the Marburg Psychological School, who studied cases of eidetism among preschoolers and younger children, concluded that it was a common and normal phenomenon for these children.

FIG. 2.1 The picture shown to children with eidetic memory in the experiments of K. I. Veresotskaia.

fact which is established by means of control questions and collation of the answers with the original picture. The child reads the text by letters, counts up the windows on each floor, describes the interrelation of objects and their parts, naming the color and describing the minutest details.

Research shows that such an eidetic image is subject to all the rules of perception. The psychological basis for such memory is, apparently, the momentum of the visual nervous excitation, which is prolonged after the stimulus that evoked excitation in the optic nerve has already ceased to have an effect. This type of eidetism is observed not only in the sphere of visual sensations, but also in the sphere of audible and tactile sensations.

Among cultural peoples, eidetism is widespread for the most part only in children; among adults eidetism is a rare exception. Psychologists believe that eidetism represents an early, primitive phase in the development of memory that the child usually outgrows by the time of puberty and that is seldom preserved in an adult. It is more widely found among mentally and culturally deprived children.

This form of memory is biologically very important in as much as it, while developing, transforms into two different forms of memory. First, as research shows, eidetic images, according to the degree of development, merge with our perceptions and impart a stable, permanent character to these perceptions. Second, they are transformed into visual images of memory in the strict sense of this word.

Researchers believe, therefore, that eidetic memory is a primary, undifferentiated stage of unity of perception and memory, which becomes differentiated and develops into two separate functions. Eidetic memory lies at the basis of any individual thought.

On the basis of all the data collected by Lévy-Bruhl (and introduced by us earlier), Jaensch came to the conclusion that the outstanding memory of primitive man bears a kinship with the eidetic form. Furthermore, the way in which a primitive man perceives, thinks, and imagines also indicates that his development is extremely near the eidetic phase. Thus, for example, the visionaries often found among primitive peoples are compared by Jaensch to two of his experimental subjects — boy-eidetics who envisioned, at times, absolutely extraordinary places and buildings.

If we take into account that the visual images of eidetics may be reinforced by effective stimulation accompanied by pharmaceutical means, we then find it highly possible to accept the suggestion made by the famous pharmacologist Lewin[22] that shamans and doctors among primitive peoples artificially induced in themselves eidetic activity. Similarly, the mythological art of primitive man approaches visionary character and eidetism.

Comparing all these data with data from research on eidetism, Jaensch came to the conclusion that everything known to us with respect to the memory of primitive man points to the fact that we are dealing with an eidetic phase in the development of his (primitive man's) memory. Eidetism, in the opinion of Jaensch, explains mythological images.

Blonskii stated:

> One must only add that similar wood goblins, mermaids, etc., emerge in corresponding circumstances under the influence of strong emotions in primitive eidetics, and are then reinforced by the sustained frame of mind which corresponds to the prolonged eidetic state. Eidetism in primitive peoples explains not only the emergence of mythological images, but certain characteristics of primitive art and language as well.

The language of a primitive man, about which we will speak more later, strikes us in comparison with languages of cultural peoples by its pictur-

---

[22]Kurt Lewin (1890–1947), a German Gestalt psychologist who later worked in the United States, a theoretician, and an experimental psychologist who attempted to apply principles of Gestalt psychology to the psychology of personality. For more information, see Vygotsky's article (1982, Vol. 1) "The Problem of Mental Retardation" where Vygotsky rather extensively analyzed Lewin's works. See also Lewin (1935).

esqueness, by its abundance of concrete details and words—by its figura-
tiveness. With respect to art, Wundt[23] also posed the question, "Why did
the figurative art of cave peoples flourish precisely in the darkness of caves?
"Maybe," Blonsky said, "this is explained by the fact that eidetic images are
brighter in darkness and with closed eyes."

Danzel[24] came to similar conclusions in his study of this question. In his
opinion, memory plays an unmeasurably greater role in the intellectual life
of primitive man than it does for us. In activity of this type of memory, we
are struck by the "unprocessed" nature of the materials preserved by
memory—by the consecutive photographic nature of its work. The repro-
ductive function of this memory is considerably greater than ours.

Primitive memory, as Danzel remarked, apart from its faithfulness and
objectivity, strikes us also by its complex character. In his memory, the
primitive man does not go laboriously from one element to another,
because his memory preserves the entire phenomenon as a whole, and not
its parts.

Finally, in the opinion of Danzel, the last feature distinguishing memory
in primitive man is that he still poorly differentiates between his perceptions
and his memories. What is objective and actually perceived merges for him
with what is only imagined and conceived. You can find an explanation for
this, of course, also only in the eidetic character of primitive man's
memories.

Thus, biological (organic) memory or the so-called mnemonic unit, the
base of which is embedded in the plasticity of our nervous system (in its
ability to store traces of external stimulations and to reproduce them),
reaches its maximal development in primitive man. It (biological memory)
cannot develop any further.

Depending on the measure of primitive man's enculturation, we observe
a tapering-off of this memory just as we observe this decrease vis-a-vis the
cultural development of a child. The question arises, what is the course of
development of memory in primitive man? Does this memory improve or
perfect itself in the transformation just described from a lower, more
primitive level to a relatively higher stage?

Research studies have unanimously shown that in reality this does not
occur. Here we must immediately point out that particular form of memory
required for the historical development of behavior, the form that memory
acquires in a given situation. We only have to look objectively at primitive

---

[23]Wilhelm Wundt (1832–1920), a German psychologist and physiologist, initiator and
spokesman of experimental psychology. No direct citation here. For information, see
references made to Wundt in volume 4 of Vygotskii's *Sobranie sochinenii* (1983).

[24]T. W. Danzel. Vygotsky no doubt has in mind here Danzel's *Die fänge der Schrift* (1912),
which Thurnwald cited in *Psychologies des Primitiven Menschen* (1922).

memory to see that this memory functions spontaneously as an elemental, natural force.

Man uses it but does not control it, in the words of Engels. To the contrary, this memory dominates him. It evokes in him unreal fantasies, imaginary images, and fabrications. It causes him to create myths that often serve as obstacles on the developmental path of his experience; his subjective inventions shroud over an objective picture of the world.

The historical development of memory begins from that moment when man shifts for the first time from using his memory as a natural force to dominating it. This domination, as with domination over any natural or elemental force, means only that, to a certain degree, the development of man accumulates—in the case at hand—psychological experience and adequate knowledge of the laws, by which memory operates and begins to incorporate these laws. It is not necessary to see this process of accumulating psychological experience leading to the control over behavior as a process of conscious experience—of intentional accumulation of knowledge and theoretical examination. This experience should be called "naive psychology," analogous to what Köhler called "naive physics" in the behavior of apes, having in mind the way an ape naively experiences the physical properties of his own body and the objects of the physical world.

From an ability to find paths, that is, from an ability to use tracks as signs that reveal and remind him of whole complex pictures—from the use of a sign—primitive man, at a certain stage of his development, arrives for the first time at the *creation of an artificial sign.*

Thurnwald[25] told about a primitive man in service that each time he was sent to the main camp with messages, he took with him "auxiliary tools of memory," in order to remember all the messages. Thurnwald believed, in spite of Danzel's view, that with the usage of such auxiliary means there is absolutely no necessity to think about their magical origin. Writing in its initial form appears on the scene precisely as such an auxiliary means, with the help of which man begins to control his memory.

Our written word has a very long history. The first tools of memory are signs, as, for example, the golden figures of West-African story tellers; each figure recalls some particular tale. Each of such figures seems to represent the initial name of a long story—for example, the moon. Essentially, the bag with such figures represents a primitive table of contents for such a primitive storyteller.

Other signs have an abstract character. A typical example of such an abstract sign, as Thurnwald said, is a knot, tied to jog the memory, as we still do now. Thanks to the fact that these tools of memory, as Thurnwald

---

[25]See Thurnwald's (1922) discussion of early systems of writing *(Schrift)* in "Psychologie des Primitiven Menschen" (pp. 243–265).

FIG. 2.2   Letter of a primitive man (Thurnwald, 1922).

said, are used identically within a certain group, they become conventional and begin to serve as the goals of communication.

Figure 2.2 (taken from Thurnwald, 1922) shows the writing system of a primitive man. This orthographic system is made out of a cane cord, two pieces of reed, four shells, and a piece of fruit peel. This letter (written) by an incurably ill father to his friends and relatives has the following contents: "the illness has taken on an unfavorable turn; it is becoming worse and worse, our only help comes from God" (Thurnwald, 1922, p. 244).

Similar signs among the Indian tribes of Dakota take on universal significance. Thus, feather "a" (Fig. 2.3, taken from Thurnwald, 1922) with a pierced hole indicates that the wearer has killed the enemy; feather "b" with a cut-out triangle means that he has cut his enemy's throat and scalped him; feather "c" with the tip cut off means that he has cut his throat. The split feather "d" means that he has wounded him (Thurnwald, 1922, pp. 244–245).

The most ancient relics of writing shown in Figs. 2.4 (taken from Thurnwald, 1922) and 2.5 (taken from Clodd, 1905) are *quipu* (knotted cords in Peruvian language), used in ancient Peru, just as in ancient China, Japan, and other countries. These are conventional auxiliary memory aids and were widespread among primitive peoples, and demanded precise knowledge on the part of the person who tied all these knots.

Similar *quipu* are used even now in Bolivia by the shepherds for counting the herds in Tibet and other places. The system of signs and counting is

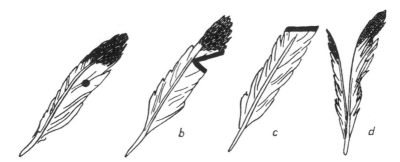

FIG. 2.3   Feather with notches (Thurnwald, 1922).

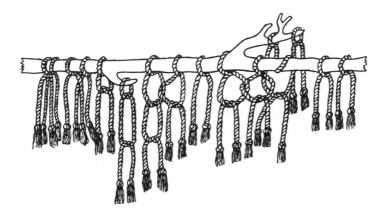

FIG. 2.4 *Quipu* (Peruvian language) for keeping score of the slain in battle (Thurnwald, 1922).

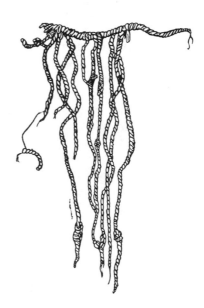

FIG. 2.5 Quipu, for reckoning (Clodd, 1905, p. 37).

connected with the economic structure of these peoples. White cords signified silver and peace, red ones warriors and war, green ones maize, yellow ones gold.

Clodd (1905) considered the mnemonic stage to be the first stage in the development of written language (p. 35). Any sign or object is a means of mnemotechnical remembering. Herodotus[26] explained that when Darius

---

[26]Herodotus (between 480 and 490 and 425 B.C.), an ancient Greek historian who gave the first systematic description of the customs and daily habits among the Scythians. Darius was Tsar of the powerful Axemenidov kingdom at that time.

ordered the Indians to remain behind to guard the bridge hanging over the river Ister, he stretched out 60 knots on a belt, saying:

> Men of Ionia. . . . do you keep keep this thong and do as I shall say: — so soon as ye shall have seen me go forward against the Scythians, from that time begin and untie a knot on each day; and if within this time I am not here, and ye find that the days marked by the knots have passed by, then sail away to your own lands. (cited in Clodd, 1905, p. 36)

Such a knot tied to jog the memory is, apparently, the most ancient record showing how man progressed from the use of this device to the control of his memory.

These *"quipu"* were used in ancient Peru for the introduction of manuscripts, for conveying commands to isolated provinces, for sending communiques about the condition of the armies, and for preserving the memory of a deceased person, into whose grave *quipu* were cast.

The Peruvian tribe of Chudi, as Tylor[27] pointed out, had a special officer in each town whose function was to tie and interpret knots (cited in Clodd, 1905, p. 38). Although these officers achieved great perfection in their art, they were rarely able to read foreign *quipu* when passed on without oral commentaries. When someone appeared from a remote province, then it was necessary for him to give explanations along with the *quipu,* regardless of whether this was a *quipu* for correspondence, for collecting taxes, for declaring war, and so forth (Clodd, 1905, p. 38).

In the course of constant practice, these officials perfected the system to such a degree that they were able to record, with the help of knots, all the most important events of the kingdom and to set down laws and ordinances. Tylor pointed out that, to date, in South Peru there still live among the Indians those who are perfectly familiar with the contents of certain historical *quipu* preserved from ancient time; however, they keep their knowledge a deep secret and guard it particularly from white people (cited in Clodd, 1905, p. 38).

Most often in contemporary times, such a mnemotechnical system of knots is used for remembering various calculating operations. The herdsmen of Peru use one strand of *quipu* to record their bulls, a second one to differentiate the milking cows from those that cannot be milked, further on come the calves, sheep, and so forth. The products of animal husbandry are recorded with knots on special cords. The color of the cord

---

[27]E. B. Tylor, *Early History of Mankind* (1964) as well as Isaac Taylor's *History of the Alphabet* (1899) is used as the basis of the formulation of Edward Clodd's own analysis of early memory-aids and picture-writing. Vygotsky leans heavily on this data presented by Clodd (1905), the president of the New York Folk Lore Society at the turn of the century.

and the various methods of twisting the knots indicate the nature of the record.

We shall not elaborate on the subsequent history in the development of writing; let us say only that this shift away from the natural development of memory to the development of writing, from eidetism to the use of external systems of signs, from mnemonic activity to mnemotechnics, constitutes an essential turning point or sudden change determining the entire subsequent course of the cultural development of human memory. External development takes the place of inner development.

Memory is perfected in as much as systems of writing — systems of signs and ways of using them — are developed. What was perfected in the Ancient and Middle Ages was called *memoria technica* or artificial memory. The historical development of human memory can basically and primarily be summed up as the development and perfection of those auxiliary means that social humans have worked out in the process of their cultural life.

Given this, it is self-understood that neither natural nor organic memory remains unchanged, but on the contrary, its changes are determined by two essential factors. The memory of man, who knows how to write down what he needs to remember, is trained and consequently develops in a different direction than the memory of a man who is absolutely unable to use signs. Inner development and perfection of memory thus are no longer an independent process, but are dependent on, subordinated to, and defined in the course of these changes originating from outside — from man's social environment.

The second and no less essential limitation is that this memory is perfected and developed very one-sidedly. It adapts to that form of writing that dominates in any given society. Subsequently, in many other respects it does not develop at all, but is degraded, and involuted, this is, is curtailed and undergoes reverse development.

Thus, for example, the outstanding natural memory of primitive man in the process of cultural development is reduced more and more to naught. Therefore, Baldwin[28] was right when he defended the position that any evolution is in the same degree in involution, that is, any process of development has included as its major component the backward processes of the curtailment and atrophy of old forms.

One has only to compare the memory of an African ambassador, who conveys word for word some long message of the chief of some African

---

[28] J. B. Baldwin (1861-1934), American psychologist, interested in both developmental, or functional, psychology and symbolic interactionism. He approached evolutionary development from the point of view of individual differences, coming up with a sophisticated hypothesis of organic selection, accounting for the new direction in evolution — this notion became known as the "Baldwin effect."

FIG. 2.6 Ojibwa love letter (Clodd, 1905, p. 53).

tribe and uses exclusively natural eidetic memory, with the memory of the Peruvian "officer of knots," whose duty consists of tying and reading *quipu,* in order to see in which direction the development of man's memory is headed as a result of cultural growth. The main thing is by what means and how it is (this development) directed.

"The officer of knots" stands higher on the ladder of cultural development of memory than the African ambassador, not because his natural memory has become greater, but because he learned to make better use of his memory, to control it with the help of artificial signs.

Let us ascend still one step higher and turn to the memory that corresponds to the following stage in the development of writing. Figure 2.6 (taken from Clodd, 1905) reveals an example of so-called "picture-writing," that is, of writing that makes use of visual images to convey certain thoughts and concepts. On birchbark, a girl (from the tribe of Odjibwa[29]) writes a letter to her beloved in White Earth, Minnesota. Her totem is a bear, his a "mud puppy" (Clodd, 1905, p. 51). These two images signify the addresser and the addressee. The two lines, leading from their posts, merge and continue on to the district that lies between the two lakes. From this line, a path branches off toward two tents. Here in their tents live three girls who have converted to the Catholic faith, which is expressed by three crosses. The tent on the left is open and from it a hand stretches out with a waving gesture. The hand, belonging to the author of the letter, makes the Indian sign welcoming her beloved. This sign is expressed with the palm turned forward and down and with the index finger stretched toward the position of the speaker, calling the attention of the one being invited to the path along which he must come. (Clodd, 1905, pp. 51–53)

At this stage, writing already requires of memory a completely different form of operations (cf. Fig. 2.7, taken from Thurnwald, 1922). Still another form arises when mankind shifts to ideographic or hieroglyphic writing, which uses symbols, the meaning of which becomes more and more removed from the objects. Mallery[30] correctly pointed out that in the majority of cases these were "merely mnemonic records, and were interpreted in connection with material objects, formerly, and perhaps still, used mnemonically" (cited in Clodd, 1905, p. 67).

---

[29]The Ojibwas are an Indian tribe that lived around Lake Superior.

[30]D. Garrick Mallery did research in the late 19th century on American Indian signs. The reference is to *Sign Language among North American Indians* (1971).

FIG. 2.7 Sample of a picto-graphic letter: letter of an Indian (c) to his son (d). The names of the father and the son are indicated by small figures above the heads (tur-tles a and b for one and a small man for the other). The contents of the letter are as follows: the father summons his son to come (the line from the fathers mouth (e) and the small figure of the man at the right hand of the son (h); the cost of the trip is 53 dollars, which the father is sending to him (the small circles (f) above (Thurnwald, 1922).

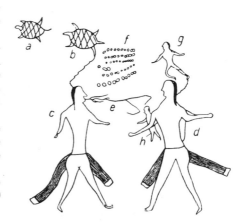

It is impossible to present a history more remarkable or characteristic of the psychology of man than the history of the development of writing, a history that shows how man tries to control his memory. Thus, a decisive step in the transformation from the natural development of memory to cultural development is the crossing from mnemonic operations to mnemo-technics — to dominance over memory — from the biological form of its development to the historical form, or, from an inner to an outer form.

Let us note that the initial forms of such dominance over memory are signs that are used not so much for one's self as for others, with social goals that only afterwards become signs for oneself. Arsenev, a famous researcher of the Ussuri[31] area, told how he visited a settlement of Udegeians located in a very remote spot. The Udegeians complained to him about the claims that they have to tolerate from the Chinese, and asked that on his arrival at Vladi-vostok, he convey this to the Russian authorities and request protection.

When the traveller left the settlement the next day, the Udegeians came out in a group to accompany him as far as the outskirts. A grey-haired old man stepped out of the crowd; he handed Arsenev a lynx claw and ordered him to put it in his pocket in order that he not forget their requests in regard to Li Tan Kuj. Not trusting natural memory, the Udegeians introduced an artificial sign having no direct relationship to those things that the traveller was supposed to remember; and it served as an auxiliary technical tool of memory, as a means to direct his remembering along the desired channel and control its flow.

At this moment, the operation of remembering with the help of a lynx's

---

[31]Ussuri, a tributary of the Amur, is a river that runs along the Chinese border, a remote region of the former Soviet Union.

claw, directed first toward another person and then to one's self, also expresses the first beginnings of that path along which the development of memory of a cultural person proceeds. All that enculturated mankind remembers and knows now, his entire experience accumulated in books, relics, monuments, and manuscripts, all of this immense expansion of the human memory — the necessary condition for man's historical and cultural development — is indebted to external memory based on signs.

THINKING IN CONNECTION
WITH THE DEVELOPMENT OF LANGUAGE
IN PRIMITIVE SOCIETY

We also observe the same path of development in another, no less central area of the psychology of primitive man — namely in the area of speech and thought. And here, as in the area of memory, we are struck from first glance by the fact that primitive man differs from a cultural man not simply because his language turns out to be more meager in means, cruder, and less developed than the language of a cultural man. All this, of course, is so; but at the same time, with respect to the language of primitive man, we are struck precisely by the huge wealth of vocabulary. All the difficulty of understanding and studying these languages first and foremost stems from their superiority over the languages of cultural peoples because of the degree of wealth, abundance, and luxury of their various nomenclatures, which is totally absent in our language.

Lévy-Bruhl and Jaensch pointed out with complete justification that these dual characteristics of language of a primitive man are closely connected with his unusual memory. The first thing that strikes us about the language of a primitive man is precisely the immense wealth of nomenclature that he has at his disposal. This entire language is filled with nomenclature. For the expression of these concrete details, he uses an enormous number of words and expressions.

"It is our aim," said Gatschet,[32] "to speak clearly and precisely; the Indian's is to speak as if drawing; while we classify, he individualizes" (Lévy-Bruhl, 1910/1926, p. 168). Therefore, the speech of primitive man actually reminds us of an endlessly complex (when compared to our language), most subtle, plastic, photographic description of some event in the minutest details.

The development of language is therefore characterized by the gradual disappearance of a great number of concrete details. In the languages of

---

[32]See also A. Gatschet (1890), *Transactions of the American Ethnological Society* (pp. 136–138). Gatshet (1832–1907) studied the Atakapa language and contributed his findings to the American Ethnological Society.

Australian peoples, for example, there is almost a complete absence of words that designate general concepts, however, they (these languages) are inundated by with a large number of specific terms that precisely discern the individual features and distinctiveness of objects.

Eyre[33] said about the Australians, "Generic terms such as tree, fish, bird, etc., were lacking, although specific terms were applied to every variety of tree, fish or bird" (cited in Lévy-Bruhl, 1910/1926, p. 179). Similarly, among other primitive peoples we observe the same phenomenon where there is no corresponding word for tree, fish, or bird, and all objects and creatures are designated by their own names.

The Tasmanians do not have words to specify such qualities as sweet, bitter, hard, cold, long, short, and round. Instead of "hard," they say "like a stone," in place of "tall"—"high feet," "round"—"like a ball," "like a moon," and they also add a gesture that explains this. Similarly, in the archipelago Bismark, there are no names for colors. Colors are designated only by naming an object with which it shares a likeness (Lévy-Bruhl, 1910/1926, p. 170).

"In California," Powers[34] said, "there are no genera, no species: every oak, pine, or grass has its separate name" (cited in Lévy-Bruhl, 1910/1926, p. 171). All of this creates an immense wealth of words for primitive peoples. The Australians have an individual name for almost every most minute part of the human body: thus, for example, in place of the word "hand," there exist in their language many separate words, distinguishing the upper part of the hand, its middle section, the right hand, the left hand, and so forth (Lévy-Bruhl, 1910/1926, p. 172).

The Maoris have an unusually complete system for the nomenclature of the flora in New Zealand. For them, individual names exist for the gender of male and female trees. They also give individual names to trees, the leaves of which change form at different moments of their growth. The *koko* bird, or the *tui,* has four names: two for the male gender and two for the female depending on the time of year. There are separate words for the bird's tail, the tail of an animal, and the tail of a fish. There are three words for the designation of a parrot's cry: a cry in a calm state, his cry when he is angry, and one when he is frightened (Lévy-Bruhl, 1910/1926, p. 172).

In South Africa, the Bawenda tribe has a special name for each form of rain. In North America, the Indians have an enormous number of precise,

---

[33]F. Eyre made expeditions to discover primitive peoples of central Australia. Lévy-Bruhl refers repeatedly to his work.

[34]Stephen Powers, American anthropologist who studied Indians in California and Nevada. His data can be found in *Tribes of California (1976, p. 419)* and are cited by Lévy-Bruhl. (1910/1926)

almost scientific definitions for various forms of clouds and for the description of the sky, which are almost untranslatable "and for which it would be in hopeless," Lévy-Bruhl continues, "to seek an equivalent in European languages." One of these tribes has, for example, a particular word for naming the sun when it shines between two clouds. It is almost impossible to count the number of nouns in their language. One of the Northern primitive peoples, for example, has a multitude of terms for designating different species of deer. There is a special term for designating a deer that is one, two, three, four, five, six, and seven years old; there are twenty words for ice, 11 words for cold, 41 words for snow in different forms, 26 verbs in order to designate freezing or thawing, and so forth. Here is why "they resisted any attempt to exchange their language for Norwegian, which is too poor from this point of view" (Lévy-Bruhl, 1910/1926, p. 172). This very phenomenon explains the large quantity of proper names that are given to the most varied individual subjects.

In New Zealand, for the Maoris, each thing has its own particular proper name. Their boats, their houses, their weapons, even their clothes; each object receives its own proper name. All of their lands and their roads have their own names; the birches around the islands, the horses, the cows, the pigs, and even the trees, cliffs, and springs. In South Australia, each mountain chain as well as each mountain has its own name. A native can tell precisely the name of each separate hill, so that it turns out that the geography of a primitive man is much richer than ours (Lévy-Bruhl, 1910/1926, p. 174).

In the area of Zambezi, each knoll, hill, mountain, and each peak in a chain has its own name. In precisely the same manner, each spring, each valley, each meadow, each part and place of the country is thus called by a special name. All of this would take a man's entire life to decipher the sense and meaning of, as Livingston said (Lévy-Bruhl, 1910/1926, p. 174).

This wealth of vocabulary is directly dependent on the concrete and precise nature of primitive man's language. In the same way that he photographs and reproduces all his experience he also recalls it, just as precisely. He does not know how to express himself abstractly and conditionally, as the cultural man does.

That is why in cases where a European may use one or two words, a primitive man utters sometimes ten; for example, the phrase: "a man killed a rabbit" in the language of the Ponka Indian tribe would literally be rendered as "man he one alive (nominative case) standing killed intentionally to shoot an arrow a rabbit him one alive (accusative case) sitting" (Lévy-Bruhl, 1910/1926, p. 140).

This precision is also found in definitions of certain complex notions; for example, in Botakud language, the word "island" is represented by four words that literally mean the following: "earth water middle is here."

Werner[35] compared this (phenomenon) with "pigeon" English, a jargon in which semi-primitive [people] created the expression "a box, when being beaten, it cries out" for the word "grand piano."

This flexible, detailed description turns out to be both the greatest advantage and the greatest drawback of primitive language. The great advantage is that such language creates a sign for almost every real object and provides the primitive man with the unique possibility of having at his disposal exceedingly exact replicas of all the objects with which he comes in contact. So it is quite clear that, given the primitive man's characteristic mode of life, for him to shift from his native tongue to a European language would mean to immediately deprive him of his most powerful means of orientation in life.

However, at the same time, this language loads thought down with endless details and particulars and does not process the data of experiences; it reproduces them not in abbreviated forms, but in the full completeness with which they were observed in reality. To communicate the simple thought that a man killed a rabbit, an Indian has to draw the whole picture of this event in full detail. That is why the words of a primitive man are not differentiated from objects, but continue to be closely connected with immediate sensory perceptions.

Wertheimer[36] described a semi-primitive man who, while being taught a European language, refused to translate the following phrase from one of the exercises: "A white man killed six bears." A white man cannot kill six bears, that is why the expression itself seemed impossible [to him]. This demonstrates the degree to which language is here understood and used only as a direct reflection of reality. It also demonstrates the extent to which it is still far removed from an independent function.

A similar case was reported by Thurnwald when he asked a primitive man to count. Due to the fact that only something definite may be counted, he counts pigs. Having reached 60, the man stops and states that it is impossible to go on counting because no owner can have more pigs.

Language operations and numeric operations turn out to be feasible only when they are connected with those concrete situations that generated them. The concrete, visual nature of primitive languages affect grammatical forms. These grammatical forms are aimed at denoting the minutest details of meaning. Thus, in the language of one of the primitive tribes', instead of the general "we" a number of individual concrete expressions can be found:

---

[35] Heinz Werner (1890–1964). German-American psychologist, specialist in developmental psychology (cf. Werner, 1961).

[36] Max Wertheimer (1880–1943), German-American Gestalt psychologist. Mostly likely Vygotsky here is referring to a passage from Wertheimer's *Über das Denken der Naturvölker. 1. Zahlen and Zahnelngebilde,* in *Zeitschrift für Psychologie,* 1912, 60, cited in volume 4 of Vygotsky's *Collected Works* (1984, p. 431).

I and thee, I and you, I and you two, I and he, and I and they. All of these expressions may also be combined with the number 2: for example, we two and thee, and we two and you. These latter (constructions) may be further combined with the plural: I, you and he, or they. In the simple conjugation of the present indicative, there are more than seventy different forms; different verbal forms denote whether the object is animate or inanimate (Lévy-Bruhl, 1910/1926, p. 141). Instead of plural and singular, in some languages forms [for groups] of two, three, and sometimes even four are used. All these things are closely connected with the concrete character of both primitive language and primitive memory.

In these languages, certain prefixes function as an expression of the subtlest nuances that are always concretely denoted by one word. The unusual richness of verbal forms in the languages of Northern Americans has been described long ago. Dobrizhoffer[37] calls the Abipone language the most terrible of all labyrinths (cited in Lévy-Bruhl, 1910/1926, p. 146). According to Veniaminov,[38] the language of the Aleutians can change a word in more than 400 ways (tense, mood, persons): each of these forms corresponds to a definite shade of meaning (cited in Lévy-Bruhl, 1910/1926, p. 146).

Many authors agree that this language is pictorial or colorful, and they see it as a tendency to "speak with the eyes"—to draw and depict what one wants to express. In this language, movement straight ahead is expressed in a different way than movement to the side, movement along an indirect route, or movement at a certain distance from the speaker. Lévy-Bruhl said: "the spatial relations which are so exactly expressed in the Klamath[39] language can be stored or reproduced in visual and muscular memory with one word."

The primacy of the spatial component is indeed the main characteristic of many primitive languages. Gatschet[40] came to the conclusion that "the

---

[37]Lévy-Bruhl (1910/1926) quotes from M. Dobrizhoffer's description of this primitive culture and language.

[38]Ivan Evseevich Veniaminov (1797–1879), Russian ethnographer and naturalist. As a missionary to the Russian-American Company (1824–1839) he studied the Aleutians and Indians of North-East America.

[39]Vygotsky's translation of this quoted statement differs in the Russian considerably when compared to the English translation of the same passage. The latter reads: "it is especially spatial relations, all that can be retained and reproduced by visual and muscular memory, that the Klamath language aims at expressing" (Lévy-Bruhl, 1910/1926, p. 147). For more information about this language, see Gatschet's *The Klamath Language* (1890 cited here from Lévy-Bruhl, 1910/1926).

[40]Gatschet studied a very large family of languages in North America known as the Klamath language. In his book about these languages, he described their main characteristics, which in Lévy-Bruhl's (1910/1926) words "obeyed a well-marked tendency which Gatschet calls 'pictorial' " (p. 147). (cf. also footnote 32 of this section)

categories of position, location and distance are of such paramount importance to the conception of uncivilized nations as are to us those of time and causality" (cited in Lévy-Bruhl, 1910/1926, p. 147–150). Any phrase or sentence must necessarily express the relationship of objects to space.

Lévy-Bruhl (1910/1926) said:

> primitive mentality does not demand *alone* [Vygotsky's emphasis] that the relative positions of things and persons in space, as well as their distance from each other, be expressed. It is not satisfied unless the language expressly specifies besides, the details regarding the form of objects, their dimensions; way of moving about in the various circumstances in which they may be place; and to accomplish this, the most diverse forms are employed. (p. 152, italics added)

The means used to this end are prefixes and suffixes denoting form and movement (form and size), the character of the environment in which the movement takes place, the position [of an object – J. K.], and so on. The number of these additional linguistic elements is unlimited. This type of detailed specification may indeed be endless in the languages of primitive people. In the language of one primitive tribe, there are ten thousand verbs; and this number can be increased with the help of a huge number of prefixes and suffixes. The Abipones have an enormous number of synonyms. They have special words to express [the following different meanings – J. K.]: to wound a man or an animal with the teeth, with a knife, with a sword, or with an arrow. They have a different word to denote fighting with a spear, with arrows, with fists, or with words. A special word is used to express [the situation where] two wives of one man are fighting because of him. Special particles are used to express the different location of the objects spoken about – up, down, around, in the water, in the air, and so on.

Speaking about the South-African tribes, Livingstone[41] said that what terrifies a traveller is not the lack of words but their abundance:

> We have heard about a score of words to indicate different varieties of gait – one walks leaning forward, or backward; swaying from side to side; loungingly or smartly; swaggeringly; swinging the arms, or only one arm; head down or up, or otherwise: each of these modes of walking was expressed by a particular verb. . . . (cited in Lévy-Bruhl, 1910/1926, pp. 157–158)

---

[41]David Livingstone (1813–1873), a Scottish missionary and explorer who had a great influence in the West with respect to the primitive peoples of Africa. Lévy-Bruhl (1910/1926) cited Livingstone's *Narrative of an Expedition to the Zambesi and Its Tributaries* (1865) and may well be Vygotsky's source.

When we examine the reasons underlying this character of (primitive) language, in addition to the flexible, eidetic memory of primitive people, we find a second cause that has the greatest significance for our explanation of the specificity of this language. This is the fact that the language of primitive man is in essence two languages in one: On the one hand, it is a language of words; on the other, it is a language of gestures. The language of primitive man conveys the images of objects in the way they are perceived by the eyes and the ears. The goal of such a language is exact reproduction.

These languages, as Lévy-Bruhl (1910/1926) said, "have a common tendency to describe, not the impression which the subject receives, but the shape and contour, position, movement, way of acting, of objects in space—in a word, all that can be perceived and delineated." This characteristic, he says, is understandable "if we note that the same peoples, as a rule, speak another language as well, a language whose characteristics necessarily react upon the minds of those who use it" (p. 158). Consequently, it determines both the mode of their thinking and the character of their oral speech.

This second language—the language of signs or gestures—is extremely widespread among primitive peoples, but is used in different situations and in different combinations with verbal language. For example, Gason[42] described how, for one tribe, sign language existed side by side with the oral language. Animals, natives, men, women, sky, earth, [the acts of] walking, mounting a horse, jumping, stealing, seeing, eating, drinking, as well as hundreds of other objects and actions have a special sign, so that a whole conversation can be conducted without a single word (cited in Lévy-Bruhl, 1910/1926, pp. 159–160).

We will not dwell on issues such as the prevalence of this language or those contexts where it may be found. We point out only the great influence that this language has as a means of thought on the very nature of mental operations. It is easy to see that language and its character determine the nature and organization of mental operations to the [same] degree that tools determine the organization and structure of any given manual task by man.

Lévy-Bruhl came to the conclusion that the majority of primitive communities possess two languages: oral speech and signs. That is why, he says, one cannot state that these languages could exist without influencing one another. Cushing,[43] in his brilliant work devoted to "manual concepts," studied the influence of manual language on oral language. He showed that

---

[42]S. Gason studied the manual languages of the Dieyerie Tribe, a native tribe in South Australia. In this section of chapter 2, the word "sign" means specifically a hand sign or gesture. Elsewhere sign conveys the general meaning of any conventional tool or technique for communication.

[43]F. H. Cushing (1979, 1990) an American anthrologist who wrote about manual concepts and sign languages of primitive people.

in one primitive language, the word order of sentences, the derivation of numerals, and so on originate from the motions generated by the hand (cited in Lévy-Bruhl, 1910/1926, p. 161).

As is well known, in order to study the mental life of primitive man, Lévy-Bruhl settled with a primitive tribe and tried to live not as a European, but as one of the natives: he participated in their ceremonies, joined their various secret societies, and so on. Patiently, with much training, he adapted his hands to primitive functions. He achieved this by using his hands to do all those things done in prehistoric times, working with those very materials and in those conditions that were characteristic of the epoch *"when the hands were so at one with the mind that they really formed a part of it"* (cited in Lévy-Bruhl, 1910/1926, p. 161).

Lévy-Bruhl stated:

> The progress of civilization was brought about by the reciprocal mutual influence of mind upon hand and *vice versa*. To reconstitute the primitives' mentality he had to rediscover the movements of their hands, movements in which their language and their thought were inseparably united. [Hence the daring yet significant expression 'manual concepts.'] A primitive man who did not speak without his hands did not think without them either. (cited in Lévy-Bruhl, 1910/1926, p. 161)[44]

Cushing showed that the extent of verb specialization found in the language of primitive man stems from the role of hand movements in the development of primitive mental activity. "He declares this to have been a grammatical necessity, and says that in the primitive mind thought-expressions, expressions-concepts, complex yet mechanically systematic, were effected more quickly than, or as quickly as, the equivalent verbal expression came into being" (cited in Lévy-Bruhl, 1910/1926, p. 162).

> Speaking with the hands is literally thinking with the hands, to a certain extent; therefore the features of these 'manual concepts' will necessarily be reproduced in the verbal expression of thought. The general processes in expression will be similar: the two languages, the signs of which differ so widely as gestures and articulate sounds, will be affiliated by their structure and their method of interpreting objects, actions, conditions. If verbal language, therefore, describes and delineates in detail positions, motions, distances, forms, and contours, it is because sign-language uses exactly the same means of expression. (cited in Lévy-Bruhl, 1910/1926, p. 162)

Originally, as the study shows, these two languages were not isolated and separated; instead, each phrase had a complex form that combined signs

---

[44]The phrase in brackets was left out of Vygotsky's citation of this passage but is in the original text of Lévy-Bruhl; we have reinstated it for clarity of meaning.

and sounds. These signs reproduced a movement that exactly depicted and described the objects or actions.

"To express *water,* the ideogram reproduces the way in which the native laps up the liquid he has taken in his hand." The word "weapon" was expressed by a menacing descriptive sign that imitated the way it [the weapon] was used.

Lévy-Bruhl (1910/1926) explained:

> In short, a man who speaks this language has at his disposal a great number of fully formed visual motor associations. [And the idea of persons or things, when it presents itself to his mind, immediately sets these associations going.] We may say that he imagines them at the moment he describes them. His verbal language, therefore, can but be descriptive also. (p. 163)[45]

Mallery[46] noted that a word in one of the Indian languages is identical with a sign and that only by studying the latter can we comprehend the language of these primitive people. He stated that one of these [two] languages explains the other and neither can be understood without knowledge of the first. The dictionary of sign language compiled by Mallery casts some light on the mental operations of those who used this language and makes clear why primitive oral language was necessarily descriptive.

German researchers called this pictographic nature "phonic pictures" that is, pictures in sounds. In one of the languages of primitive tribes, Lévy-Bruhl counted 33 verbs denoting different manners of walking. Moreover, according to him, this does not include the variety of all the adverbs that, when added to the verb, serve to describe different nuances of a gait.

According to Junod, listening to conversations among black [people — J. K.] might lead one to conclude that they have a childish manner of speaking. In fact it is just the opposite: In this picturesque language, words convey shades [of meaning — J. K.] that would be impossible to render in

---

[45]Vygotsky left out what is in brackets and we have reinserted it to make the text understandable.

[46]D. Garrick Mallery conducted research in the late 19th century on American Indian signs. His major work is *Sign Language among North American Indians* (1971), Vygotsky's knowledge of Mallery obviously comes from Lévy-Bruhl's (1926) discussion of this study on sign-language in *How Natives Think* (p. 163). Compare this passage with a similar passage from *How Natives Think:*

> Mallery tells that the words of an Indian language which are synthetic and undifferentiated parts of speech are strictly analogous in this respect with the gestures which are the elements of sign-language, and that the study of the latter is valuable of the purpose of comparison with the words. The one language explains the other, and neither can be studied to advantage if the other be unknown. (p. 163; cf. also footnote 30)

more highly developed languages. There is no reason to say that this character [the seemingly childish manner – J. K.] of a primitive man's language strongly influences the whole structure of his thinking (cited in Lévy-Bruhl, 1910/1926, p. 167).

Thinking in this sort of language, just as the language itself, is completely concrete, picturesque, and image laden. Similarly, it is full of details and deals with directly reproduced situations – with contexts extracted from real life. Lévy-Bruhl (1910/1926) pointed out both the limited abstraction [occurring – J. K.] with the use of this language and the specific "inner pictures" or images concepts that serve as the material for this type of thinking (pp. 167–168).

We have all the grounds to argue that the thinking of a primitive man using such a language is eidetic. On the basis of his own data, Jaensch[47] also came to the same conclusions. He found in this type of language an indication of sensory memory that has at its disposal an extreme multitude of optical and acoustic impressions. This "pictorial function" of the primitive language seems to him a direct indication of the eidetic character of the primitive man. In the course of cultural development of thinking and language, the eidetic character fades into the background and, at the same time, language loses its tendency to express individual concrete details.

Humboldt[48] quite reasonably said that in these languages one feels as if transferred to a completely different world because, when prompted by this type of language, perception and interpretation of the world differ profoundly from the manner of thinking that is characteristic for an educated (cultural) European.

Thurnwald, in complete agreement with these data, said that with respect to the number of words, the language of primitive man can in no way be said to be limited in expressions. From this point of view, that is, concreteness of expression, the language of primitive people surpasses the language of the cultural man. "However, it (the language of primitive man) is too closely connected with a specific activity occurring in a small space and with the living conditions to which the small group using this language is confined. Characteristics of the life of this group are reflected in a primitive man's language, as if in a mirror."

The language of those who toiled the earth turns out to have an enormous number of names for the coconut in the different stages of its flowering and ripening; the same variety of words exists for different kinds of maize. The

---

[47]E. R. Jaensch (1883–1940), a German psychologist who is best known for his work on eidetic memory. See also Jaensch (1911/1927).

[48]Wilhelm von Humboldt (1767–1835), a German philosopher. For Humboldt, language originated historically when nature and the idea became connected. From Humboldt, we have the notion of Völkerpsychologies or ethnopsychology.

language of Central Asian nomads distinguishes between horses by differences in sex and color. In the same manner Bedouins distinguish between camels, not having any generic name for these animals. So, too, other people classify dogs (by sex and color). Thurnwald says that the concreteness of a primitive utterance determines its force and expressiveness, as well as its connectedness, that is, its inability to express something separate or general or to denote a relationship to other (unconnected) things. In the absence of abstraction, this language is dominated by the enumeration of objects.

The reverse influence of thinking on language, a phenomenon described by Thurnwald, is of enormous significance. We noted earlier the degree to which the structure of mental operations depends on the means of language used. Thurnwald showed that in cases when one group of people borrows a language from another, or when languages are mixed, the stock of words is easily transferred from one language to the other without changes, but the grammatical structures are profoundly altered by the "techniques of thinking" used by those who adopt the [new] language. The very processes of thinking greatly depend on the means of thinking.

The primitive man does not have concepts; abstract, generic names are completely alien to him. He uses the word differently than we do. A word may acquire a different functional usage. The way it is used will determine the thinking operation to be realized with the help of this word.

A word can be used as a noun—as a sound associated with this or that individual object. For primitive man, it is a proper name and it is used to perform a simple associative operation of memory. We have seen that, to a large degree, primitive language is precisely at this stage of development.

Let us remember the number of proper names we found in the languages of primitive people, as well as the tendency toward maximal specification of each individual feature and object. The way an individual uses a word defines in any given case the way that individual thinks. That is why thinking in a primitive man indeed takes a second seat when compared to the activity of his memory.

The second stage in the development of word usage is that stage when the word appears as an associative sign not for an individual object, but for an aggregate or group of objects. The word becomes similar to a family or group name. It performs not so much an associative function, but a mental task; for with its help, different individual objects are categorized and combined into a certain aggregate [collective representation].

However, this combination still remains a group of individual objects, each of which, upon entering the new combination, preserves its individuality and uniqueness. At this stage a word becomes a means of forming a complex. A typical example of such a phenomenon in our languages is the family name. When I talk about a certain family, "the Petrovs," for example, I use this word to denote a definite group of persons not because they have some common feature, but because they definitely belong to a certain common group.

A complex[49] differs from a concept by the relationship established between the individual object and the group name. Looking at an object, I can state absolutely objectively whether it is a tree or a dog, because "tree" and "dog" stand for the designations of concepts, that is, general, generic groups to which different individual objects can be referred on the basis of certain essential features. Looking at a human being, I cannot say whether or not he is a Petrov. To do this, I must simply determine in *fact* whether or not this person belongs to this family. Thus, in the complex, the individual is retained as such. In the complex, different elements are combined not on the basis of some intrinsic substantial bond, but on the basis of the real, concrete contiguity that actually exists between them in one way or another.

It is at this stage of thinking in complexes that the primitive man primarily stands. His words are proper or family names, that is, signs for individual objects or signs for complexes. The primitive thinks not in concepts, but in complexes. This is the most essential feature that distinguishes primitive thinking from ours.

When Lévy-Bruhl (1910/1926) defined the thinking of the primitive man as prelogical thinking, where the most heterogeneous connections are possible at the same time, he pointed out the main characteristic of this thinking—"the law of participation [heterogeneity]" (p. 76). According to this law, primitive thinking does not follow the laws of our logic, but has its own primitive logic, based on a notion of connections that are quite different from ours. This specific type of connections, characteristic for primitive logic, implies that one and the same object can coexist in various complexes [aggregates—J. K.], that is, be an element in completely different relationships.

Thus, the law of the excluded third[50] is not valid for primitive man. For him, the fact that a human being can be included in the "human being" complex does not mean that he cannot also be a parrot: he may be at one and the same time both a "human being" and a "parakeet." Thus, Indians of the Bororo tribe boast that they are red parakeets. This does not mean that after death they become parakeets, or that parakeets are metamor-

---

[49]Lévy-Bruhl (1910/1926) used the terms *aggregate* or *collective presentation* (p. 76-77) to describe this stage in primitive thinking, however, we have chosen the term *complex,* already established by previous translators of Vygotsky's texts (cf. for example, Vygotsky, 1986, pp. 112-113). In this later text, Vygotsky described the same phenomenon as the second stage in the development of child thinking.

[50]Lat.: *lex exclusi tertii sive medii inter duo contradictoric.* One of the main laws of formal logics, according to which one of the two contradictory statements given at the same time and in the same relation is definitely true.

phosed Bororos, and must be treated as such.[51] This type of connection is inconceivable according to the laws of concept-based logic. According to this logic, a human being by the mere fact that he is a human being can simply not be a parrot (cited in Lévy-Bruhl, 1910/1926, p. 77).

This type of thinking and this type of logic, as we see, is based on complexes with concrete bonds, and of course one and the same object may have an exorbitant number of these bonds. The same person may enter different "familial groups." From the point of view of his kinship he may be a Petrov, from the point of residence he may be a Moscovite, and so on.

All the characteristics of primitive thinking can be reduced to this main fact, that is, to the fact that instead of notions, it operates with complexes. According to Werner[52] "any primitive thinking is at the same time visual thinking."

Leroy (1927) rightfully warned against making judgments about the abstract or concrete manner of primitive thinking on the basis of the external structure and character of language. One should analyze not only the tool, he said, but the way it is possibly or actually used. For example, an abundance of special terms is not the exclusive characteristics of primitiveness. This is also found in our technology; this reflects the need for exactness in the technical operations of a fisherman or a hunter. For example, in his language, a primitive man differentiates between different kinds of snow because in reality they are different things in his activity. He *has to* differentiate between them. In this case, the wealth of vocabulary reflects only the wealth of experience, and this wealth of experience is necessitated — either adapt or perish. That is why, as Leroy put it, a primitive man cannot risk an exchange of his language for Norwegian, "in which contact with objects has become very distant."[53]

Thus, technical needs and life's necessities, not the characteristics of thinking, are the real source of these features of language. For example, sign language, as it was demonstrated by Leroy[54], appears in certain economic and geographic conditions; it is created by need (when a tribe has to live among unfamiliar tribes, when chasing prey, when those living on the

---

[51]The Bororos are a tribe in Northern Brazil studied by K. von den Steinen.

[52]Heinz Werner (1890–1964), German-American psychologist and specialist in developmental psychology. As Kozulin (Vygotsky, 1986) pointed out, Werner's "views on mental development closely resembled those of Vygotsky" (p. 267). Although no citation is given here, Vygotsky is no doubt quoting from Werner's *Comparative Psychology of Mental Development* (1961). The German original (*Einführung in die Entwicklungspsycholgies,* 1900) is cited in other Vygotsky works.

[53]Although no citation is given by Vygotsky, this seems to be a statement made not by Leroy, but by Keane in his description of the Lapps and their origin and quoted by Lévy-Bruhl (1926): "The (the Lapps) resist any attempt to exchange their language for Norwegian, which is much more limited in this respect" (p. 173.)

[54]Leroy. No reference given by Vygotsky. In all probability, he is referring to Leroy's (1927). *La raison Primitive.*

plains have to communicate over long distances). *That is why all the characteristics of this language and thinking can not be considered primary in an absolute sense.* If some tribes lack generic terms for "tree," "fish," "bird," others (Queensland tribes) have generic denominations for "bird," "fish," and "snake." Often these generalizations and generic names are different from those in our languages. For example, in the language of Pitta-Pitta[55] tribe the root "pi" is found in all of the words denoting objects moving in the air: For example, bird, boomerang, moon, star, lightning, and falcon.

An analogy with our technical language where one can often see our same tendency to introduce a variety of concrete terms instead of a few abstract ones and our widespread habit of naming colors by objects (tobacco color, straw color, cherry color, coral, etc.), will convince us that it is not the primary features of primitive thinking alone — and in any case not these features in and of themselves — that determine many of the characteristics of primitive language and thinking. These characteristics are also the result of a need for "direct contact with objects" and of the requirements of technical activity.

Thus, we see that primitive thinking, which is connected with primitive language, can be characterized by the same developmental specificity as memory. Remember that development of memory is associated with a transition from the perfection of organic memory to the development and perfection of mnemotechnical signs used by memory. Similarly, the development of primitive thinking is in no way an accumulation of more and more details, of an ever-increasing vocabulary, or of a more and more sophisticated reproduction of details. The very essence of this type of primitive thinking undergoes changes, shifting to the development and perfection of language and its usage, that is, to the development of this fundamental means for facilitating the perfection of thought.

The main progress in thought development affects a shift from the first mode of using a word as a proper name to the second mode, where a word is a sign of a complex, and finally to the third mode, where a word is a tool or means for developing the concept. Just as the cultural development of memory was found to have the closest connections with the historical development of writing, the cultural development of thinking is found to have the same close connection with the history of the development of human language.

NUMERIC OPERATIONS AND PRIMITIVE MAN

A study of primitive man's numeric operations gives us the most explicit example of his thinking development and of the dependence of this

---

[55]Pitta-Pitta — Australian aborigines.

development on the perfection of external signs that govern and realize development. Many primitive peoples have no numbers for counting beyond 2 or 3.

However, it would be wrong to infer from this that they cannot count beyond 3. This means only that they lack abstract concepts extending beyond these numbers. They cannot use those operations that are characteristic of our way of thinking, Lévy-Bruhl (1910/1926) says, but "by the processes which are peculiar to them they can obtain the same results to a certain extent" (pp. 181–182).

These operations depend to a greater degree on memory. Primitive man counts in a way that is different from our way (of counting)—a way that might sooner be termed *concrete*—and with this concrete method (of counting), primitive man again surpasses cultural man. In other words, the study of the calculation processes in primitive man shows that here again, as with memory and speech, primitive man is not only not inferior (poorer), but in a certain sense superior (richer) to cultural man. Thus, it would be more correct to speak here not about quantitative differences, but about the *qualitatively* different way in which primitive man counts.

If we want to characterize in one word the specificity of the primitive man's numeric operations, we may say that he has primarily developed a natural arithmetic. His calculation depends on concrete perception, on natural remembering, on comparison. He does not resort to the technical operations created by cultural man to facilitate calculation. If we do not count in any other way but with the help of numbers, then we are ready to admit that those who do not have numbers above 3 cannot count beyond 3. "But are we obliged to take it for granted that the apprehension of a definite plurality of objects can take place in one way only?" Lévy-Bruhl asked. "Is it impossible for the mentality of primitive peoples to have its own peculiar operations and processes to attain the end we reach by numerations" (Lévy-Bruhl, 1910/1926, p. 182). The primitive perceives a group of objects in its quantitative aspect. In this case, the qualitative characteristic appears as the known, immediately perceived quality distinguishing this group from other groups. And the primitive can judge by the outward appearance whether the group is complete or not. It must be said that this immediate perception of quantities can be found in cultural man as well, mainly in cases of perception of ordered quantities. If a performer were to omit one bar from a piece of music, or someone were to "steal" one syllable from a poem, immediately, without resorting to calculations, we would conclude on the basis of the immediate perception of the rhythm that a bar or a syllable is missing. On these grounds Leibniz[56] called music an unconscious mathematics.

---

[56]Gottfried Wilhelm Leibniz (1646–1716) a German philosopher, mathematician, physicist, and linguist. In *Monadologie* (1714/1991), Leibniz postulates that the world consists of

Something of the same sort takes place in the primitive when he perceives groups with a different quantity of objects; for example, a group of twelve apples in their immediate impression differs from a group of three apples. The difference between these two quantities can be perceived concretely without counting. This in no way astonishes us because in this respect we have the same ability to judge by eye which of the two groups is bigger.

What usually struck the researchers was the level of sophisticated differentiation the primitive man reached in this art. Researchers tell us that on the basis of his outstanding memory, the primitive refines this immediate perception of quantities to the greatest degree. Collating the present impressions with an image in the memory, he detects the absence of one object in some large group.

Dobrizhoffer said about the primitives [the Abipones]:

> They are not only ignorant of arithmetic, but they dislike it. Their memory generally fails them. . . . they cannot endure the tedious process of counting. . . . When they return from an excursion to hunt wild horses . . . none of the Abipones will ask them, 'How many horses have you brought home?' but 'How much space will the herd of horses which you have brought home occupy?' (cited in Lévy-Bruhl, 1910/1926, p. 183)

When the primitives prepare for a hunt, they glance over their many dogs and immediately notice if one is missing. In just the same way, the primitive man can detect the absence of a single animal in a herd of several hundred animals. This precise differentiation is essentially a further development of the same immediate perception of quantities that we notice in ourselves.

If distinguishing between the group of 12 apples from the group of 3 apples is as easy as differentiating the color red from blue, then differentiating a herd of 100 animals from a herd of 101 animals, let us say, is just as difficult as distinguishing between one shade of the blue and another that may be just a little darker. However, this is the same operation but developed to a greater differentiation through practice.

It is interesting to note that modern cultural man also has to resort to visual concrete perception of quantities whenever he wants to vividly and clearly perceive a difference between some quantities. From this point of view, Wertheimer (1912) was correct when he said that the natural arithmetic of primitive peoples, like their thinking in general, is at the same time both *more and less* than ours: it is *less* effective, because certain

---

countless "psychic" energetic substances — monads. Their interelationship is one of a preestablished harmony that expresses itself through music and mathematics. According to Leibniz, man possesses inherent mental or "psychic" abilities to perceive these higher forms of harmony.

operations turn out to be completely inaccessible for the primitive man and his abilities in this area to be much more limited than ours (pp. 274–275).[57] This natural arithmetic is *more* effective, because his thinking is always anchored in the context of reality. It lacks abstraction and immediately reproduces a live concrete situation; and often, as is so in our everyday life and art, these concrete images turn out to be much more real than abstract representations.

When a modern pacifist wants to give a vivid notion of the great number of people killed at war and make you feel it, this person transforms the abstract mathematical sum into new concrete albeit artificial representations. The pacifist may say: "If the corpses of all those killed at war were placed in a row shoulder to shoulder, they would extend from Vladivostok to Paris." With this graphic image, the pacifist wants to convey an immediate sense, as in a visual perception, of the huge magnitude of this number.

In just the same way, when trying to represent with a typical diagram something simple such as the quantity of soap consumed in China and in Germany, we draw for this purpose a huge Chinese man and a small German, which symbolizes the number of times the population of China is bigger than the population of Germany. Under these figures we would draw one small and one huge piece of soap, so that this whole picture—this diagram—tells us directly more than the abstract mathematical data will. It is these pictures—these graphic means—that are used in primitive arithmetic of primitive man.

Lévy-Bruhl (1910/1926) described the attitude of the primitive peoples to our numeration: It is "an instrument the need for which they can not recognize, and the use of which is unfamiliar to them. They do not want numbers, apart from the totals which they can count so easily in their own way" (p. 184).

This concreteness or visual nature of primitive counting is manifested in a number of characteristics. If a primitive wants to denote 3 or 5 men, he does not designate the sum of men, as Thurnwald said, but calls everybody he knows personally by name; if he does not know the name, then he counts them using some other concrete feature: for example, a man with a big nose, an old man, a child, a man with sick skin, and a small man are all waiting—and all this instead of saying "five men came."

A total is perceived initially as an image of some picture. The image and the quantity are still merged in a single complex. That is why, as we showed before, abstract calculation for a primitive mind is impossible; a primitive calculates only as long as his calculation seems to him to be associated with

---

[57]See also Wertheimer's (1912) investigation of numeric operations of primitive people in his "Über das Denkens der Naturvölker, Zahlen und Zahlgebilde."

reality. Thus, a number to primitive peoples is always a name, which denotes something concrete; it is a numerical image or a shape, used as a symbol for a certain sum. Very often in these cases we are simply speaking about an auxiliary means of memory.

The crucial role, however, is played not by this factor but by the direction that the development of calculation takes. This development does not follow a path of further improvement [refinement — J. K.] of natural arithmetic, but develops in the same way as primitive memory and thinking does, that is, by the creation of specific signs that facilitate the switching from natural arithmetic to cultural arithmetic.

True, for primitive peoples this usage of signs still bears a concrete and visual–optical character. The simplest way of enumeration for a primitive man is an association with body parts, which he compares with this or that group of objects. Thus, the primitive man at the highest level of his development no longer simply sizes up at a glance a certain group of objects, but performs a quantitative correlation of one given group with another, for example, with five fingers. On the basis of one certain aspect, namely quantity, he compares the group of objects to be counted with some *tool for enumeration.*

In this sense, the primitive took a most important step toward abstraction and initiated a most important transition to absolutely new ways of development. However, in its initial usage, the new tool still remains purely concrete. Primitive peoples continue to calculate solely in a visual manner. They touch one after one their fingers, parts of the hand, arm, eyes, nose, and forehead; then, they touch the same body parts on the other side, thus equating in a purely visual way the number of objects with their own body parts, which are enumerated in a certain order.

At this step, there are no numerals in the proper sense. As Lévy-Bruhl noted, here we find a concrete method [of counting], an operation of memory, which aids the determination of a given sum total. According to Haddon,[58] this system is used as an auxiliary aid in counting; it is used like a knotted string, but not like a series of actual numbers (cited in Lévy-Bruhl, 1910/1926, p. 184). It is sooner a mnemonic device than a numeric operation. At this step, there are neither numeral names nor numbers in the proper sense. Lévy-Bruhl called attention to the fact that in this method of counting, one and the same word may denote different quantities, for example in New Guinea the word "ano" (neck) is used to denote both the numbers 10 and 14 (cited in Lévy-Bruhl, 1910/1926, p. 186).

Similarly, for other primitive peoples the words denoting a finger, an

---

[58]A. Haddon (1901–1935) studied the West Tribes of Torres Straits and edited a six-volume study devoted to the anthropological expeditions to this area. His work is repeatedly cited in Lévy-Bruhl (1910/1926).

arm, and a hand stand for different quantities depending on whether they are associated with the process of calculating with the right or left side [of the body — J. K.]. From this, Lévy-Bruhl (1910/1926) concluded that the terms used do not designate numbers. He asks: "How could the word 'doro' stand for for 2, 3, 4 and for 19, 20, 21 alike if it were not differentiated by the gesture which indicates the special finger of the right or left hand?" (p. 188).

We present an excellent example, given by Brooke,[59] about the way a native from Borneo tried to remember an errand. He had to visit 45 villagers, who had rebelled and had been subjugated, and inform them about the amount of penalty they were to pay. How did he set about this errand? He brought a few dry leaves, which he divided into parts. His chief exchanged these for pieces of paper. The man arranged them on a table, placing one piece after the other, and at the same time counted them with his fingers. Then he put his foot on the table and with the help of his toes started counting the remaining pieces of paper, each of which served as the sign for a village name, the name of its chief, the number of its warriors, and the amount of the fine. When he was through with the toes, he came back to the fingers, ending his counting with 45 pieces of paper laid out on the table (cited in Lévy-Bruhl, 1910/1926, pp. 188–189).

Then he was asked to repeat his errand, which he did. In doing so, he went over the pieces of paper and touched upon his fingers and toes as before. " 'Now,' he said, 'this is our kind of letter; you, white men read differently to us.' Late in the evening he repeated them all correctly, placing his finger on each paper and then said: 'Now, if I recollect them tomorrow morning it will be all right; so leave these papers on the table.' " Then he mixed the papers in a pile. In the morning he arranged the papers in the same order as the day before and repeated all the details with perfect accuracy. For a month, going around the country from one village to another, he never forgot even one of the different amounts (cited in Lévy-Bruhl, 1910/1926, p. 189).[60]

Lévy-Bruhl noted: "The substitution of pieces of paper for the fingers and toes is particularly noteworthy, for it is a clear case of abstraction, still really concrete, with which the prelogical mind is familiar" (cited in Lévy-Bruhl, 1910/1926, p. 189). It is indeed hard to imagine an example that could better serve as a more striking demonstration of the most essential difference between human and animal memory. Once he encountered a task that surpasses the natural resources of his memory, the

---

[59]Rajah Brooke wrote a study of his 10 years in the Sarawak working with the Dayaks of Borneo.

[60]In this long quotation, the quotations marks in the Vygotsky text were placed only around the actual speech of the natives.

primitive resorts to paper and to fingers and toes—to the creation of external signs.

He tries to exert influence on his memory from outside. He organizes the internal processes of memorizing from without, substituting internal operations for external activity, which most easily yields to his control. By organizing external activity he gains control of his memory through the use of signs. Herein lies the essential difference between human and animal memory. At the same time, this example shows how closely the primitive's operations of calculation are tied to memory operations.[61]

Roth[62] asked a primitive man how many fingers and toes he had and asked him to mark their number with the lines on the sand. The man started to turn his fingers down in twos and, for each pair, drew a double line on the sand. This practice is used by the tribe elders to count the men. It is in this phenomenon that we see an indirect instrumental method used to create the perception of quantity with the help of signs. As we can see, the transition from a natural arithmetic based on the direct perception of quantities to a mediated operation realized with the help of signs is found already in the very first stages of man's cultural development.

This method of counting with the help of body parts—this concrete enumeration—gradually becomes semi-abstract (semi-concrete) and constitutes the first stage of our arithmetic. Haddon said, " 'N*abiget*' can hardly be said to be the name of the number five, but that there were as many objects referred to as there are fingers on one hand" (cited in Lévy-Bruhl, 1910/1926, p. 190). Hence, at the base of such calculation is an unspoken image or pictorial comparison, *a manual,* or, according to Haddon, a visual *conception,* without which the development of primitive numeric operations would be incomprehensible.

---

[61]We should note the importance of these ideas for the other theoretical and experimental studies conducted by Vygotsky's students, reflected, for example, in A. N. Leontiev's (1931, 1981) research on the development of higher forms of memory. These studies were conducted within the framework of *the cultural historic theory* and dealt with the forms and development of *mediation* both in ontogenetic and phylogenetic aspects. See also Vygotsky (1928).

[62]Compare with

I have often had a practical demonstration of the fact [that the Pitta-Pitta aboriginal has visible conceptions of higher numbers] by asking him to mark the number in the sand. He commences with the hand open, and turns his fingers down by two, and for every two he will make a double stroke on the sand. . . . This method of counting is common throughout the district, and often practiced by the elders of the tribe *to ascertain the number of individuals in camp* (cited in Lévy-Bruhl, 1926, pp. 189–190).

This passage was written by W. E. Roth (1897) Ethnological Studies among the N.W. Central Queensland Aborigines. The italics are Lévy-Bruhl's. According to Lévy-Bruhl, Roth compiled "a fairly detailed dictionary" of the Copper's Creek natives.

This visual origin of numeric nominations is displayed in the primitive's tendency to count not by units, but by distinctly different groups; for example, by twos, fours, fives and so on. For this reason, although he often possesses a very small number of numerals, he nevertheless can calculate extremely large quantities [number totals—J. K.], repeating the same numerals several times.

The same concrete character is indicated by the various enumeration systems that many primitive tribes have for counting different objects, for example, for flat or round objects, for animals or people, for time, for long objects and so on. Different objects have to be calculated in different ways. So, for example, in the Mikir[63] language there are different calculation systems to count people, animals, trees, houses, flat or round objects, and body parts. A numeral is always a number of a definite object.

We can see traces of this in our culture preserved in the different methods for counting objects. Pencils, for example, up to this day are counted by dozens, grosses, and so on. Of particular interest in this respect are those auxiliary words that many primitive peoples use when counting. The purpose of these auxiliary words is to visualize the consecutive stages of an arithmetic operation. When in this language they say, for example, 21 fruits, it literally means: above the 20 fruits I put 1 on the very top. When they say 26 fruit, it is expressed like this: above two groups of 10 fruit each I put 6 on the top. Here, as Lévy-Bruhl said, we see the same pictorial arithmetic, a feature we have seen in the general construction of the language (Lévy-Bruhl, 1910/1926, p. 200).

However paradoxical this conclusion may seem, it is nevertheless true: In the lowest [most primitive—J. K.] societies, people calculated for centuries without numbers. It would be a mistake to believe that the human mind created numbers in order to count; on the contrary, people began counting before they managed to create numbers.

Wertheimer gave an excellent explanation of the link between numeric operations and the concrete situation. He illustrated how those very numeric images that the primitives used are connected to real possible situations. What is impossible in reality is also impossible for them in their numeric operations. Where there is no real concrete connection between objects, for these people no logical relation can exist. For example, for the primitive, 1 horse + 1 horse = 2 horses; 1 man + 1 man = 2 men, but 1 horse + 1 man = 1 rider.

Wertheimer (1912) posed the general question, how do these people behave when they face those mental problems that we solve when operating

---

[63]The Mikir language is of the Naga group of the Tibeto-Burman family and uses generic prefixes with the terms for these words in order to indicate numbers (Lévy-Bruhl, 1910/1926, p. 198).

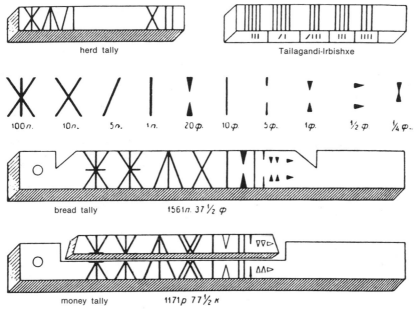

FIG. 2.8 Tallies of the Buryats in Irkutsk. Special signs in the wood, indicating the number of cattle, bread, money, and so on. The tallies serve as a primitive record, a receipt, or a promissory note, substituting an inadequate system of numbers and letters (Khoroshikh, 1926).

with numbers? It turns out that the primitive faces this type of problem very often. In such cases, at the lowest stages of development, he operates with immediate [direct] perceptions of quantities, and at the highest levels—with numeric images, still having a purely concrete character, which he uses as signs or tools.

At an early stage, small stones, fingers, and sticks were used as signs or auxiliary tools; subsequently these became tallies (Fig. 2.8, taken from Khoroshikh, 1926). Finally, when a primitive runs out of fingers, he calculates with the help of his friend's fingers, and, if necessary, he involves a third party; and sometimes the fingers of every new comrade stand for the next numeric category (tens).

In the calculation of primitive peoples, we often find signs approximating those of the Romans. For example, the Zuñi[64] express all numbers with the help of knots: a simple knot stands for 1, a more complex one stands for 5, a still more complex knot stands for 10. A quantity of 2 is expressed by 1 + 1. Five preceded by a simple knot stands for 4; 5 followed by a knot means 6. This system of designating smaller quantities by subtraction of one

---

[64]Zuñis, Australian aborigines.

from the larger quantities shows that the arithmetical orientation of the primitive was based on complete, whole, natural ensembles (fingers of a hand, etc.).

One researcher[65] gave an excellent example of the way a primitive man counts.[66] This example sheds some light on the development of numeric systems. A primitive first calculates with the fingers on one hand, saying at the same time: this is one, and so on; coming to the last finger, he says, 1 hand. Then he counts the fingers on the other hand, and then the toes on his feet. If he is not through with his calculations, then "1 hand" is taken as a unit of higher value. From then on, as he counts his fingers and toes, he counts in "fives," that is, he counts his hands as whole units.

This operation may be simulated in a purely experimental way. Imagine that a group of educated people were asked to count 27 objects, being warned that, like certain primitive people, they are unable to calculate beyond 5. As our experiments show, part of the group cannot solve the problem at all, others solve the problem, but do it ignoring the conditions of the task; finally, a third sector solves it absolutely correctly and identically.

They count the objects, all the while repeating the row from 1 to 5, then they start counting the "fives" and give the result in the following way: there are 5 "fives" plus 2. The study shows that enumeration in our decimal system is based exactly on this method of counting. This calculation always has, so to say, two strands: first we count the objects themselves and then we calculate our calculations, that is, groups of these objects. Thus, for example, when I count 21, 22, 23, and so on, then 31, 32, 33, in fact I am counting the objects only with the help of the numbers 1, 2, and 3. The words twenty, thirty, added each time, show me that the calculation is performed within limits of a second or third [group of — J. K.] ten.

Experimental studies have produced an extremely interesting conclusion, demonstrating that our system of calculation counts for us. The bifurcation of attention that a primitive had to accomplish by first calculating with his fingers and then with his hands, using the same fingers, is done for us by the decimal system. That is why psychologists say that when we calculate, from a psychological point of view this is not counting at all, but recall. We use our system of calculation automatically; we reproduce the sequential number line and, reaching a certain point, we have the ready result. What we see in an adult cultural man in hidden, automatic, and already-

---

[65](J. K., V. G.) Vygotsky noted in his introduction that this material and the subsequent diagram were taken from the work of P. P. Khoroshikh.

[66]Pavel Pavlovich Khoroshikh was a famous archaeologist and ethnographer who studied illiterate and semiliterate people in the area of Lake Baikal, mainly the Buyat and Yakut peoples.

developed form exists in the primitive still in bare-faced form, in a developing state.

It is interesting to note that these specific auxiliary means are used not only for simple calculations, but also for complex arithmetical operations. Wertheimer (1912) told about a remarkable way of counting found among the Kurds who live at the Russian–Persian border. Having no abstract operation for counting, Kurds multiply in the following way. The numbers from 6 to 10 are represented by bending one, two, three, four, and five fingers (implying plus five). Multiplication from 5×5 to 10×10 is performed so that the bent fingers are totalled as tens, whereas the straight fingers are multiplied as ones.

For example, one has to multiply 7×8. To do so, it is necessary to bend two fingers on one hand $(2 + 5 = 7)$ and three fingers on the other hand $(3 + 5 = 8)$. Then it necessary to put two hands together, total up the bent fingers $(2 + 3 = 5)$, and multiply the stretched fingers—this makes six $(2 \times 3 = 6)$. The result is 56.

Leroy pointed out that cultural peoples also have numeric multiples or numeric images (century, year, week, month, squadron—these are all numeric images). He asked: "In what way is the word *kogo,* meaning one hundred coco-nuts in the Fiji language, more primitive than the word *century* which means one hundred years?" If we have 10 soldiers walking separately, this is just 10 men, but if they are walking with a corporal in a formation, we have a platoon: here Leroy saw an analogy with the fact that in the primitive languages, a number "describes special conditions [contexts]" in which calculation takes place.[67]

Leroy's main conclusion seems to us irrefutable; one cannot equate primitive enumeration with "the counting" of animals, that is, all primitive arithmetic cannot be reduced to an immediate perception of quantities. The most characteristic feature of this arithmetic is the fact that this "embryonic scale of notation always has to resort to the help of *concrete mnemotechnics* (use of fingers, sticks) in order to get beyond certain limits." A combination of natural arithmetic (immediate perception of quantities) with mnemotechnical [calculations—J. K.] is the most specific characteristic of the primitive system of counting. Leroy correctly compared this arithmetic with the way that illiterate people calculate, on the one hand, and with use of visual numbers (diagrams) in our culture [on the other—J. K.].

Subsequent development of "cultural mathematics" has been very closely connected with the evolution of signs and the means of their usage. This applies not only to the lowest, but also to the highest stages of the development of scientific mathematics. Newton, when explaining the

---

[67]Vygotsky gives no citation, however, more than likely he is citing from Leroy's *La raison primitive* (1927).

essence of the algebraic method, said that in order to solve problems involving numbers or abstract relations among values, one must first translate the problem from English or any other language in which it is presented into an algebraic language capable of conveying our notions about the correlation of values.

Sheremetievskii brilliantly assessed this role of signs as tools in his essay "The History of Mathematics." He said, "As regards a strictly mathematical analysis, one characteristic feature transforms it into a real thought machine, performing its work with the speed and precision of a well tuned mechanism. I mean here the technique of symbolically registering all the results of the analysis with an algebraic sign."

In his comparison of modern sign-based algebra with the rhetorical algebra of ancient people, Sheremetievskii concluded that all the psychological work entailed in problem solving is transformed under the influence of these new means of denoting operations. He said about ancient mathematicians:

> They lacked a symbolic system which makes reasoning mechanical [automatic] and represents the great advantage of modern algebra. In their non-symbolic rhetorical algebra one had always to strain the memory and imagination to be able to keep in mind all the logical threads linking the final conclusions with the conditions of the problem. The ancient mathematician had to develop that specific frame of mind which is characteristic of chess players who play blind without looking at the board. Such operations required a 'super-human comprehension.' That Euclid did not find himself any followers and the theory of incommensurables[68] remained in this form for 1800 years testifies to the exceptional strength needed for abstract thinking required with this type of operation.

PRIMITIVE BEHAVIOR

Thus, we see that the primitive has already made the most important step [forward — J. K.] in his development when he switches from natural arithmetic to the use of signs. We noted the same phenomenon in the development of the spheres of memory and thinking as well. We are

---

[68]Sheremetievskii is referring to Euclid's systems of 465 theorems, which constitute on axiomatic deductive method. According to this method, the truth of the derived theorems follows from the truth of the axioms and postulates that are offered as self-evident. However, the parallel postulate was less self-obvious. Here, instead of the result of one self evident truth, two alternative outcomes were shown to be possible, existing side by side without contradiction. Consequently, nonEuclidean geometry emerged to allow for this phenomenon.

justified in saying that the overall path of the historic development of human behavior stems from this very step.

Just as the increasing supremacy of man over nature is based not so much on the development of his natural organs but on the perfection of his technology, so too the continuing growth of his behavior stems primarily from the perfection of external signs, external methods and ways that develop in a certain social context under the pressure of technical and economic needs.

All of man's natural psychological operations are reconstructed under this influence as well. Some of them die out, others develop. But most important, most crucial, and most characteristic for the whole process [of the development — J. K.] is the fact that its perfection comes from outside and is determined in the end by the social life of the group or a people to which the individual belongs.

If with the ape we find the phenomenon of tool use but an absence of sign usage, then with primitive man we see the phenomenon of labor that develops on the basis of primitive tools as the foundation of his existence. We also find a transition from the natural psychological processes (such as eidetic memory, immediate perception of quantities) to the usage of cultural signs, to the creation of specific cultural devices that help primitive man regulate his own behavior.

However, in this respect, there is one feature that characterizes the developmental stage reached by the primitive. When we wish to characterize the primitive with one word, we usually speak about magic or magic thinking as the most characteristic feature of his [existence — J. K.]. This word, as we will now try to show, characterizes not only his outward behavior, which is concentrated on gaining control over nature, but also his inner behavior, concentrated on gaining control over himself.

Any of numerous simple examples will easily reveal what a magical act is. A man wants it to rain. With this purpose in mind, he imitates rain through a special ritual: he blows, imitating wind, waves his hands, imitating lightning, beats a drum, imitating thunder, and pours out water; in a word, he imitates rain — he creates a visual picture similar to the one he wants to call forth in reality. The primitive or semiprimitive resorts to the same type of magic based on analogy, when he performs the sexual act on a sown field, wishing in this way to bring fertility to the land.

As Danzel (1912) correctly pointed out, the primitive performs the ritual of fertility in those cases where we would use technological agricultural means. The analysis of these simplest examples readily shows that the primitive uses magical operations in cases where he wishes to gain control or domination over nature — to invoke a certain phenomena with the help of these magical operations.

This is why magical activity is really strictly human behavior. This is also why it is wrong to consider magic to be exclusively a deficiency in thought development. On the contrary, in a certain sense, it represents a great step forward in comparison with animal behavior. It reflects man's maturing tendency to gain control over nature, that is, his tendency to make a transition to a principally new form of adaptation.

Magic reflects not only an attempt to dominate nature, but an equally strong attempt to control one's self. From this point of view, we find in magic the embryo of another, purely human form of behavior: an attempt to gain control over reactions. In principle, magic produces an identical effect on the natural elements and man's behavior. Magic, to the same degree, casts a spell on love and rain. That is why we see in magic in its undeveloped form both the future technique for controlling nature and the cultural techniques for controlling man's own behavior.

That is why Danzel said that in contrast to the objective practical usages of our technology, magical behavior can be seen as the use of subjective, intuitively used psychological devices (psycho-technology). Danzel saw the point of departure and the most essential line of man's cultural development in this undifferentiated state of the objective and subjective and in the gradual polarization of the two.

Indeed, complete differentiation of the objective and subjective becomes possible only on the basis of a developed system of techniques that help man in his ascendancy over nature become cognizant of it as something extraneous, having its own specific laws. In the sphere of his own behavior, as man accumulates certain psychological experience, he becomes aware of the laws regulating that behavior.

Man produces an impact upon nature by combining its forces, making some of them act on others. In the same way, he exerts an influence on his own [behavior — J. K.], combining external forces (stimuli) and bringing them to bear an influence on himself. This experience of exerting an influence by means of intermediate external forces, this path of using "tools," is, from a psychological point of view, identical for both technology and behavior.

Bühler and Koffka were quite right when they said that the appearance of a child's first word as a sign to denote an object is an absolute psychological parallel of the chimpanzees' use of a stick in their experiments. Observations of a child show that, from a psychological point all of view, the characteristics of the process we saw in the chimpanzee are repeated here. The distinctive feature of the primitive's magical thinking is that his attempts to control nature and his attempts to control himself have not yet become differentiated.

Reinach[69] defined magic as a strategy of animism. Other authors —

---

[69]Salamon Reinach (1853-1932), a French archiologist who investigated the history or

Hubert and Mauss[70] — defined magic as techniques of animism. Indeed, the primitive who perceives nature as a system of animated objects and forces interacts with these forces in the same way that he does with an animate creature. Therefore Tylor (1874, 1877) correctly saw the essence of magic in the erroneous promotion of the ideal over the real.

Frazer[71] was right when he said that magic equates control over one's thoughts with control over objects; natural laws are replaced by psychological law. For the primitive, what is brought together in in the mind is also brought together in reality. This is the basis of imitative magic. One can easily see in the examples of the magic practices introduced earlier that power over nature is established according to the law of simple association by similarity.

Because the ritual being performed resembles rain, it should therefore call forth rain in nature; because the sexual act results in fertility, it should provide for a good harvest. Such practices are feasible only on the basis of a conviction that the laws of nature coincide with the laws of thinking. This identification of the laws of nature with the laws of thinking underlies other magic practices, for example, the intention of causing someone harm by stabbing, wounding, or tearing the person's picture, by burning that persons hair, and so on.

Our description of the magic behavior would be incomplete if we did not mention that man is found to show the same magic attitude not only in relation to nature, but also in relation to himself.

Words, figures, and knots, used to remember, gradually begin to play the role of magical means because the primitive has not yet acquired sufficient control over his own behavior to understand the real laws of language, numeration, or mnemotechnical signs. The success achieved with the help of these means seems to him to be magic; hence, savages attribute to some magical power the ability of white people to convey their thoughts to each other with a note.

However, it would be the gravest mistake to make, as Lévy-Bruhl did, the magical character of primitive thinking and behavior an absolute and to ascribe to it the significance of a primary, independent trait. Studies show, as Thurnwald said, that magic is not significantly widespread among the most primitive peoples. Its development takes root only among semideveloped primitive people and flourishes among the highest [most developed — J. K.] primitives and ancient, cultural [civilized — J. K.] people. Substantial

---

religion and art and who wrote about scientific expeditions to Tunisia (1884–1888). No indication given in Vygotsky's text about which work by Reinach he read.

[70]cf. Hubert and Mauss, "Esquisse d'une Théorie Générale de la Magie," *Année Sociologique* or *Mélangies d' Histoire des Religious* (cited in Lévy-Bruhl, 1910/1926, pp. 99, 134–135, 237, 366).

[71]See Sir J. G. Frazer (1890), *The Golden Bough*. Vygotsky does not give a direct reference.

cultural development is the necessary prerequisite for the appearance of magic.

Thus, we see that primitive and magic behaviors do not coincide completely and that magic is not the primary feature of thinking, but one which appears comparatively late. Leroy (1927) said: "Lévy-Bruhl finds in magic the main sphere for support of his ideas. However even some cultural peoples have magic, and magic as well as belief in magic powers do not necessarily mean a kind of thinking which avoids the laws of logic." The latter is particularly important because it provides for an understanding of the true place and importance of magic in primitive thinking. We have already quoted Thurnwald's excellent analysis, where he showed that the magic ceremony of driving spirits out of a sick man is quite logical from the point of the primitive's understanding of the causes of the disease.

Thurnwald then showed that a certain development of technical power in the hands of the primitive is a necessary prerequisite for the appearance of magic. This development of primitive technology[72] and thinking is the necessary precondition for behavior to acquire a magical character. Therefore, it is not magic that generates primitive technology and the mode of primitive thinking, but technology and, connected with it, technical means of primitive thinking that generate magic.

This becomes particularly clear if we take into account not only the later appearance of magic and its relative independence from primitivity, but also the fact that even in those cases where magic is widely developed, it hardly acquires absolute domination over the primitive's behavior and thinking; it does not color his entire behavior. Rather, as studies show, magic is only *one* aspect of his behavior, only *one* plane or dimension of behavior, and only *one* sphere that, of course, is closely connected with the other spheres but does not replace or merge with them.

We have already referred to the view of one researcher, according to which the the primitive would die within a day, if he really thought as Lévy-Bruhl described. This is really true. Any adaptation to nature, any primitive technical activity, hunting, fishing, war — in short, *everything* that constitutes the real foundation of his life would be impossible on the grounds of magic thinking alone. Similarly, no regulation of behavior, no mnemotechnics, no writing or numeration, and no use of signs, would be possible on the basis of magic alone. Control of the natural elements and one's own behavior requires not imaginary but real thinking, not mystical but logical thinking, not magical but technical thinking.

We have already pointed out that the magical meaning attached to the first mnemotechnical means, words and numbers — signs in general — is of later origin and in no way is an initial or primary phenomenon. The

---

[72]Vygotsky means here the development of a system of external means, techniques, or tools.

mystical meaning of numbers, as Leroy accurately states, contains nothing primitive. This refers to other later appearances of magical forms as well. Magic in no way serves as the initial point in cultural development, as a synonym for primitiveness, or as the start of thinking. However, even when magic does appear, it does not, as has been said, overlay all behavior.

Leroy (1927) said: "The primitive lives on two different planes—the natural experimental and the supernatural, or mystical plane. This refers both to the primitive's mind and his life. These planes may merge but such a combination is not the rule, as Lévy-Bruhl says." If the importance of magicians should not be underestimated, then, as seen by Leroy in another light, it should also not be overestimated. And most essential is that the significance of magic must be discussed in its own realm: "In other words, one cannot argue that the primitive mind constantly mixes magic power and technical skill" (Leroy, 1927). A chieftain, for example, is not a magician, but one who in his old age possesses experience, courage, and the gift of an orator.

Lévy-Bruhl's major mistake was that he underestimated the primitive's technical activity, his practical intellect, and his use of tools, which is infinitely more superior than but genetically connected with the chimpanzee's operations and has at its roots nothing in common with magic. Lévy-Bruhl often erroneously equated the thinking of a primitive with his instinctive and automatic activity.

Àpropós of this, Leroy (1927) said:

One cannot compare, as Lévy-Bruhl does, the technical activity of primitive people with the adroitness of a billiard player. Such a comparison might be possible in reference to the way the primitive swims, climbs trees, but making a bow, or an ax cannot be reduced to instinctive operations: it is necessary to select the material, find out its properties, dry it out, soften it, cut it etc. In all of these operations adroitness may give the movements greater precision but it can neither render them meaningful nor combine them. It may be that a billiard player is in no way a mathematician, *but the designer* of a billiard had to possess something greater than instinctive adroitness. Does the absence of an abstract theory mean the absence of logic? Why does a savage, who sees a boomerang returning to him, not attribute this to the activity of a ghost? He must see this as the effect of a form and isolate the useful details of this form in order to be able to reproduce them later.

Our goals do not include an extensive analysis of this problem. The question of magic goes far beyond our topic and requires more than a psychological study and interpretation. We would, however, venture a theoretical hypothesis that magical thinking that embodies the disparity between the need for and the possibility of gaining control over natural powers is not only called forth by an insufficient development of technology and reason, accompanied by an overestimation of one's own strengths, but as a rule appears at a certain stage of technology and thinking development as the necessary product of his predisposition to regulate nature and his own behavior, not yet distinguishable from the primitive unity of "naive psychology and physics."

In our analysis, we have continually tried to show how the means of thinking, with which the primitive mind is armed, inevitably result in complex thinking, thus preparing the psychological ground for magic. Division of the stream of development into a practically functioning intellect, technical thinking, and verbal thinking constitutes the second necessary prerequisite for the appearance of magic. The need to develop technical thinking early on, to adapt, and to bend the natural elements to his will constitutes the most important feature differentiating the primitive's intellect from that of the child.

The third theory of cultural–psychological[73] development, which we mentioned at the beginning of this chapter and the essential aspects of which we have attempted to develop in our essay, holds that the major factors in the primitive's psychological development are the development of technology and, corresponding to it, the development of a social structure. Magic does not give birth to technology, but a certain level of technological development *under the specific conditions of primitive life* generates magic thinking.

This primitive unity of a "naive psychology" and a "naive physics" becomes especially clear in primitive labor practices, which we unfortunately had to leave out of our analysis, but which reveal a real clue to an understanding of the whole behavior of the primitive. This unity finds its material symbolic expression in the unification of tool and sign often seen in primitive peoples. Bucher[74] said: "On the islands of Borneo and Celebes special sticks for digging were found, on the upper part of those sticks there was a smaller one. When the stick was used for hoeing the soil while sowing rice, the smaller stick produced some sound." This sound, being something like a work cry or a command, had the purpose of rhythmically organizing work. The sound of the device attached to the stick served as a substitute for the human voice. A tool used as a means to have an impact on nature and a sign used as a means for stimulating behavior are in this case combined in the same gadget, out of which later a primitive shovel and drum will develop.

---

[73]Here Vygotsky uses the term *cultural–psychological,* whereas later the term *cultural–historic* appears.

[74]K. Bucher (1847–1930), a German economist and statistician who represented a "new historical school" and gathered vast material on the numbers of populations, towns, and artisans organizations in the Middle Ages.

An act of magic unites man's attempts to control nature and to regulate his own behavior. This union, although distorted by its reflection through magic, represents the beginning of cultural development — man's highest status, according to Thurnwald. This combination is the most characteristic feature of the primitive personality. Subsequent cultural development, determined by man's growing domination over nature, follows a path of separating these two tendencies. Advanced technology results in the separation of the laws of nature from the laws of thought, and magical acts begin to die out.

Paralleling a higher level of control over nature, man's social life and his labor activity begin to demand still higher requirements for control over his own behavior. Language, calculation, writing, and other technical means of culture develop. With the aid of these means, man's behavior ascends to a higher level.

3 The Child and Its Behavior

APPROACHES TO THE PSYCHOLOGY OF AN ADULT

If we wish to study the psychology of an adult cultural man, we have to bear in mind that it developed as a result of a complex evolution that combined at least three courses: the course of biological evolution from animals to the human being, the course of historical cultural evolution, which resulted in the gradual transformation of primitive man into modern cultural man, and the course of individual development of a specific personality (ontogenesis), as a result of which a small newly born creature passes through a number of stages, turning into a schoolchild and then into an adult cultural man.

Some investigators (proponents of the so called "biogenetic law") believe that we should not study analytically each of these courses of development. They assert that, in the process of its development, the child repeats the essential features of genus development, covering in the few years of its individual life the path that this genus covered in many thousands and tens of thousands of years.

We do not share this point of view. We believe that each of these evolutionary courses — the development from ape into human being, from primitive man into a representative of the cultural era, and from child into adult — follows its own individual path that is influenced by specific factors and passes through specific, often idiosyncratic forms and developmental stages.

That is why when analyzing the adult cultural man, in addition to the evolution of the behavior of the animal and of primitive man, we must also study the development of child behavior.

Consequently, we try to dwell upon the features of child behavior and trace the paths of development of the child's psychology.

ADULT AND CHILD: THE PRINCIPLE OF METAMORPHOSIS

One inaccurate concept has become deeply rooted in the general consciousness; that is the notion that a child differs from an adult only quantitatively. We only have to shrink the adult, make him weaker, reduce his skills, and make him a little less intelligent and we will have a child.

This concept of a child as a small adult is very widespread. Very few people have contemplated the thought that the child is not always simply a miniature replica of the adult, and that in many respects the child radically differs from the adult — that the child is quite a different, unique creature.

Why people usually do not give this a thought and remain certain that the child is only a small adult can be explained very easily. The fact of the matter is that the simplest way to judge objects and their laws is by analogy with the self ("anthropomorphically"); primitive man ascribed his own characteristic features even to animals and plants. He endowed all the environment with his own features, with feelings of joy and grief; he found plants and inanimate nature to have a mind, wishes, and will; he communicated with them as if with his own likeness. No doubt, primitive man always treated the child as his double, ascribing to him all those characteristics of an adult that he knew from his own personal experience.

This attitude toward the child is particularly clear as seen in the way the children are often drawn.

Figure 3.1 contains the drawings of an adult and a child made by an adult

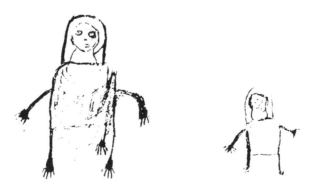

FIG. 3.1   Drawing of a child and an adult by an adult Uzbek woman from a remote village.

Uzbek woman, a resident of a remote *kishlak* (a village in Central Asia), who was characterized by a low cultural level of development.[1] The Uzbek woman was asked to draw a woman. The left part of Fig. 3.1 is her primitive drawing of a woman. "But every woman must have a child" — remarked the woman, and drew the figure of the child on the right. If we look carefully at both drawings, we see that they are indeed exactly identical, differing only in size. The head, arms, legs, shawl on the head, and even the necklace on their necks are similar; the child drawn by this semicultural woman in fact represents only a smaller adult.

This notion of a child persisted for centuries, and in any picture gallery you can see tens of madonnas holding in their laps infants whose body proportions bear a strong resemblance to adults. All those baby Jesuses, small knights, and dukes attired as adults in the portrait galleries of German castles are in effect adult dwarfs; are they not proof of the fact that humanity for centuries took the child as a small adult? For centuries, people underestimated the fact that the child both in physical appearance and psychological characteristics is a very special type of creature, who qualitatively differs from an adult and whose laws of life and activity should undoubtedly be studied with particular attention.

Indeed, not only does the child think in a different way, perceiving the world differently from an adult, not only is the child's logic based on qualitatively different principles, which are characterized by great specificity, but in many aspects the structure and functions of his body differ greatly from those of the adult organism.

Several simple examples will convince us of this. The metamorphoses that the child passes through affect the most important attributes usually considered to be stable in man — his body build, proportions of the limbs, and construction. If one adult differs from another by the proportions of his body parts, height, scull formation, and so on, how much greater these differences would be for a child in comparison with an adult! Strictly speaking, we have the right to argue for a specific *child constitution,* which a child, once born, grows through before becoming an adult. This "child constitution" is characterized by completely different proportions than those we usually see in an adult: a larger head, a barely visible neck, and short arms and legs. These features are specific to a small child, and its further development involves a crucial reconstruction of these characteristic proportions: the neck becomes visible, the limbs grow longer, the ratio between the head and body size decreases, and by the age of 15–16 we have quite a different human being with different proportions and shapes. If we take a look at a sketch depicting the body build of the child at different ages and that of the adult (Figs. 3.2 and 3.3, taken from K. Bühler,

---

[1](A. L.) We acknowledge Dr. T. N. Baranova from Central-Asian University who kindly permitted us to use this drawing.

FIG. 3.2 The bodily proportions of the newborn infant and the adult (after Stratz (1922), cited in Bühler, 1930, p. 38).

1919/1930)[2] we will see that, in the course of development, the child's appearance passes through a number of metamorphoses.

Of course, underlying these metamorphoses are crucial changes in the processes determining child development. We are not going to dwell on these processes and discuss such phenomena as development of internal secretion or growth of separate parts of the nervous system; the main thesis that the development of a child's organism is a complex system of metamorphoses has been confirmed by a great number of studies.[3]

If such crucial constitutional changes characterize a child's growth and transition to adulthood, then the metamorphoses in the mechanisms of child behavior turn out to be even more outstanding.

We know that perhaps the most essential feature characterizing adult behavior is the periodical alternation of dream and wakefulness; in fact, all of us lives a double life and each of these lives (wakefulness and dream) is concentrated and occupies a compact interval of time. Nothing of the kind occurs in the new-born infant. As it has been shown by the studies of a number of researchers (e.g., the recent such study by Shchelovanov[4] in Leningrad), a newborn infant lives neither in a state of dream, nor in wakefulness. For the child, dream and wakefulness are broken up into small

---

[2](V. G., J. K.) Stratz (1909/1922), *Der Körper des Kindes*. Vygotsky most likely took these illustrations from K. Bühler's (1919/1930, pp. 36, 38) *The Mental Development of the Child;* the Russian translation of K. Bühler's (1927, 1919/1929) work is cited by Vygotsky elsewhere in other manuscripts.

[3](A. L.) See the collection of data in Blonskii (1911).

[4](V. G., J. K.) Shchelovanov — not able to identify.

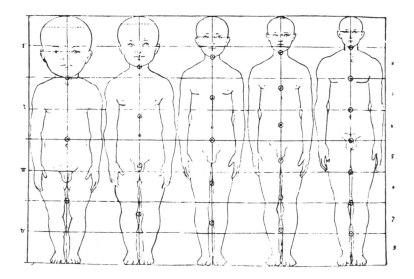

FIG. 3.3 The development of the bodily proportions (after Stratz (1922), cited in Bühler, 1930, p. 37).

alternating periods that replace one another, interweaving and resulting in some intermediate state, a state of irradiated arousal and inhibition. A newborn infant is a very unique creature with very distinctive body proportions and a completely different organization of activity. Let us take an even closer look: We try to distinguish those threads that connect the infant to the environment. If we ask ourselves about the child's world, we will get know him as he is.

THE INFANT AND HIS WORLD

An adult is not only connected with the environment by thousands of the most intimate bonds, he himself is its product; his essence is found in the essence of the environmental conditions. It is not the same in the case of a newborn. Everything that for the adult serves as a bridge between himself and the environment, everything that brings him each signal from the external world—that is, his vision, hearing, and all his organs of perception—is almost nonfunctional in a newborn. Imagine a man in whom all the links connecting him with the environment are cut off one after another; he turns out to be completely isolated from the world, a lone person amidst the world of things that do not exist for him. This is the condition resembling that of a newborn. Though this world is filled with noises and splotches, the child's organs of perception do not yet function for him: He does not have isolated perceptions, does not recognize objects, and does not single out anything of this general chaos. For him there does not yet exist a world of habitually perceived things, and he lives like an anchorite. Perhaps the first things the child begins to perceive and single out include the position of his own body, stimulations of instinctive character (e.g., hunger) and those things which comfort him. While the adult is connected with the world mainly through the eyes, the child is connected through the mouth. Sensations of hunger and of his mother's breast, appeasing hunger, are perhaps the first psychological phenomena that we can observe in the child. The bond with the environment begins at the mouth, and it is here that the initial primitive sensations, primary psychological reactions, appear.

Of great, determining importance for the adult are those behavioral functions that connect him with the environment and that by themselves are the product of this social, cultural influence, that is, his perceptions, his skills, and his intellect. For the infant, the dominant role is played by organic sensations restricted to the body (primitive drives, stimulations from the mucous membrane of the mouth, etc. — constant internal stimuli). Those things that are most essential in the behavior of the adult are missing in the infant. The primitive phase of an infant's development is characterized by different values, different proportions, and different laws; in certain respects, the infant differs from the adult no less than a chrysalis from a butterfly (Werner, 1926; see also Bühler, Hetzer & Tudor-Hart 1927).

Reality starts to exist for the child in those forms that we perceive in a rather late period of his development. For example, only after 1½ months does an infant show coordinated eye movements; it is only from this moment that the child is capable of shifting his eye-gaze from one object to another and from one part of the object to another; and, as we well know, exactly these coordinated eye movements are the necessary condition for seeing. However, a child at a month and a half still has almost minimal access to the world perceived visually; accommodation of the eyeball — adaptation to external stimulations — appears around the age of 2 months, absolutely correct recognition of faces comes at the age of 2½ to 3 months, and we can consider that only by 4 to 5 months does the "visible world" become accessible to the child. Of course, this development makes an entire revolution in the child's life: from a primitive being with only organic sensations, from a non-seeing and non-hearing being, immersed only in his organic life, he turns into a being who for the first time encounters reality, starts to interact with it, begins to actively react to stimulations coming from it, and finds himself facing the necessity to gradually, in primitive ways, adapt himself to it. The first "organic" principle of existence begins to be replaced by a second principle — the principle of external and, what is most important, social reality.

So the child begins his entrance into life. However, it would be amazing if this being, establishing his first relations with the world, had in the slightest degree the same attributes that the adult has, this is, if he possessed those characteristics that appear only in the process of prolonged adaptation. On the other hand, it would be wrong to think that the child, having already covered some distance along the path of development (a very specific path which differs from that of the adult), has no forms of nervous-psychological activity, however primitive they may be. It would be wrong to believe that the child is a blank sheet of paper that is to be gradually filled by a text drawn up by life. This sheet of paper is already covered by letters inscribed during the first weeks and months of the child's life, and this sheet begins to frantically fill up with the letters from the time the child has established contacts with the world. However, these are letters in quite a different language, which we often understand rather badly; they often remind us of some language that has died out, the language of the primitive man. It is absolutely wrong to think that a child, for example a 2- or 3-year-old, is simply more stupid than the adult—that the child is simply an underdeveloped man. The child is intelligent in his own way, but compared to us he perceives the world in a more primitive way; he treats it in a different way, he thinks differently from us.

PRIMITIVE PERCEPTION

The child begins to see the world after having lived an entire period of his life as an "organic being," cut off from the world and immersed in his own organic experiences. The child, before birth (the child of the intrauterine period), is a being completely isolated from external stimuli; the child of the first weeks of life is almost the same. No wonder that when his eyes begin to see they do not see like ours. The child's perceptions, including the perceptions of time and space, are still primitive and distinctive, and much time will pass before they turn into the perceptions that are characteristic for the adults.

Let us start with the simple. The child, who at the beginning of life had only organic sensations (of rest or anxiety, of tension and calm, of pain, touch, warmth, and primarily of stimulations from the most sensitive areas), lacks, of course, *the perception of space* that we possess. Helmholtz said that in his childhood (3 to 4 years), when he was passing by the church tower he took the people on the gallery for puppets and asked his mother to get them down for him, thinking that it would be enough for her to stretch out her hand to do it (cited in K. Bühler, 1919/1930, p. 66).[5] Everyone must

---

[5](A. L.) "The example is taken from Bühler's *Dukhovnoe razvitie rebjonka* [Spiritual development of the child] (1927, p. 161). The data on child's perception of space can be found in Troshin's (1915) *Sravnitel'naia psikhologija normal'nykh i nenormal'nykh detei*" [Comparative Psychology of Normal and Abnormal Children] (p. 1).

(V. G., J. K.) This example was originally cited by Bühler from *Physiology of Optics* (1901) by H. L. Helmholtz (1821–1894). In 1868, Helmholtz was a German scholar at the St.

have seen a child reaching his hands toward the moon hoping to grasp it or trying to catch a bird in the sky and so on. A 2- to 4-year-old child has no perspective. The principles underlying the visual perceptions of the child are different: they are much more primitive, the world is seen in a primitive way, it is perceived usually as something near at hand, within the child's reach, touch, grasp, or groping, that is, all these primitive forms of possession. It is the predominance of these primitive forms of contact with the world that gave Bühler the grounds to distinguish three stages in the development of a child's spatial perception and to speak of the acquisition of oral (connected with eating, sucking), tactile, and visual control of space *(Mundraum, Tastraum, Fernraum)*. Indeed, the child first begins to know the world with his mouth, then with his hands; and only after that does his vision lay the corner stones for perceptions that develop fully much later.

If indeed the organs of perception, which connect the child with the external world, such as the eye, ear, and so on, become active rather late, then it is clear that the child perceives the whole picture of the world differently from the adult.

We know that perception in the forms observable in an adult is formed by means of slow evolution. The example from Helmholz's biography just described is easily explained physiologically; the fact of the matter is that every visual stimulation leaves a trace on the retina. It is only natural that the image left on the retina from the perception of a man standing up close will be large whereas the one left by a man standing on the church tower will be comparatively smaller. In order that the small image of a man standing in the distance be perceived as a large man, one additional component is necessary — a long-standing skill, or habit. This constancy in evaluation of the size of individual objects independently of their distance — the so called "invariance" of perception — develops in the course of prolonged training. The physiological trace left on the retina by a perceived object has to be processed and evaluated from the perspective of previous experience; a simple successive image (Nachbild) has to merge with the images left by previous experiences (Vortstellungsbild); an adequate orientation in space is necessary whereby the distant objects will not be perceived as small ones and closer objects — as large ones simply because of their nearness. The child does not yet have this function that is very important for adaptation. The child's experience is so meager that his vision functions in the most primitive manner; the child naively trusts the images appearing on his retina. Thus, he reaches toward people on a church tower, mistaking them for puppets, or he thinks that he can play with the small house on a faraway hill.

Petersburg Institute of Man, Academy of Sciences, therefore his work became known to Russian physiologists and psychologists. His major works were devoted to physics, biophysics, physiology, and psychology.

We have all the grounds to think that the child's perception of the world is unstable and variable, so that the slightest change in the distance to an object (we omit the other factors) is enough for the object to be perceived in quite a different way. The problem of adapting these perceptions to a changing world arises — this is the necessity of transforming perceptions from one naive-physiological stage to another stage, where previous experience will introduce a correction in the physiological image of an object. One could say that our physiological perception must to a certain degree be corrected, it has to be "spoiled" by previous experience so that the organism might indeed effectively adapt to the conditions of the external world.

This is exactly the task undertaken by the mechanism, later called "eidetism" (see Bonte, Liefman, & Rössler, 1928; Jaensch, 1930). The point is that every visually perceived object leaves a certain aftereffect on the child. Some children are characterized by an ability to see objects quite vividly after the latter have disappeared from their visual field; such individuals are able to describe an image in all its detail after it has disappeared, and this phenomenon is far from being a simple act of memory. They vividly see the image as if it were quite real; they just describe what is still soaring before their eyes.

It is absolutely understandable that the mechanism involved in perception corrects in a certain way the external sensations; the child begins to see the external world not simply with his eye as a perceiving and conducting apparatus — the child sees with all of his previous experience, and in doing so somewhat alters the objects perceived.[6] A specific type of perception emerges — the undifferentiated world of purely physiological perceptions is substituted by the world of "visual images," perceived by the child with unusual brightness. In these images external impressions are mixed with and corrected by the images preserved from previous experience. Naturally, it is this very phenomenon that helps the child shift to the next stage of perceiving, to develop a stable, "invariable" picture of external perceptions of the world in place of unstable sensations that are susceptible to any incidental influences.

However, this primitive mechanism of "visual images," which is of enormous biological importance, helping the child to cope with accidental influences of external environment, brings about a substantial reconstruction of the child's entire psychology.

What the child had perceived earlier as a number of accidental, separate, and fluctuating scraps (we have a similar impression when we scrutinize an unknown map or walk along a street of a strange city or analyze an unfamiliar

---

[6](A. L.) In our recent studies devoted to children's drawing, we had an opportunity to visually trace this phenomenon. Further on we dwell upon this in more detail, supporting the argument with a number of facts.

preparation) now begins to be perceived as a series of whole pictures. Because "visual images" remain in child's mind, previous experience merges with actual stimuli and the world acquires an integral character.

But this is not achieved at a cheap price. In perceiving the world holistically, the small child at the same time often loses the boundary separating reality from fantasy, the present from the past, what exists from what is desired.

One researcher, Major (1906), tried to conduct special experiments to clarify the above arguments; he offered colorful pictures to children of different ages and observed their behavior with respect to these pictures (p. 251). It turned out that children at different ages behaved differently in this situation and three specific stages can easily be distinguished in the child's attitude toward a picture. At first, the child does not treat the picture as a portrayal (first stage): he treats it simply as a motley piece of paper, he snatches it, tears it. The second stage comes when the previously described mechanisms seemingly begin to dominate: the child begins to perceive the picture's contents as an image and begins to treat the things, depicted in the picture, *as real.* He tries to snatch them, to speak to them, – in a word, he does not make any distinction between the real things and their depiction. Much later the third stage starts: the child begins to distinguish real things from their depictions, and his attitude toward both begins to differ greatly. However, this third stage begins rather late and we can say that the psychological life of the child at the first steps of his development is particularly characterized by the manifestations that are similar to the behavior noted here and stem from the child's poor differentiation of stimuli.

It is necessary to say that this just-described stage of primitive perception of the world, governed by "visual images," lasts rather long; the child continues for a long time to confuse dreams with reality, to hatch up unusually vivid fantasies, which for him are often a substitute for reality.

This feature of primitive psychology is particularly vividly displayed in children's play. Anyone may well see a small child most seriously feeding a wooden stump, fighting some invisible enemies, or playing with made-up friends. No actor is able to "play" so convincingly as the child does. Indeed, the child looks at the wooden stump but sees a doll, the child ascribes to the most primitive objects those qualities that are dictated by his wishes, his experience, and his fantasy. For the child, the primitive picture of the world is undoubtedly a picture where the boundaries between real perceptions and fantasy are erased; much time has to pass before these two will become differentiated and will not be confused.

Child speech and thinking will have to develop; his experience, aimed at reality, will have to become firmly established and acquire enough independence; the vivid "eidetic" visual images, which play such an important role in the child's mind, will have to fade away. In short, a significant cultural reconstruction has to take place in order for the child to shift from the stage of primitive perceptions to the next one—to the stage of competent forms of adaptation to the external world.

PRIMITIVE THINKING

The first years in the child's life are years of a primitive isolated existence and of establishing the most elementary, most primitive[7] connections with the world.

We have already seen that the child, in the first months of his existence, is an asocial, "solely organic" being, cut off from the external world and wholly restricted to its physiological functions.

For an infant, the whole world is restricted first of all to his own body and to everything that can bring him comfort; he still has had almost no encounters with the external world. Living mostly in the conditions of "parasitic" circumstances, he in fact has not yet encountered the boundaries and obstacles of reality. His perception of the world is in many aspects passive. As we have just seen, he still confuses the primitive activity of his imagination and the rudiments of previous experience with reality.

All this can not but influence the child's thinking in a most definite way, and we have to argue resolutely that the thinking of a 3- to 4-year-old child has nothing in common with adult forms of thinking that have been created by culture and a long cultural evolution, by multiple and active encounters with the external world.

Certainly, this does not mean that child thought has no laws of its own. On the contrary, there are quite definite laws of child thought that differ from the laws of thinking in adults: a child of this age (3–4) has his own primitive logic, he has his own primitive modes of thinking; all of them are determined by the fact that this thinking unfolds on a primitive base of behavior, which has not yet had sufficiently serious encounters with reality.

It is true that these laws of child thinking were barely known up to the most recent time, and only in the very last years have we become acquainted with its main features as a result of studies by Piaget.

We have made a really interesting discovery. After a number of studies, we have found out not only that the laws underlying child thinking are different from those that characterize the cultural adult, but that there are deep-rooted differences in the structure of this thinking; it uses different means.

---

[7](V. G.) Here it is particularly clear that for A. Luria, "primitive" often means *fundamental, basic, primary.*

If we analyze the functions of adult thinking, we will quickly find that it *organizes our adaptation to the world in particularly difficult situations.* It regulates our attitude toward reality in particularly complex conditions where simple instinct or habit is insufficient. From this point of view, the function of thought is to adequately adapt to the world; the form [thinking takes] is the organization of our influence on the world. This function determines the whole construction of our thinking. In order that thought makes possible an efficient influence on the world, it must function with a maximum of correctness: it must be faithful to reality without merging with fantasy. Each step in our thinking must be checked by practice and pass this test. Indeed, the thinking of a normal adult meets all these requirements and only in those who have some mental or neurological illness does thinking acquire different forms that are not connected with life and reality and do not organize an efficient adaptation to the world. Quite a different picture can be seen in the initial stages of child development. Often it does not matter for the child how accurate or efficient his thinking is in its first test, that is, its first encounter with reality. Often his thinking is not aimed at regulating and organizating an efficient adaptation to the external world. When sometimes his thinking does function in this way, it still does so primitively with those imperfect tools that a child has at his disposal and that require prolonged development to become effective.

Piaget characterized the thinking of a small child (3 to 5 years) with two main features: *egocentrism and primitivism.*

We have already said that the young child's behavior is characterized by disassociation from the world, and concentration on the self, concentration on his own interests and pleasures. Try to watch a child of 2 to 4 years playing alone: he pays no pay attention to anyone, he is completely immersed in himself, he arranges something in front of himself, he addresses himself and answers himself. It is very difficult to distract the child from this play; if you address the child, he will not immediately tear himself away from his occupation. A child of this age can play perfectly well alone, completely preoccupied by himself.

We present the transcript of a child at 2 years, 4 months during such play:[8]

---

[8](A. L.) The record is taken from the materials kindly presented by V. F. Schmidt.

(V. G., J. K.) There is no clear indication here whether Luria is speaking about a relatively unknown Soviet colleague, a German pedagogue, or the ethnographist and linguist, Wilhelm Schmidt (1868–1954) who was, according to Prokhorov (1985), "one of the founders of the *cultural–historical school*" (p. 1512). W. Schmidt (1904) was referred to earlier in chapter 2 of this book. Schmidt was known for his studies of the languages of southeast Asia, Melanesia, and Australia. However, Luria does indicate later in this text that the conversations transcribed here were recorded in a children's laboratory residential home. Elsewhere, Luria does refer to the work of F. Schmidt (1904) in Leipzig.

Marina, 2y.4m., was deeply immersed in play: she was pouring sand onto her legs, she was pouring it mostly on her legs above the knees, then she took the sand and rubbed it with her whole palm onto her leg. Finally she began pouring sand on her thigh after that she covered it with a kerchief and smoothed it around her leg with both hands. She had an expression of pleasure on her face, often smiling to herself.

During her play she says to herself: "Mama here . . . here . . . more . . . more . . . Mama, pour more . . . mama more . . . Mama, pour, Mammy, pour more . . . OK . . . It is my aunt . . . Aunt, more sand . . . Aunt . . . doll must have sand more . . ."

This egocentrism of child thinking can also reveal itself in another way. Let us try to note when and how a child *speaks,* what goals he pursues in his talk, and what forms his speech acquires. If we look closely at the child, we will be astonished to find how often the child's speech does not serve the purpose of communication. One gets an impression that a child's speech often is not used for the social purposes of mutual communication and the sharing of information, as it is for adults.

Following is another transcript of a child's behavior, taken from the same source. Notice how the play of the child (2y. 6m.) play is accompanied by "autistic" speech, speech addressed only to the self:

Alik, 2y.6m. (on entering his mother's room) began playing with ash berries, he began picking them and putting into a slop basin: "[I] must pick the berries quicker . . . These are my berries — they are lying in a little bed. (Notices a biscuit wrapper.) No more biscuits? Only a wrapper left? (Eats a biscuit.) Biscuit [is] tasty (eating). Biscuit [is] tasty. [It] dropped! A little bit dropped! It is such a small . . . A big . . . a small block . . . It can sit, a block . . . It can also sit . . . It cannot write . . . [The] block cannot write . . . (he takes a milk-jug). [We] will put matches there and give them a little pie (Takes a cardboard circle). Many little pies" . . .

It was Piaget, already quoted earlier, who discovered that the most characteristic form of child speech is *a monologue,* speech for the self. This form of speech is preserved in children even in a group, where it acquires specific, somewhat comical features. Even in a group each child speaks for himself, keeps developing his *own* topic, paying minimal attention to his "conversational partners" who (if they are of the same age) also speak for themselves.

Piaget (1923) noted: "The reason why the child speaks this way — not usually caring whether his collocutors are listening to him — is simply the fact that he does not address his speech to them. The child in general does not address anybody. He speaks aloud for himself in the presence of others" (p. 28).[9]

We have become accustomed to believe that speech in a collective connects people with each other. However, often we do not observe this in children. Here is one more transcript. This time the transcript represents the conversation of a child (6.6 y.o.) in a group of peers playing, that is, drawing (Piaget, 1923, pp. 14–15):

Pie, 6 y.o. (to Ez who is drawing a tram-car with carriages in tow):

23. "But the trams that are hooked on behind don't have any flags. (No answer.)

24. (Talking about his tram). They don't have any carriages hooked on. (He was addressing no one in particular. No one answers him.)

25. (To B.) " 'T'sa tram that hasn't got no carriages. (No answer)

26. (To Hei), This tram hasn't got no carriages, Hei, look, it isn't red, d'you see . . . (No answer)

27. (L. says out loud: "A funny gentleman," from a certain distance, and without addressing himself to Pie or to anyone else). Pie: "a funny gentleman! (Goes on drawing his tram.)

28. "I am leaving the tram white."

29. (Ez., who is drawing next to him says: "I'm doing it yellow.") "No, you mustn't do it all yellow."

30. "I'm doing the stair-case, look." (B. answers: "I can't come this afternoon, I've got a Eurithmetic class . . .") (Piaget, 1957, p. 30)

The most characteristic feature of the entire conversation is that one cannot find the main thing that we usually notice in a group conversation, that is, a mutual crisscrossing of questions, responses, and opinions. This feature is almost absent in the above fragment. Every child speaks mainly about himself and for himself, without addressing anyone and without expecting a response from anyone. Even if a child expects an answer from someone and does not get it, he quickly forgets about it and shifts to another "conversation." Speech for a child of this age serves as a tool for mutual communication only in one respect, in another it is not yet

---

[9](V. G., J. K.) This is a translation from the Russian. The closest passage in the English translation is: "When the child utters phrases belonging to the first group, {i.e. to the ego-centric — V. G.} he does not bother to know to whom he is speaking nor whether he is being listened to. He talks either for himself or for the pleasure of associating anyone who happens to be there with the activity of the moment." (Piaget 1957, p. 32).

And a little further: "The child talks to himself as though he were thinking aloud. He does not address anyone" (Piaget 1957, p. 32).

"socialized," it is "autistic," egocentric; as we shall see later, it plays quite a different role in the child's behavior.

Piaget and his colleagues also pointed to a number of other speech forms bearing an egocentric character. A careful analysis revealed that even a child's questions in many cases are of an egocentric nature; the child asks a question knowing the answer beforehand, doing it only to disclose himself. It turned out that there are rather many such egocentric forms in child speech; according to Piaget, their number is on average between 54% and 60% at the age of 3 to 5 years, and 44% to 47% at 5 to 7 years. Based on prolonged and consistent observations of children, these figures show how specific the thinking and speech of a child are, and to what degree child speech serves absolutely different functions, greatly distinguishing it from the character of adult speech.[10]

As a result of a number of special experiments, we have obtained only just recently proof that egocentric speech exhibits absolutely definite psychological functions. These functions include first of all the planning of certain actions self initiated. In these cases, speech begins to play an absolutely specific role; its relations to other behavioral acts acquire a functionally special character. It is enough to look through the above two fragments to be convinced that the child's verbal activity here is not solely a manifestation of egocentric speech, but exhibits obvious planning functions. An outburst of such egocentric speech can be easily evoked by impeding some [psychological] process in the child (Vygotsky, 1929a; A. Luria 1929b).

The primitive egocentrism of child thinking is manifest not only in the forms of speech. Features of egocentrism are even more observable in the contents of a child's thinking, in his fantasies.

Perhaps the most expressive manifestation of child egocentrism is the fact that a young child lives completely within his primitive world, the touchstones of which are comfort and discomfort. His world has still been only barely affected by realty. As far as we may judge by the child's behavior, this world is characterized by the existence of an intermediate state between the child and reality; this semi-real world, so highly characteristic for the child, is the world of egocentric thinking and fantasy.

Each of us adults encounters the external world when we are pursuing some need and we realize that it has not yet been satisfied. In this case, the adult organizes his activity in such a way that by a series of consecutive steps

---

[10](A. L.) Russian data, obtained in the course of prolonged study by S. O. Lozinsky, have shown a much lower percentage of egocentrism in children attending children's educational establishments. This is yet further proof that supports the idea that different environments bring about significant differences in the structure of a child's mind [psychology].

the goal might be achieved and the need be satisfied; or reconciling himself to the inevitable, he gives up satisfying his need.

It is quite a different story with a small child. Being unable to perform sequenced actions, the child follows a particular path of minimal resistance: If the external world proves unable to supply the child with something real, he compensates for this shortage with his fantasy. Unable to adequately react to some obstruction to his goal, the child reacts inadequately by creating for himself an illusory world where all of his wishes are realized, where he is the complete master and the center of the created universe; the child creates the world of illusory egocentric thinking.

This "world of realized wishes" is preserved in an adult perhaps only in his dreams, sometimes in daydreams; for the child it is a "live reality"; as we have pointed out, the child is completely satisfied in substituting real activity with play or fantasy.

Freud reported a boy whose mother had deprived him of cherries: the following morning, upon awakening, this boy claimed to have eaten all the cherries and to be very happy about it. The wish, unsatisfied in reality, found its illusory satisfaction in a dream.

However, a child's fantasies and egocentric thinking are manifest not only in dreams. They are especially sharply exhibited in what may be called a child's "daydreams" and what often easily merges with play.

It is this phenomenon that we often take for a child's lie, and from this phenomenon comes a number of specific features of child thinking.

When in answer to the question, "why is it light in the daytime and dark at night," a 3-year-old child says: "because the day is the time for dining and the night is the time for sleeping." This is, of course, a manifestation of the same egocentric–practical set, which may explain everything as an adaptation for the child himself, for his benefit. The same is true for the naive notion, characteristic for children, that everything around them — the sky, the sea, the rocks — is produced by people and may be presented to the child;[11] the same egocentric set and an absolute belief in the omnipotence of an adult can be seen in a child who asks his mother to give him the pine forest in the village B. where he wanted to go, or when he asks his mother to cook spinach in such a way that it becomes potatoes, and so on (Klein, 1925, pp. 25–26).

When little Alik (2 y.o.) happened to see a passing car, which he liked very much, he insistently began to beg his mother: "Mother, again!!" Marina (also about 2) reacted in the same manner to a crow flying: she was

---

[11](A. L.) It should be noted, however, that these data are characteristic for the children who grew up in the environment in which they were examined by Piaget. Our children, developing in a different environment, may show different results.

sincerely convinced that her mother was able to make the crow fly by again.[12]

This tendency tells us in a very interesting way about children's questions and answers. This can be illustrated by a transcript of one conversation with a child:[13]

Alik, 5y.5m.
In the evening he saw Jupiter through a window.
— "Mother, what for does Jupiter exist?"
I tried to explain to him. but was unsuccessful. He again pestered me.
— "Well, really what for does Jupiter exist?"
Then not knowing what to say I asked him:
— "And for what do you and I exist?"
To that I got an immediate and confident answer.
— "For ourselves."
— "Well, Jupiter too.
He liked this, and he said (looking satisfied):
— "And ants, and bugs, and mosquitoes, and nettle — are they also for themselves?"
— "Yes."
And he laughed happily.

The primitive teleologism, seen in this talk, is extremely characteristic for a child. Surely Jupiter must exist for some reason. And for the child this "what for" often substitutes the more complex "why." When the answer to this question turns out to be difficult, the child nevertheless finds a way out. We exist "for ourselves" — this answer is typical for the child's specific teleological thinking, which provides the child with a possible solution for the question, "what for" do other things and animals exist, even those that are unpleasant for the child himself (ants, bugs, mosquitoes and nettle).

Finally, we able to capture the affect of the same egocentric thinking in the child's characteristic attitude toward the conversation of others and toward the phenomena of the external world: He is sincerely confident that there is nothing incomprehensible for him, and we almost never hear the words "I don't know" from a 4- to 5-year-old child. Further on we will see that it is very difficult for the child to hold back the first solution that came to mind, and that it is easier for him to give an absurd answer than acknowledge his own ignorance.

Holding back immediate reactions — the ability to appropriately delay an

---

[12](A. L.) Reported by V. F. Schmidt.
[13](A. L.) Reported by V. F. Schmidt.

answer—is the product of development and education and appears only much later.

After everything said about the egocentric character of child thought, it will not be surprising if we say that a child's thinking differs from that of the adult in *its logic* as well, and that it (child's thinking) is based on the "primitive logic."

Of course, we are in no way attempting to present in this small chapter any complete description of this primitive logic characteristic for the child. We need dwell only on certain separate features that are so clearly seen in a child's conversations and a child's judgments.

We have already mentioned that the child who has an egocentrical attitude toward the external world perceives its objects concretely, holistically, and first of all from that angle that addresses the child himself, from that aspect that affects him directly. The child still has not developed an objective attitude toward the world, an attitude that allows him to disengage from an object's perceived concrete features and that directs his attention to the objective correlations and laws. The child accepts the world the way he perceives it; he does not care about the connections among the individual pictures he perceives, nor about the construction of a systematic picture of the world and its phenomena. This sort of picture is necessary for the cultural adult whose thinking must regulate his interactions with the world. It is exactly this logic of relations, causative connections, and so on that is missing in the child's thinking and is substituted by other primitive logical devices [of thinking].

Let us return to child speech and analyze the ways a child expresses those linkages in his thinking. Many authors have noted that a little child almost never uses subordinate clauses; children never say: "When I went for a walk, I got soaked, because a thunderstorm began:" instead he would say: "I went for a walk, then it started raining, then I got soaked." Causative connectives are usually absent in child speech; the connections expressed by "because" or "as a result of" are substituted by the conjunction "and." Therefore, it is quite clear that such absences in speech formation cannot but also be reflected in the child's thinking: a complex systematic picture of the world, an arrangement of its phenomena according to their connections and causative relations is replaced by a simple "glueing" together, a primitive combining, of the isolated features. These methods of child thinking are very well reflected in a child's drawings where the child uses precisely the same principle: He simply strings out the individual elements without making any particular connection between them. That is why in a child's drawing one can often find eyes, ears, a nose drawn apart from the head located beside it but without any connection to it. The drawing fails to provide any organization of these parts into some general structure.

The following are several examples of such drawings. The first drawing

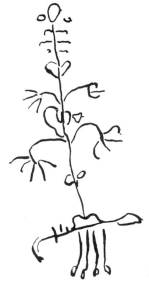

FIG. 3.4 Drawing of horse ride by a barely literate Uzbek woman.

(Fig. 3.4) is not a child's, but belongs to an Uzbek woman with little cultural background, however it reproduces the typical characteristics of child thinking with its similar unusual vividness. Thus, we took the risk of introducing this example here.[14] The drawing is supposed to represent a rider on a horse:

Even at first glance one can see that its author did not copy reality, but drew according to some principles other than logic. A careful examination of this drawing reveals its main distinctive feature, that is, that it is constructed not according to the system "a-man" and "a-horse," but according to the principle of glueing, of adding on the separate features of a man without synthesizing them into an integral image. We see in this drawing a head drawn separately and an ear also drawn apart and below [the head]; then we see the eyebrows, the eyes, the nostrils—all are presented without a trace of their real interconnections. They are simply strung together one after another as some sort of individual parts. The legs are drawn in the bent manner in which a rider *feels* them, the genital organ is depicted separately from the body, — everything is represented in a naively glued, strung together manner.

The second figure (Fig. 3.5) is a drawing of a 5-year-old child.[15] The child

---

[14](A. L.) The drawing is borrowed from the collection of T. N. Baranova, who kindly offered it for this book.

[15](A. L.) The drawings are submitted by V. F. Schmidt and are taken from the materials of the Children's Home laboratory.

(V. G., J. K.) In the authors' introduction to this book, there is no mention of where this

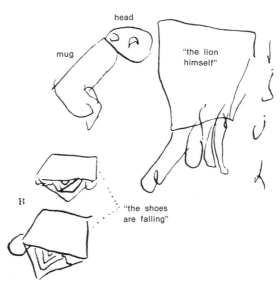

head

mug

"the lion himself"

B

"the shoes are falling"

FIG. 3.5   Drawing of a lion by a 5-year-old child.

tried to draw a lion and included the appropriate explanatory labels; separately, he drew a "muzzle," then a "head," and finally the rest of what he called "the lion itself." Of course, the number of details is far fewer in this drawing than in the first (this is complete accordance with the abilities of child perception at this age), however the "glued together" phenomenon is here quite obvious. This phenomenon is particularly expressive in those drawings where a child tries to represent some complex combination of objects, for example, a room. Figure 3.6 presents an example of 5-year-old's attempt to draw a room in which a stove is burning. We can see that characteristic for this drawing is the "glued-together character" of the individual objects, all having something to do with the stove: here is the prepared firewood, then the stove doors and dampers, and a box of matches (its huge size is in agreement with its functional importance); everything is given as an additive combination of individual objects arranged one after another, strung one on top of another.

According to Piaget, it is this phenomenon of "being strung" together with its absence of strict regulating laws and ordered relations that characterizes child thought and logic. The child has almost no knowledge of the categories of causality and combines consecutively in one chain without any order and effect both the causes and consequences as well as individual phenomena having nothing to do with these relations. As a result, the cause

illustration came from. Moreover, it is not mentioned among those that were supplied by Soviet colleagues. Therefore, it was no doubt lent to Luria by the German child psychologist and linguist Schmidt (see Schmidt, 1904).

FIG. 3.6   Drawing of a room by a 5-year-old child.

often changes places with the result and, when confronted with a conclusion beginning with the word "because," the child who knows only this primitive, precultural thinking turns out to be helpless.

In his experiments, Piaget gave a child a phrase ending with the word "because" and asked the subject to insert the reason. The results of these experiments were rather characteristic for a child's primitive thinking. Here are several examples of such judgments (the children's answers are given in italics):

> Ts. (7y.2m.) A man fell down in the road because . . . *he broke his leg and had a bit of wood stuck on* [a wooden leg].
> K. (8y.6m.) A man fell from his bicycle because . . . *he broke his arm.*
> L. (7y.6.m.) I had a bath because . . . *afterwards I was clean.*
> D. (6y.) I've lost my pen . . . *because I am not writing.* (Piaget, 1928, p. 17)

We see that, in all the above cases, the child mixes cause and effect, and it turns out to be almost impossible for him to get a correct answer: thinking that correctly operates with the category of cause seems to be completely alien to the child. Significantly closer to the child is the category of goal— this is quite understandable if we remember the child's egocentric set. Thus,

one of Piaget's young subjects generated a phrase that reveals the picture of
child logic at its core:

D. (3y.6m.): A want to make a stove . . . because for the heating. (Piaget,
1928, p. 18)

This example quite vividly illustrates both the phenomenon of "stringing"
together separate categories and the phenomenon of replacing the alien
category of causality with the more kindred category of goal.

This phenomenon of "stringing together" disconnected representations in
the child's primitive thinking is exhibited in yet another interesting way: the
child's notions are not arranged in a certain hierarchy (e.g., a broader
notion, a component part, a still narrower component, according to the
typical scheme: genus, species, family, etc.), but the individual representations prove to be similar for the child. For example, a town, a province, and
a country do not differ in principal for a small child. Switzerland for the
child is something like Geneva, but a little further away; France is also
something like a familiar town, but is still further away. The fact that a
resident of Geneva is at the same time a Swiss is incomprehensible for the
child. Below is a short conversation presented by Piaget; it illustrates this
peculiar "flatness" in a child's thinking. The talk takes place between the
parents and a young subject (8 years, 2 months):

—What is a Swiss?
—They live in Switzerland.
—Is Friburg in Switzerland?
—Yes, but I am not a Freibourgeois [resident of Freiburg] and then Swiss . . .
—And those who live in Geneva?
—They are Genevans.
—And Swiss?
—I don't know. No, it's like me. I live in Freiburg which is in Switzerland, but
I am not Swiss. It's the same thing for the Genevans.
—Do you know many Swiss people?
—Not many.
—Are there any Swiss people?
—Yes.
—Where do they live?
—I don't know. [From "Are there any Swiss people" to the end of this
quotation is missing. We have reinstated to give the complete dialogue—J. K.]

This conversation clearly confirms that the child cannot yet think
logically and consistently enough to see that concepts associated with the
external world can be located on several levels and that an object can belong
to both a narrower and a larger class at one and the same time. The child

thinks concretely, perceiving an object from that aspect that is more familiar to him; he cannot yet separate himself from this aspect and cannot realize that, if at the same time you take other characteristic features into account, this object can fit into different categories. From this point of view, one can say that the child's thinking is always concrete and *absolute*. Thus, using the child's primitive thinking as an example, we can demonstrate the specificity of the primary, prelogical stage of thought development.

We have already mentioned that the child thinks by means of concrete things, grasping the relations among them with difficulty. A 6- to 7-year-old child firmly differs his right hand from the left one, but the fact that one and the same object simultaneously can be on the right in relation to one thing and on the left in relation to another is completely incomprehensible for him. Equally strange for him seems to be the fact that if he has a brother, it means that he himself is a brother to the first. When asked, how many brothers he has, a child answers that he has one brother, whose name is Nick. Then we ask the child: "How many brothers does Nick have?" The child keeps silent and then declares that Nick does not have any brothers. We can be certain that even in such simple cases, the child cannot think in terms of relativity, that primitive forms of thinking are always absolute and concrete. Thinking that is able to abstract from these absolute [notions], that is, relative thinking, is a result of high cultural development.

We should note one more specific feature of a young child's thinking.

It is quite natural that a large number of those words and concepts that the child encounters turn out to be new and unknown. However, adults use these words and in order to catch up with them and not seem inferior or more stupid, the small child develops a rather unique way of adapting. In this way, the child spares himself the feeling of inferiority and makes it possible for him to master, if only in appearance, those expressions and notions that he does not yet know. Piaget, who has extensively studied this mechanism of child thinking, called it *syncretism*. This term denotes an interesting phenomenon, traces of which can be found in the adult but which flourish in the child's mind [psyche — J. K.]. The essence of this phenomenon is the following: Concepts that have only one external aspect [in common — J. K.] are brought together with extreme ease and an unknown concept is replaced with a more familiar one. Such substitutions of the unknown with the understandable, such mixtures of meanings, are found in child speech fairly often. In his interesting book Chukovsky (1925/1968)[16] presented a number of rather expressive examples of such syncretic thinking.

---

[16](J. K.) Chukovsky's book has been published in Russian at least 17 times. It was first published with the title *Young Children* in 1925. Luria refers to the Leningrad edition (1928) also entitled "Young Children" *(Malen'kie deti); later* editions, however, were entitled *From Two to Five.*

When little Tanya was told that she has a "rust spot" *(rzhavchina)* on her pillow, she exerted no effort thinking about this word which was new for her and came out with the utterance that that it was her horsie "neighing" *(narzhala)* at her. A horseman *(vsadnik)* for small children is a man who works in a garden *(sad);* a loafer *(lodyr')* makes boats *(lodki),* a poor house *(bogadel'na)* is the place where they make God *(bog).*[17]

The mechanism of syncretism proves to be very characteristic for child thinking, and the reason is clear; in fact, it is the most primitive mechanism without which it would be very difficult for the child to cope with the first steps of his primitive thinking. At every turn the child encounters new difficulties, new unknown words, ideas, and expressions. And certainly the child is not a laboratory scientist or a theoretical researcher — he cannot always poke through a dictionary or ask an adult. He can maintain his independence only by means of primitive adaptations, so syncretism is that form of adaptation that a child's inexperience and egocentrism promotes.[18]

So how does thinking proceed in a child? What laws underlie a child's inferences, and how does the child construct judgments? After everything that has been said above, it is clear that developed logic with the limitations it imposes on thinking, with all of its complex conditions and regularities, cannot exist for the child. A child's primitive, precultural thinking is constructed in a much simpler way: it is an immediate reflection of the naively perceived world, and for the child one detail, one incomplete observation, may be enough for a corresponding (though a completely inadequate) inference. Thinking in adults proceeds according to laws of complex combination involving the accumulation of experience and inferences from generalizations. It follows the laws of inductive–deductive logic, whereas thinking for the young child is, according to Stern (1914), "transductive" (pp. 272-275). It develops neither from the general to the specific nor from the specific to the general; it simply infers from one episode to another, guided each time by new features that catch the child's

---

[17](J. K.) This translation directly from the Russian text, because it is one of the many difficult passages from Chukovsky's *From Two to Five* that is missing from Miriam Morton's translation (Chukovsky, 1968). For example, it is difficult to convey the word *vsadnik* in English and maintain both the meaning of the root "sad" (garden), the prefix "v-" (in), and the suffix "*-nik,*" which conveys the meaning of someone or something doing something. We have chosen to give a literal translation and include the Russian words so that the reader can see that the little girl tended to create her own words as rhymes based on her understanding of both the root and the suffix of the new unfamiliar adult words.

[18](A. L.) It is interesting to note that there is one case where syncretic thinking may be reactivated and thrive in adults: This happens in cases of learning a foreign language. One may say that when an adult reads a book in a foreign language that he does not know well enough, a very important role is played by a syncretic, not exact understanding of individual words. The primitive characteristics of a child's thinking are repeated.

attention. The child immediately finds a corresponding explanation for each phenomena and does it directly without any logical intermediate steps, without any generalizations.

Here is an example of this type of an inference (cited in Piaget, 1928, p. 181):

> M., an 8 year old child is shown a glass of water, then a pebble is put into it, the level of water rises.
> In answer to the question why the level of the water had risen the child answers: "because the pebble is heavy." Then another pebble is taken and shown to M. He says: *"It is heavy. It will make the water go up."*
> "And this one?" [a smaller one]
> "No."
> "Why?"
> "It is light."

We see that the inference here is made immediately, from one specific case to another, the basis [for the inference] being one of the artificially chosen features. The fact that there is no inference from some general notion is supported by the continuation of the experiment:

> The child is shown a piece of wood.
> "Is this piece of wood heavy?"
> "No."
> "If it were put in the water would it make it rise?" —
> *"Yes, because it isn't heavy."*
> "Which is heaviest, this wood or this pebble" [a small pebble and a large piece of wood]? —
> *"The pebble"* [correct].
> "Which will make the water rise highest?"
> *"The wood."*
> "Why?"
> *"Because it is bigger"* [because it has more volume than the pebble].
> "Then why did the pebbles make the water rise just now?"
> *"Because they are heavy"* (cited in Piaget, 1928, pp. 181–182)

We see how easily the child abandons one feature (weight), which in his opinion causes the water to rise, and replaces it with another one (size). Each time, he makes an inference from one episode to another, and absence of the general explanation escapes him. Here we approach another interesting fact: *There are no contradictions for the child,* he does not see them, contradictory judgments can coexist not excluding each other.

The child can argue that in the first instance the water rises because the object is heavy, in the second — because it is light. The child can argue that the boats float because they are light, while the ships float because they are heavy, and in so doing the child will sense no contradiction. Here is the complete protocol of such a conversation:

T. (7y.6m).
"Why does wood stay on the water?"
"Because it is light and the little boats have sails."
"And those that have no sails why do they not sink?"
"Because it is light."
". . . And how about big boats?"
"Because they are heavy."
"Then heavy things stay on top of the water?"
"No."
"Does a big stone?"
"No, it sinks."
"And big boats?"
"They stay because they are heavy."
"Is that the only reason?"
"No."
"What else?"
"Because they have big sails."
"And when these are taken away?"
"Then they are less heavy."
"And if the sails are put on again?"
"The same thing happens. They stay [on the water] *because they are "heavy"* (Piaget, 1928, pp. 181–182).

This example shows perfectly clearly the child's complete indifference to contradictions. The child draws a conclusion from one episode and then from another, and if his inferences are contradictory, this does not bother him. This is because the child still does not possess those laws of logic that are rooted in objective experience — in encounters with reality — and based on a validation of assumed suppositions, that is, on the laws of logical thought developed by culture. That is why there is nothing more difficult to do than to derail a child with the realization of the contradictory character of his inferences.

Because of this trait noted in the thinking of a child who as a rule easily makes inferences on the basis of one particular case, then on another, without stopping to fully comprehend the real relationships, we have an opportunity to observe in the child the forms of thought that, in their specific forms, can be found only in adult primitive people.

Encountering phenomena in the external world, the child inevitably begins to form his hypotheses on the basis of causality and relationships among individual things, and these hypotheses inevitably acquire the primitive forms that correspond to the specific characteristics of child thinking. Making the inferences on the basis of one episode then of another, the child in his hypotheses of the external world shows a tendency to connect one phenomenon with any other, thus connecting "everything with everything." The child knows no barriers on the basis of which he can establishing causal dependence, that is, barriers that exist in reality and that in some natural way become clear for the cultural adult only after long familiarization with the external world. In the child's understanding, one thing can influence another independently of distance, time, or complete absence of any connections between them. This character of understanding may result from child egocentrism. Remember how the child who poorly differentiates between reality and fantasy achieves illusory satisfaction of his wishes in cases when reality cannot provide it for him.

Influenced by this attitude toward the world, the child gradually develops the primitive notion that the same is also true about nature—any phenomenon can be connected with any other and any thing by itself can influence any other. This primitive and psychologically naive character of child thinking has become particularly obvious to us after a number of experiments that were performed by Piaget, whom we have already cited, and in Germany by Raspe (1924).

The latter performed the following experiments: he presented the child with an object, which after some time changed its shape as a result of certain causes. It might be a shape producing an illusion under certain conditions, a shape that seemed bigger if presented against a differing background, or a square, which, once turned on edge, (Fig. 3.7) produced an impression of increased size. Whenever such an illusion appeared, the child was intentionally presented with another outside stimulus, for example, a bulb might be switched on, or a metronome started. And when the child was asked to explain the cause of the illusion, that is, to explain why the square increased in size, the child invariably pointed to the new simultaneously appearing stimulus as the cause. The child said that the square increased because the bulb was switched on, or because the metronome clicked, though, of course, there were no evident connections between these phenomena.

The child's belief that these phenomena are connected, his *"post hoc—*

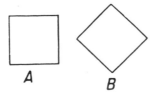

FIG. 3.7 The illusion given by a square turned out its edge.

ergo propter hoc" logic is so firmly ensconced that if you ask the child to change the phenomena back — to make the square smaller — he, without reflection, will approach the metronome and stop it.

We reproduced such experiments in our laboratory and inevitably got the same result in 7- to 8-year-old children. Only several of them were able to inhibit this primary spontaneous response and to construct a different hypothesis or acknowledge their ignorance. A significantly greater number of children showed much more primitive characteristics of thinking, arguing that phenomena occurring simultaneously are interconnected and that the connection is that of causality. Simultaneousness means causality; this is one of the main suppositions of child thinking, and one can therefore imagine the kind of picture of the world this primitive logic creates.

It is interesting to note that this primitive character of judgments is preserved in older children, and Raspe's (1924) data prove it: out of ten 10-year-old children, eight argue that the shape grew bigger as a result of starting the metronome, one constructed another hypothesis, and only one refused to give an explanation.

This mechanism of "magic" thinking is particularly expressive in 3- to 4-year-olds. The observations of these children readily show that a purely external evaluation of some phenomenon causes the child to make a hasty inference about its role. One of us had the opportunity to observe a girl who noticed that she did better with the small tasks given to her by her mother when the latter repeated two or three times what the girl was supposed to do. After several days, the following episode occurred: When the girl was sent to the neighboring room on a small errand, she demanded: "Mother, repeat it three times" and without waiting for her mother's repetitions, she rushed to the other room. A primitive, naive attitude toward her mother's words is quite clearly seen here and hardly requires further explanation.

This is the general picture of child thinking at the stage when the child stands either before the ladder of cultural influence or on its lowest rungs.

Beginning his life journey as an "organic creature," the child preserves his introversion and egocentrism for a long time. Prolonged cultural development is necessary in order for a primary weak connection with the world to become established and the harmonious apparatus, which we call cultural adult thinking, to finally replace primitive thinking.

STEPS TO CULTURE

We have recounted the features that are characteristic for a young child's primitive perception and way of thinking. A child speedily develops, however, and moves ahead, shifting to new forms of activity. An infant turns into a child and a child turns into an adolescent, whereas an adult has only reminiscences of how at one time he lived through childhood experiences and of how he at that time thought, felt, and perceived the world in a significantly different way.

New "adult" cultural forms of behavior gradually replace primitive childhood ones. New skills, new forms of thinking, logic, and new attitudes toward the world develop. It is natural therefore that science should ask questions about the ways in which the primitive child mind transforms step by step into the mind of an adult cultural man.

In the process of his development, the child not only grows, not only matures, but at the same time—and this is the most essential thing that we can note in our analysis of the evolution of the child's mind—the child acquires a number of new skills, a number of new forms of behavior. In the process of development, the child not only matures, but also *becomes rearmed*. Precisely this "rearmament" causes the greatest development and change that we observe in the child as he transforms into a cultural adult. This is what constitutes the most pronounced difference between the development of human beings and that of animals.

Indeed, let us trace the paths of animal development, the ways an animal adapts to the conditions where it lives. We can say that in the evolutionary process, all the changes that take place in animal behavior come down to two main components: the development of natural, innate features and the appearance of new skills, acquired in the course of an individual life, that is, "conditional reflexes."

If we take an animal, which had to adapt to the conditions of the woods, we will see how all its organs of perception are sharpened, helping it to avoid dangers. We will see how its vision is sharpened, how amazingly developed its scent is, and what an astoundingly beautiful hearing it has. On the other hand, we see how all these perceptive organs unite with the motor functions into a highly sophisticated and flexible system, we see how they are mobilized and activated by any sign that becomes habitual for the animal.

This is how the animal becomes adapted to nature—by altering its organism, by refining all its organs of perception, and activating all of its motor resources.

One would think that because in the process of evolution and transition to higher and higher stages of development all these natural abilities (vision, hearing, scent, memory, etc.) become more and more perfected, we might expect all these functions to be unusually developed in the human being.

However, we will be deeply disappointed if we expect anything of the kind. A thorough analysis of a number of inherent abilities in the human being will inevitably cause us to acknowledge that many of these abilities not only have not undergone strong development and perfection when compared to animals, but are at best completely dormant; moreover, in the majority of cases, we have grounds to speak of their deterioration, degradation, or even regression.

Indeed, how can one compare human vision with that of an eagle or hawk, human hearing with that of a dog that distinguishes rustles and pitches of tones that no cultural adult could ever perceive.[19] Finally, how can one compare a human being's sense of smell or his tactile and motor systems with the development of these systems of perception in the lower biological species?

Moreover, if we compare these processes in a cultural man — say an average modern Parisian — with those in an Australian who is at a very primitive stage of development, we will see that the cultural man is inferior to the latter with respect to almost all the simplest psychological functions. Reports of travellers and ethnographers are filled with stories about the amazingly developed hearing and vision of primitive people, about their surprising memory, and about their extraordinary ability to perceive many objects simultaneously and to estimate quantity (for example, when one sheep is missing in a big flock). In all these natural functions, the primitive man is incomparably superior to the cultural man, and nevertheless we still know that the mental life of the latter is much richer, that he is much more powerful, and that often he is much better oriented in his environment and controls the environmental phenomena.

What is the key to the puzzle of the evolution of psychology from animal to human being, from primitive to cultural man?

We believe that the answer is to be found in the evolution of those conditions of existence, in which we all live, as well as in the evolution of those forms of behavior that are determined by these external conditions. Modern man does not have to adapt to the external environment in the way that an animal or primitive man does. Modern man has conquered nature and what the primitive man did with his legs or hands, his eyes or ears, the modern man does with his *tools*. Cultural man does not have to strain his vision to see a distant object — he can do it with the help of eyeglasses, binoculars, or a telescope; he does not have to lend an attentive ear to a distant source, run for his life to bring news, — he performs all these functions with the help of those tools and means of communication and transportation that fulfill his will. All the artificial tools, the entire cultural environment, serve to "expand our senses" (Viner, 1909). Modern cultural man can allow himself the luxury of having the worst natural abilities, which he amplifies with artificial devices thus coping with the external world better than the primitive man who used his natural abilities directly. The latter broke a tree by beating it on the stone, modern man takes an ax

---

[19](A. L.) Studies that were conducted in Pavlov's school objectively demonstrated that a dog unerringly distinquishes 1/8 of a tone, [a feat] that not every adult is able to do.

or a frame-saw and does this work quicker, better, and with less energy wasted.

However, this does not exhaust the differences between cultural and primitive human beings. The industrial and cultural environment gradually changes them and that every human being we know today is a stone repeatedly cut and altered under the influence of the industrial and cultural environment.

Because of external conditions, the ape rose on its posterior extremities, its trunk straightened up; the same conditions caused the differentiation of the extremities, that is, development of the hand, which later on became the human hand. Engels associated this moment of the ape's transformation into something resembling man with this fact.

However, the influence of the industrial and cultural environment did not end here. The changes in the hand were to be followed by changes in the brain resulting in more sophisticated, more dynamic forms of human adaptation to the environment. It is natural that new conditions required new forms of adaptation, and such forms were developed in the course of time. Under the immediate pressure of the external conditions, man in his active struggle with the external world learned not to directly use his natural abilities in the struggle for existence, but to first develop more or less complex *methods* to help him in this struggle. In the process of evolution, man invented tools and created a cultural industrial environment, but this industrial environment altered man himself; it called forth complex cultural forms of behavior that took the place of the primitive ones. Gradually, the human being learns to *use* natural abilities rationally. The influence of the environment results in the appearance of new mechanisms unprecedented in the animal; the environment, so to speak, becomes interiorized [internalized — J. K.]; behavior becomes social and cultural not only in its contents, but also in its *mechanisms,* in its means. Instead of immediately memorizing something of particular importance, the human being develops a system of associative and structural memory; language and thinking develop, abstract notions appear, and a number of cultural skills and means of adaptation are created — as a result, a cultural adult emerges in place of a primitive one. Although natural, inherent functions are similar in both primitive and cultural man, or in some cases even may deteriorate in the course of evolution, cultural man differs enormously from primitive man by the fact that a huge inventory of psychological mechanisms — skills, forms of behavior, cultural signs and devices — has evolved in the process of cultural development, as well as by the fact that his entire mind is altered by the influence of the complex conditions that created him.

We deliberately digressed from our analysis of a child's mind. Our aim was to show where we are to look for serious and deep-seated changes in the behavior of a child as he turns into an adult.

We have noted before that we are no way inclined to think that there is a similarity or even a strict parallel between the evolution of the [human — J. K.] species, which we have just analyzed, and the development of the child. The child is born to an already existing cultural–industrial environment, and this fact constitutes the crucial, critical difference between the child and the primitive man. However, the matter is that the new-born child is cut off from this environment and is *not immediately integrated into it.* Integration into the cultural context is no way similar to putting on a new dress: This process entails deep transformations in behavior and is accompanied by the development of major specific mechanisms of behavior. So it is quite natural that every child necessarily must have his own precultural primitive period; this period lasts for some time and is characterized by its specific characteristics in the child's mental life, by particular primitive features in perception of thinking.

Once integrated into an appropriate environment, the child undergoes quick changes and alterations: This is a surprisingly rapid process, because the pre-existent social cultural environment stimulates in the child those necessary forms of adaptation, which were created long ago in the adults surrounding him.

The child's entire behavior becomes reconstructed; the child develops the habit of refraining from immediate satisfaction of his needs and drives and of retarding immediate reactions to external stimuli, so that by using indirect ways and acquiring the necessary cultural skills he could gain easier and better control over the situation.

It is this inhibition of the primitive functions and the development of complex forms of adaptation that constitute the transition from primitive forms of child behavior to adult forms.

ACQUISITION OF TOOLS

Already at the highest stages of pre-human animal evolution, we noted a very interesting fact: In some cases, the ape adapted to new and difficult conditions not directly, but by using external tools (sticks, boxes, etc.).[20]

We still do not observe in infants such phenomena that would suggest a rather high level of development of behavioral forms. The child must grow to between 1, year 6 months and 2 years before he develops the initial ability to use objects as tools, before he first proves able to treat a certain object not simply as a thing, but as an object *with the help of which* one can achieve some goal. The first *functional* attitude toward an object is the first

---

[20](A. L.) See chapter 1.

step on the path of establishing an active, and not purely mechanical connection with the external world.

It is no wonder that the child — just beginning to familiarize himself with the external world that appears strange and often filled with fantastic phenomena — proves to be barely able to exert any organized influence on this world and to use individual external objects as tools for achieving his own goals. In order to be able to enter into such complex relations with objects of the external world and learn that these objects may serve not only for immediate satisfaction of the instincts (an apple, which can be eaten, a toy, with which one can play), but also as *tools* for achieving a certain goal, the child has to go a long way in his development. For this it is necessary to replace instinctive, immediate activity with intellectual activity guided by complex intentions and translated into the organized action.

Let us take a look at those initial situations when the child first begins to use objects in the external world as tools and in so doing makes his first steps in the transition to complex intellectual behavior.

We know that a little child already eats with a spoon, uses a plate, and wipes [dries] himself with the towel. But these are cases when he only imitates adults, whereas his spontaneous use of objects as tools is most insignificant, almost null. In all the above cases the spoon, the plate, and the towel are so inseparably fused with the acts of eating or washing that they constitute a single habitual unitary situation. However, we all know how difficult it is to train a child who is 1 year, 6 months old to use a spoon, to cut with a knife (instead of breaking [the bread] with his hands), and so on.

If we want to trace the process of mastering tools in its pure form and to understand what prevents a child from using them, we have to turn to experiments.

A number of researchers in Germany have conducted experiments devoted to clarification of the ways a child functionally uses things as tools to achieve some goal. These were performed, for example, by the same Köhler whose studies were described earlier and who discovered tool use by apes; these experiments were repeated by K. Bühler (1929) and Peiser (1914) with older children, as well as by the two German psychologists Lipmann and Bogen (1923) who described these experiments in a very interesting book.

The simplest of these experiments was conducted with quite young children in the following way. A child was brought to a table on which an apple had been placed. The child could not reach the apple with his hand, but there was a thread attached to the apple and the end of this thread was left on the edge of the table. He only had to pull the thread to get the apple.

However, the child K. Bühler examined the child at the age of 9 m., 1 y.3 m., 1 y.9 m.) proved unable to learn that he does not have to reach directly for the apple, but should pull the thread. The child invariably reached directly for the apple; if it was necessary, he would go around the table to get the apple from the other side, but he could not guess that he should use the thread as an auxiliary tool for getting the apple. An understanding of [the relationship between — J. K.] the goal and the means for its achievement was completely absent in the child.

It is true that, after many experiments, Bühler managed to reach the point when the child took hold directly of the thread to pull the apple (or a cookie) toward himself, but the way the child came to this method of achieving his goal was indeed a peculiar one. The child's wish to take hold of the apple was so strong and persistent that he performed a number of pointless motions with his hand and, with some of those movements, casually brushed the thread, thus moving the apple. Here this pseudo-intellectual activity of the child is explained by the repetition and reinforcement of those successful accidental movements, but not by any organized activity. The child does not perceive the thread as an object connected with the apple, that is, as a possible means for achieving the goal; it will take about a year before this connection becomes accessible for the child.

Some researchers organized the experiment in a different way: We will describe it here to demonstrate the process of the initial acquisition of tool use.

Some toys that interest the child were placed on the upper edge of the classroom blackboard. Not far from it, by the wall, were a chair and a long stick. The child's task was to get the toy that was placed too high; the only way to do this was to use the stick as a tool. The experiments were conducted with children of different ages and at different levels of mental development, and the most interesting fact was that the result of the experiment proved helpful for assessing a child's mental retardation. This task was solved without any difficulty by the normal child of 7 to 8, but proved to be beyond the abilities of the retarded child; the possibility of using the stick functionally as a tool was an idea that never crossed the child's mind.

To illustrate this, we will present two parallel transcripts demonstrating the outcome of the same experiment with two different children attending the school for the mentally retarded (Lipmann & Bogen, 1923):

Subj. P. (8y.2m.)

Subj.: "[I] can't get it." Exper.: "Think, how you can reach it." Subj.: "[I] must climb the stool." This attempt fails because the subject is too small to reach the top of the blackboard from the stool. Exper.: "Can you get it in some other way?" Subj.: "[I] can climb a ladder." Exper.: "We don't have a ladder." The subj. climbs the stool again and tries to get a toy but with no success. Exper.: "Can't you do it in some other way? Try to do it, look around." Subj.: "The stick can be used. . . ." Takes the stick, climbs the stool and gets the toys . . .

Subj. B. (8y.6m.)

The Subj. stops in front of the blackboard and begins to jump up unceasingly stretching both hands towards the toy. He seems not to understand that he will not achieve his goal in this way. Experim.: "You will not get anything like this . . ." The subj. continues to jump up. Experim.: "I say, this won't work, try some other way." The Subj. climbs a desk, which is 0.75 m. away from the blackboard and stretching his body tries to reach the toy with his hands. Experim.: "Well, what can you use to get the toy?." The subject looks at the Experim. in embarrassment, not knowing what to do. Experim. casually takes the stick and puts it near the blackboard. The subject looks at the latter, but does not do anything. Experim.: "You may take anything in this room that you can use to get the toy." The subj.: '[I] don't know, [I] can't get it . . ."

These two parallel transcripts demonstrate quite clearly the specific features characteristic for the behavior of the two children, and we can easily guess that the first of them has a milder [form — J. K.] of mental retardation, whereas the second is severely mentally retarded. Indeed, let us carefully analyze the transcript. From the beginning of the experiment, the first child begins to combine and make active use of the surrounding objects in order to get the toy. It is true that he does it with difficulties (we should not forget that he is a mentally retarded); however we see that he pulls a stool toward the blackboard and says that you can get the toy with the help of a ladder, and at last, true after the experimenter's instigation, he turns to the stick.

Quite a different picture is seen in the case of the other child. His behavior from the beginning is characterized by a refusal to use any tools, a rejection of any complex, mediated solution to the task. He begins with incessant jumping up, and trying to get the toy in this way, he then jumps onto a nearby desk, stretches his body, and still does not get the toy; he does this in spite of the obvious absurdity of his attempt (the desk was almost a meter away from the blackboard). It does not occur to this child to make any changes with those things around him and in this way use these auxiliary changes to solve the task. He cannot do this in spite of obvious hints from the experimenter, he still has no idea that an external object, that is, the stick, can be used for this purpose.

It is clear that this child is severely mentally retarded, his behavior is still on the stage of primitive development and has not yet shifted to the stage of cultural forms, which are primarily characterized by active acquisition of external objects as tools.

The ability to make use of tools turns out to be indicative of the level of psychological development. We can confidently state that it is these processes of tool acquisition together with the specific development of internal psychological methods and the skill of functionally organizing one's behavior that characterize the cultural development of a child's mind.

CULTURAL DEVELOPMENT OF SPECIAL FUNCTIONS: MEMORY

We have seen how a very young child, for whom the world of external objects at first was altogether strange, gradually draws nearer to this world and begins to gain control over these objects; he begins to use them functionally, that is, as tools. This is the first stage of cultural development, when new forms and means of behavior develop to assist both natural movements and the simplest acquired movements.

The second stage of cultural development is characterized by the emergence of mediated processes in child behavior. These processes reconstruct behavior on the basis of the use of sign stimuli. These modes of behavior, acquired in the course of cultural experience, also reconstruct the child's basic psychological functions, they [modes — J. K.] equip these functions with new arms, developing them.

In a number of experiments, we had the opportunity to trace the development of the cultural techniques connected with child *memory,* that is, to observe how a child's memory grows, becomes stronger, and rearms, thus gradually reaching the level of an adult.

How a child's memory develops seemed to remain a rather vague, almost mysterious question for a long time. Does a child's memory really develop? Is adult memory better than that of children? These questions prove to be not as simple as they might seem at first glance.

All of us, particularly those of us who have had to encounter people seeking personal advice ([those of us who are] medical professionals or psychologists), often heard our patients complain of a failing memory. The majority claimed that they had a good memory in childhood, that they could [then — J. K.] memorize several pages after reading them only once and remember them for a long time. However, in the course of time, their memory began to fail and, now that they are already adults, had become quite bad.

Do these complaints, which we hear from almost every one, have real grounds, or are they only a result of over-anxiety and morbid self doubts?

We have to acknowledge that in many respects, these complaints are well-founded. If memory is understood as the natural plasticity of the neuropsychological apparatus that allows a perceived impression to become fixed or, so to say, imprinted, then these people are not far from the truth. One may submit that this natural plasticity of the neural-brain tissue (which many Western writers call the "mnema" or "mnemic function," to use the terms of Semon[21]) does not in all likelihood develop substantially in the course of an individual life; and in some cases (in cases where the nervous system experiences exhaustion and extreme stress, etc.) it even regresses and becomes weaker. It is sufficient to compare this natural ability to remember in a normal child and in nervous, overstrained adults (whose numbers are great among the inhabitants of cities), in order to see that this is really so.

Even if we compare the average number of words mechanically memorized by children of different ages and by adults, we will be surprised not to find any significant development of this function.

The data presented below were obtained by Norsworthy.[22] She studied the ability of different-aged children to memorize words and found the following results:

8 y.o. recall on the average	11.1 words
9 — " — " — " — " — " — " — " —	12.2 — " —
10 — " — " — " — " — " — " — " —	12.2 — " —
11 — " — " — " — " — " — " — " —	12.8 — " —
13 — " — " — " — " — " — " — " —	13.5 — " —
14 — " — " — " — " — " — " — " —	13.7 — " —
15 — " — " — " — " — " — " — " —	13.7 — " —
16 — " — " — " — " — " — " — " —	14.0 — " —
Adults — " — " — " — " — " — " —	12.8 — " —

As it turns out, the development of memory in childhood and adolescence progresses rather slowly, and if the data characterizing this process are compared with those for adults, it will be clear that an adult remembers on the average fewer words than a teenager of 13- to 14-years old. It seems as if memory hardly develops at all and that by the age of maturity we have to acknowledge even a certain deterioration.

However, we all know that the memory of an adult is often extremely strong and extensive. We know that a scientist remembers vast diverse materials in his specific area; each of us stores in his head a tremendous quantity of different kinds of information, terms, figures, and so on. We know cases when an adult proves able to learn a foreign language very

---

[21](V. G., J. K.) No information available on this author.

[22](A. L.) Norsworthy (1906) *The Psychology of Mentally Deficient Children.* (cited in Wipple, 1914).

quickly. We often are amazed by the order and organization of the memory of some of our friends.

How is one to solve this contradiction? Which position is correct and who has a better memory — a child or an adult?

We can solve this problem only after looking at the ways memory develops from child to adult and after analyzing the features that characterize this development.

If we start with an analysis of the differences between the memory of a 5- or 6-year-old and that of a school age child, we will have to acknowledge that we observe in these children *different ways of using their memory.* The 6-year-old child remembers the material immediately, naturally, whereas the school-age child has a whole number of techniques [methods — J. K.] that he uses to memorize the necessary material; the latter connects this new material with his previous experience, relies on the whole system of associations, and sometimes uses some notes and so on. Both children have similar memory in general, but they use it in different ways: they both have memory, but the older one knows how to use it. It is this transition from natural forms of memory to the cultural ones that constitutes development of memory from child to adult.

Indeed, let us remember that primitive people stopped relying on the simple natural function of memory. Earlier, we pointed out[23] that a primitive man, who had to remember the quantity of cattle or measures of grain, instead of remembering this in the natural way, invented tallies. He used them to mark the necessary quantity and achieved two objects simultaneously: By employing this primitive method, he was able to recall the necessary material more firmly than in the natural way, and at the same time he relieved his natural memory of a redundant burden.

We can say that the child follows a similar path, the difference being that primitive man invented his systems of memorizing himself, whereas the developing child most often acquires ready-made systems that help him remember. The only thing the child has to do is to acquire them and learn how to use them; thus, once he has acquired the systems, he transforms his natural processes by using them.

Under these experimental conditions, we had the opportunity to see that the use of such methods constitutes the basis for this transition to cultural forms of memory and that these methods can to a great degree augment memory in a short period of time.

We asked a 6- to 7-year-old child to remember a list of numbers that were read to him. When the child was asked to recall the figures, it turned out that he could recall two, three, or, at the most, four figures.

When the child was convinced that it was indeed very difficult to

---

[23](A. L.) See chapter 2.

memorize 10 figures, we altered the experiment. The child was given some object to hold in his hands, for example, a piece of paper, rope, or wooden shavings, and so on, and was told that this object would help him remember the numbers to be read. We gave the child the task of using the object as a means to achieve a certain goal, that is, as a means to remember the figures.

Usually, the following picture unfolded before us: At the beginning, the child cannot understand how he can functionally use a piece of paper to help him remember. It does not occur to him that a piece of paper, on the one hand, and the figures, on the other, can have something in common. The child can still scarcely comprehend the notion of functionally using things, that is, of the fact that some thing can be used artificially to signify some process or some purpose. It is true the child can use a spoon for eating, or a towel for drying, but all of these behaviors are habitual processes, where an object constitutes a necessary part of the structure of the process; the child does not yet have the means to invent the use of the auxiliary tools in those cases when some "unfamiliar" object is used to realize some process. A still greater problem for the child is the use of psychological auxiliary tools.

This is why a child of this age often refuses to perform this task, pointing out that a piece of paper cannot help him remember figures. We are still faced with the task of getting the child to master this material as a means of memorization, of getting him to *discover* the functional use of some sign for the purpose of memorization.

Usually, we achieve this goal only after some time, which may be longer with some children and shorter with others. After several attempts, a child guesses that he can make some signs on a piece of paper, he gets animated, takes the paper in his hands, and begins to make some marks on it. Usually, it is a system of rips (slight tears) or a number of torn off pieces of paper where the quantity of torn off pieces corresponds to the number of units represented by the given figure. As a result, the child ends up with a particular system of notation resembling a "tally-like" system of numeric marks. Figure 2.8 illustrates typical tallies used by primitive people (in this case — by the Buriats). Figure 3.8 represents the "tally-like" notation, invented in our experiment by a 6-year-old child. We see that they [the tallies — J. K.] are similar in their formal functional roles, that under the conditions of the experiment, the child invented the system of notation, used by primitive people.

This child's system, of course, depends on a great many factors and primarily on the material offered to the child.

If we give the child a piece of paper or wood, the notation will resemble a "tally-like" system; if we give him a rope, the child will end up with something like writing with knots; finally, if we give the child individual

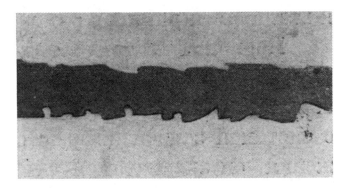

FIG. 3.8   Notched tally by a six year old child.

objects (grains, shot, feathers, a nail), then the notation will be that of grouping these objects, and so on.

In all these cases *the child manipulates the external objects to gain control of the internal memory process;* this *is* characteristic of the first cultural technique that emerges to facilitate the natural mental functions.

However, the child does not achieve success with identical ease in all cases. We observed some situations where the child invented the method of tearing off pieces of paper to correspond with the sum of units contained in a given list of numbers. Then, he collected all the small pieces into one pile but found himself in a rather difficult position when asked to recall the figures read to him one after another. In such cases, a second invention was necessary to solve the task: The child had to guess that he was supposed to group the torn off pieces into separate piles and calculate them one after another. In these cases, the task was performed successfully.

In all these experiments, one essential factor must be noted: Transition from a system of immediate recall to a system of "notation," using certain marks, resulted in a significantly increased effectiveness of memory. We would say that this notation system resulted in a certain *fictitious development.* The child, who memorized three to four figures by using the natural method of recall, in fact, proves able to recall spontaneously an unlimited number of figures when he switches to the "notation" technique. His natural memory is replaced by the new artificial methods that he invented. His memory begins to work in a new manner, thus achieving maximal results: In order to remember, the child tears off pieces of paper that he organizes in piles, or he uses matches, feathers, and so on, putting aside each time a certain amount of these objects.

In the experiments we have just described, the child himself invents a system of certain marks, then uses it to transform his natural mechanism into a cultural one, thus increasing the power of his memory many times. However, it is clear that this system turns out to be very primitive, cumbersome, and clumsy. Thus, subsequent development means not improvement in natural memory, but substitution: *substitution of primitive methods by other, more effective ones, which appeared in the process of historic evolution.*

Let us return to the experiment where the child had to remember a list of numbers that were read to him, but this time let us conduct an experiment not with a 6-year-old child, but with a first grader. This child has already learned the system of numeric notation, that is, the system of symbolic representation of numbers. He knows the system that has been developed over many centuries and translated for the child in school classes. So when we offer this child the same task of remembering a list of figures and ask him to use the same auxiliary material (paper, ropes, grains, small shot, feathers, etc.) for this purpose, we see that he behaves quite differently. Usually, the school child does not revert to the primitive methods characteristic for the preschooler; he demonstrates no desire to make incisions or tear off pieces of paper and pile them [in groups] later. He takes a sheet of paper and tears out *the shape of a number.* This tendency to construct numbers proves to be very strong in children of this age, and even when they have to use a string, they try to make a symbol out of it, difficult as this task may be. The new cultural techniques acquired at school turn out to be so strong that they suppress the older primitive methods. For example, even when using an object "better suited" for a quantitative, nonsymbolic notation the child does not return to the ólder "tally-like" notation. Even with grain or small shot, he constructs the shapes of the figures, that is, in order to memorize the digit 1, he does not *set* aside one pellet, but makes, albeit with difficulty, the shape of the digit 1.

Here is an example of such a notation (Fig. 3.9). In this case the, child used pieces of paper, wood shavings, or just anything, but no matter what the material was, he always made signs in the shape of numbers.

If we increase the speed of presentation of the figures, the child would invent a new, simplified system of notation, still resorting to the system of making up symbols for numerals or their elements.

The result was the same: A tremendous increase in the number of items recalled.

The above examples clearly show us that, in the course of his development, the child does not simply train his memory, but rearms it, shifting to new systems, as well as to new techniques for remembering. If during this time, the natural "function of remembering" remains on the average the same, the mnemonic devices continually develop, resulting in maximal effectiveness.

In fact, each of us remembers quite differently than a child. We all possess vast material, consisting of the traces of our previous experience, which we actively use in each act of remembering. In order to remember

FIG. 3.9   Paper cut-outs representing numbers.

something new we associate it in our minds with something from previous experience, with something we know and remember very well. It is said that we use the mechanism of association, that is, associatively connecting the new with the known; it would be more correct to say that we actively create a structure: The new elements take their place along side the well-known, previously stored components. When recalling a meaningful (previously known) picture, we also now store a new object or a word that we are supposed to keep in mind.

Each of us has an entire complex mechanism serving memory, and, if somebody is particularly good at remembering something, it often means that the person knows how to make good use of his memory, that is, he knows how to well-organize his psychological repertoire; he is able to create good auxiliary structures, using them as a means to remember.

In our experiments, we were able to ascertain that the development of a child's memory is tied primarily to the development of these psychological auxiliary means, to gaining control over individual associations and images, as well as to learning how to use them functionally for the purpose of remembering.

In order to be able to observe this phenomenon in experimental conditions, we of course had to study objectively the internal mnemonic devices, and to do this, we had to "bring them to the outside." The experiments were organized in the following way: A number of typical lotto picture cards were laid out in front of a child; the cards contained pictures of animals, objects, and so on. A list of words was read to the child and he was asked to select for each one a card that in his opinion might help him remember the word better. The cards the child had chosen were put aside, and once this part of the experiment was completed, the child was asked to recall the words looking at the selected card. It goes without saying that the set of cards did not contain the given words, but required a certain skill to connect them with the words (e.g., the word "dog" appeared in the word list, yet among the pictures there was no picture of a dog, but pictures of a house, a kennel, a wolf, etc.). In more complex experimental settings, there were no picture prompts whatsoever, and the subject had to actively and artificially connect the given word with picture. So the task was to stimulate the subject to use a picture functionally for the purpose of memorizing.

The experiments show that not all the children were equally successful in their ability to use the tool suggested to them.

When young children of 4 to 5 years were offered the cards and asked to use them to remember the words by establishing the most primitive connections, often this proved unsuccessful. The child refused to use the cards for remembering; it never occurred to the child that the cards can have some auxiliary role in memorizing the words. The child did not understand that the cards could be connected with the words, for example, that the picture of a dog collar could help him to remember the word *dog*.

Children of this age turn out to be unable to master the functional use of auxiliary signs; the cultural use of memory is inaccessible for them, they resort to simple immediate imprinting. This, of course, does not refer to especially gifted children, whose mental development is ahead of their biological development.

But let us take one step further. Let us try to encourage such a child to use pictures for the purposes of remembering (this proves to be quite possible) or take a child of 6 to 7 years. This child will be able to use pictures to remember words. It is true that this process will not be accessible for the child in all cases. The child proves able to remember the word with the help of a picture only when the picture and the word are in some rather simple way related. The simplest cases of such mediated remembering are those when the picture and the word are already connected in the child's previous experience, for example, the words "tea" or "milk" are easily memorized if the corresponding pictures are those of a cup or a cow; the process of establishing connections on the basis of similarity (the word "bird"—the picture of "airplane") or functional links (the word "knife"—the picture of "watermelon," because a watermelon is cut with a knife) is somewhat more difficult, although sometimes possible; however, more complicated connections prove already inaccessible for these children. In those cases, when the picture and the word are not connected in a child's previous experience and the association of these two images requires certain mental engagement, children of this age proved completely unable to use a picture as an auxiliary means for remembering.

Quite a different picture is seen with older children, say in 10- to

11-year-old schoolchildren, particularly when a child is sufficiently well developed. In these cases, quite a different mechanism is revealed. At this stage of development, the child already proves able in the course of remembering not only to reproduce familiar situations from his previous experience, *but to actively connect the proposed word and the picture thus creating a new situation,* which helps the child imprint the given word in his memory. The picture selected by such older children may have nothing in common with the word to be remembered, but is actively tied to the word in a certain situation that can help him firmly remember this word. Here are some examples of such connections made by a 10-year-old boy:

1. The child is asked to memorize the word "theater"; he picks up a picture with a crawfish at the seashore; then, after this part of the experiment is over, he correctly recalls the word "theater" looking at the picture. Explaining his choice he says: "the crawfish is sitting at the seashore and looks at the pebbles under the water: they are beautiful — and this is a theater for the crawfish."

2. The child is given the word "shovel;" he selects the picture with chickens pecking in a dung hill; later on the child correctly recalls the word. His explanation: "the chickens dig the ground with their bills [beaks] like [we do] with shovels . . ."

3. The word given is "wish;" the child selects the picture of airplane; correctly recalls the word; explanation: "I want to fly by airplane."

We have presented here three ways of linkage in one structure, which help the child remember a number of words he would have never been able to memorize without these auxiliary means. We can see that all of these examples have various kinds of rather complex connections.

Our task did not include a detailed analysis of such connections; they are of a rather primitive character in young children and become very rich and complex in adults. The difference between a child's and an adult's memory cannot be reduced simply to natural "strengthening" of memory, but lies in "the cultural" acquisition of still newer and newer methods of memorizing, in the ability to use conditional signs for remembering, that is, by using mediated means, a child manages to improve his memory several times. After we suggest to a child that he shift to a method of memorizing words with the help of pictures, we attain some sort of an "artificial memory development": using different techniques in the same conditions, the child, who could remember four to five words, now begins to remember up to 20 to 30 words. We can achieve an even greater "increase" of memory in adults. Thus, memory in the child and in the adult differs according to the "cultural methods" used. The following short table illustrates this statement.

TABLE 3.1
Development of Natural and Mediated Memory in Children and Adults

Subjects	Natural memory	Mediated memory	Coefficient of mediated memory
Preschoolers I (4–5 y.o.)	2.12	2.85	0.33
Preschoolers II (5–7 y.o.)	4.55	8.25	0.81
Schoolchildren I (7–12 y.o.)	6.75	12.03	0.93
Schoolchildren II (12–15 y.o.)	7.88	13.09	0.66
Students (20–30 y.o.)	10.03	14.28	0.42

Children of different ages were asked first to recall 10 words immediately, and then to remember the same number of words using auxiliary pictures.

The results can be summarized in the following way:[24]

An analysis of the data presented in table 3.1 shows that younger preschoolers remember extremely few words: Out of the 15[25] words presented, they remember [on the average] only 2.12 words. At the same time, the pictures given to these children produce almost no increase in recall. It is clear that the memory of preschoolers is predominantly mechanical; it does not go beyond simple natural imprinting (and this fact clearly substantiates the extensive development of graphic eidetic memory in young children [i.e., remembering in images]). It is natural that a child is unable to remember meachincially a significant number of the words presented; it is also natural that, being unable to use auxiliary signs, the child in the experiment with pictures continues to use a mechanical method of remembering: pictures often do not help, but hinder recall. Thus, when the auxiliary pictures are strange [unfamiliar to the child] and not connected with the stimuli [target words], we often see a decrease in the number of the words remembered. The results are much better in the older preschoolers where the use of auxiliary signs reveals up to 81% increase in the number of words remembered. We also observed a still greater increase in the ability of older preschoolers to remember, connected with the shift to mediated memory in the first school-age group, where the use of external signs results in a twofold increase of the number of words remembered. Subsequently, the use of auxiliary methods remains efficient, but together with it there begins a significant development of memory that does not resort to external auxiliary means.

---

[24](A. L.) The materials are borrowed from the work by A. N. Leontiev (1931) "Development of memory in children" (the study was made in the psychological laboratory of the Academy of Communist Education).

[25](V. G., J. K.) There is a discrepancy between the number reported here and what was said earlier where the children were reported to have been presented with 10 words.

If we draw a diagram for the data presented in table 3.1, we will get the graph presented in Fig. 3.10. The first [beginning] part of the diagram is characterized by the sharp ascent of the upper curve that denotes memory employing external auxiliary means; in its second half (older school age and adults) the upper curve slows down its ascent, whereas the lower line, denoting the number of words memorized without external auxiliary means, ascends more saliently. As a result, we get a picture that may be conditionally called "a memory parallelogram" and that we may interpret as [the manifestation of] unequal mechanisms of memorization at younger and older ages. The young [preschool] child was completely unable to use external auxiliary means, whereas in the first school-age group, their use reaches a maximum; the second school-age group is characterized by another phenomenon: the use of the external means begins to change also the *internal* processes. Memory in younger children was purely mechanical without external means, whereas the schoolchild begins to use some *internal modes* [of remembering], the latter remembered not mechanically but with the help of associations, logically. Properly speaking, the "natural" memory of the older schoolchild loses its natural character and turns into "cultural" memory; it is in this cultural transformation of the primitive processes that we are inclined to see the explanation of the significant development that is characteristic for the "natural" development in childhood.

To determine how these means can increase the effectiveness of memory, you can make an experiment yourself: Memorize some system of 100 words, for example, 50 Russian writers in chronological order and 50 names of towns and stations along some river or railway track. Of course it will require certain effort, but we know very well that it is not so very difficult to memorize a number of elements belonging to one system (e.g., parts of

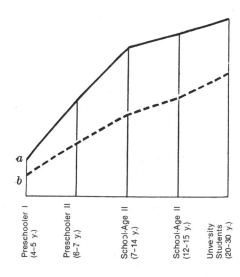

FIG. 3.10 *a* = the curve of the development of mediated memory. *b* = the curve of development of natural memory.

Preschooler I (4–5 y.)

Preschooler II (6–7 y.)

School-Age II (7–14 y.)

School-Age II (12–15 y.)

University Students (20–30 y.)

some mechanism, body parts, etc.). With this list in your memory, you can memorize without great difficulty any 100 words and recall them in the order they were read to you. This task, amazing at first glance, can be realized by a simple method that is invisible to the outside observer: You will simply have to associate each new word with a corresponding element in the sequence you had prepared before, as we did in our experiments with pictures. Having such a number of internal auxiliary signs, one can increase the "effectiveness" of natural memory 5 to 10 times or more, thus producing what we can call the appearance of "fictitious memory development."

This is how culture acts, developing in us newer and newer methods, thus transforming natural memory into "cultural" memory; the effect of school is similar: It creates a resevoir of experience, engraphs a number of sophisticated and complex auxiliary methods and opens up a number of new potentials for natural human function.

We have purposely dwelled on a more detailed analysis of memory because this function allows us to illustrate with a concrete example the interrelation of natural, inborn forms of psychological activity and the cultural ones, that is, those that are acquired in the course of social experience. It is by this example that we understood that development is not a simple maturation, but cultural metamorphoses, cultural re-armament. And if we wish to analyze the memory of an adult person, we would have to examine it not in the form nature gave it, but in the form that culture created. Indeed, it would be completely wrong to limit memory to those laws of reinforcement and reproduction of experience that are embedded in the natural mnemonic functions.

If psychology wishes to study the laws of memory in modern cultural man, it has, on the one hand, to include in this study those methods and means he employs, those external signs that created the conditions of social environment and cultural development: his notebook, his ability to extract and make notes—his entire more or less rationally organized system of external signs that assist memory. On the other hand, psychology has to take into account those fundamental changes that occur in the internal psychological mechanisms as a result of culture, as a result of the use of certain methods and means for remembering.

When we study the memory of cultural man, strictly speaking, we do not study an isolated "mnemonic function"—we study all the strategies and techniques aimed at fixing experience in memory and developed in the course of cultural maturation.

CULTURAL DEVELOPMENT OF SPECIAL FUNCTIONS: ATTENTION

We would like to dwell very briefly, literally with a few words, on the stages of development of child attention.

We know that attention plays the most important function in the organism's life. This function deals with the organization of behavior, with the creation of a certain set, preparing man for perception or activity.

If it were not for the function of a set, man would not be able to perceive in any order the stimuli coming from the environment or to differentiate the most important ones; he would not be able to organize his reactions into a corresponding system discerning and ordering the most important actions.

The phenomenon of attention can be observed from earliest childhood. Natural attention is seen in the first weeks of a child's life and is elicited by some sufficiently strong stimuli. It is quite clear that a strong external stimulus — bright light, a loud noise, and so on, — correspondingly organizes all the child's behavior: the child turns his head toward its source, a specific expression of attention appears, and so on. Strong instinctive internal stimuli operate in the same manner. Even in the youngest child, the state of hunger elicits a number of specific reactions. Instead of a nondifferentiated state, that is, the state intermediate between sleeping and vigilance, some coordinated movements appear: a child reaches for his mother's breast, all the peripheral movements recede into the background, all the child's behavior organizes itself in accordance with this dominant stimulus. Such is the simplest natural form of attention that is usually called instinctive-reflectory attention.

This type of attention is characterized by its nonintentional, nonvolitional character: Any strong and sudden stimulus immediately attracts the child's attention and reconstructs his behavior. On the other hand, once the stimulus (e.g., an internal, instinctive stimulus) becomes weaker, the organizing role of attention disappears and organized behavior again gives way to chaotic and nondifferentiated behavior.

It is quite clear that with this type of natural attention no long-term, stable form of organized behavior can appear. Every new stimulus would destroy the previous set over and over again and continually bring about new reconstructions of behavior. It is clear that such conditions can satisfy an organism only while it is outside social demands, outside the collective, outside work. However, when an individual faces certain demands, when a certain organized task (primitive as it may be) has to be done, then primitive nonvolitional attention is not sufficient, and different, more stable, forms of attention become necessary.

It is quite evident that further evolution of attention cannot pursue the path along which involuntary attention developed; to be able to solve a given task, an individual has to work out a manner of behavior that is exactly opposite to the previous dominant manner. At the earlier developmental stages, each strong stimulus could organize behavior by bringing about a certain set, whereas at the later stages this ability has to be extended also to weaker stimuli that can be biologically or socially important and require a long-term chain of ordered reactions. Natural forms of attention cannot satisfy this condition and it is evident that alongside these forms there have to develop some other mechanisms, which would now be artificially acquired, in response to the above requirement. Artificial, voluntary, "cultural" attention must emerge and is the most necessary condition for any work.

Let us try to trace the transition to such forms of attention by taking some examples of problem solving. Here, none of the conditions involved in the processes of voluntary, natural attention influence the school child. The proposed tasks do not in and of themselves serve as a stimulus strong enough to hold the child's attention; they do not find fertile ground among any of those instinctive processes that are able to organize the entire behavior of a personality. Still, a pupil may work on such tasks in an organized fashion for a sufficiently long time, concentrating only on them and not wandering off. From the point of view of natural forms of behavior, this may seem to be an unexplainable puzzle. This puzzle will be solved only when we discover the specific strengths that hold attention on a given job and that continue to be effective over a certain prolonged period.

Traditional psychology attempted to explain voluntary behavior as the activity of the will and considered it to be a typical example of willful behavior. Needless to say, in essence this does not appear to be an explanation, because the appearance of "will" also requires an explanation and does not appear to be a final, independent factor.

One may surmise that the unfolding experiences in a child's life can by themselves create certain new additional stimuli, with which the child was not born and that acquire further meaning beyond that stimulated by natural behavior. Cultural conditions (that understandably include a rather wide range of social conditions in the environment, school, and profes-sional and vocational settings — all factors influencing the child) begin to produce a certain type of "quasi-needs" (Lewin, 1926/1935), that is, certain states of stress that push the child into certain activity and disappear only when the given organized activity is brought to an end. This artificial cultural stimulation of behavior forms a powerful apparatus affecting the personality and organizing its activity. The child begins to learn to act in accordance with the posed task and to set such tasks for himself. Each of these tasks introduces serious changes in the structure of behavior; they produce a certain tension, pushing the person into a series of actions, aimed at the realization of this task. Emotionally tinged traces of former experience strengthen this cultural stimulus. The clearer the problem, the more precise the scheme in which it is formulated; the more definite the forms outlined for the paths of realizing this task, then the more persistent and stronger the stimulus becomes, pushing toward its organized realiza-tion. A series of experiments, conducted recently in the Berlin Institute of Psychology, demonstrate that even if some activity aimed at a certain goal is interrupted and not given the possibility of full realization, then already by this very start a certain tension is artificially evoked, making the individual undertake the realization of this problem at the first opportunity and overcome serious obstacles on the way.

A certain series of cultural stimuli is produced, allowing the person to concentrate on the given activity, sometimes even conquering serious distracting obstacles. However, along with the complication of dynamic conditions and the creation of new demands bearing the character of culturally grafted "drives," the influence of the historical environment is at work organizing attention in still another way. *Specific devices* are created in the child, allowing him to regulate his psychological operations, to differentiate between the essential and the non-essential, to perceive how difficult situations submit to certain fundamental, central factors. Developing culturally, a child gains the opportunity to *create himself those stimuli that in the future will influence him, organize his behavior,* and attract his attention.

The first of these factors, as we were repeatedly able to see, are unquestionably signifying gestures[26] and speech. At first, a child takes in the picture of his surroundings in a diffuse manner; however, his mother only has to point out some object and name it in order that the object stand out from its surroundings precisely in the way the mother pointed it out and in order that the child turn his attention particularly to it. For the first time, the process of attention begins to function as a cultural operation. However, attention becomes a real function only when the child himself masters the means of creating the additional stimuli that focus his attention on individual components of a situation and that eliminate everything else from the background. After externally manipulating the environment, the child at a certain moment begins to organize his psychological processes with the help of these manipulations. How does this complicated cultural activity of attention proceed? To what measures does the child go in order to keep his attention on a specific activity, and what structure does this act of "voluntary" attention acquire?

We try to analyze one example that will help us to decipher this process. We take it from the experiments of our colleague, Leontiev, which he conducted in our laboratory.[27]

An 8- to 9-year-old child is given a problem requiring his prolonged attention and concentration on a specific process: He is asked a series of

---

[26](J. K., V. G.) A term that A. Luria most likely is borrowing from George Meade; here Luria means those cues or signifying gestures that some adult, usually the mother, uses to call a child's attention to a certain object in his environment or in play.

[27](A. L.) Leontiev's work *Research on Mediated Attention in Children* was printed in *Works of the Psychological Laboratory of the Academy of Communist Education.*

(J. K.) Full reference not given. See Leontiev (1965, 1981) for more information.

questions, some of which require him to answer by naming a specific color: "Do you go to school?" "What color is your desk?" "Do you like to play?" "Are you often in the countryside?" "What color can grass be?" "What color are robes?", and so on.

The child must answer the question as quickly as possible, observing the following instructions: he cannot name the same color twice, and there are two colors he may not name (for example, white and black). The experiment is set up in such a way as to make this all possible, but the task demands continuous, intense attention.

The experiment demonstrated that the child was not able to solve this task without turning to some auxiliary methods. He invariably wanders missing some aspect of the instructions given him and . . . loses the game, not being able to sufficiently organize his behavior in conformity with the task for a prolonged period.

What means may be used to increase the child's attention, to help him master his behavior so that he does not overlook a single condition presented to him? The experiment demonstrated that the only path to this end is, it turns out, a switch-over from *direct to indirect behavior* that utilizes certain external methods to accomplish the task.

In order to help the child accomplish his task, we offer him colored cards to use as markers, as external conditions for organizing his attention. Consequently, we make available to him a definite technique and, as it turns out, the child quickly familiarizes himself with the cards. External actions help him organize his behavior. Operating externally with the help of the cards, he organizes his inner processes in the same way.

The result quickly becomes apparent. Immediately, or after one or two tries, the child achieves the necessary level of organized behavior and successfully wins the game. What conditions are needed to meet all the demands put on the child during the experiment? Thanks to the external introduction of auxiliary attention-getting devices, we gain the opportunity of establishing this with sufficient objectivity.

In one series of instances, the child responds to the task "Don't say white or black" in the following way: He arranges the cards in front of him (Fig. 3.11, *A*), then selects the white and black ones, laying them aside and turning them face down in order to remove them from his sphere of attention *(B)*. As a rule, however, this psychological method of organizing his attention does not lead to the desired result. In order to achieve success, the child should not remove the forbidden elements from the sphere of his attention, but *should make the process of attention mediated;* he must fix his attention specifically on the forbidden elements. Ordinarily, the subjects quickly guess that they should do this: They take the two cards with the forbidden colors and lay them down directly in front of themselves (*C*, rows *a* and *c*). In these instances, this process takes the following course: When

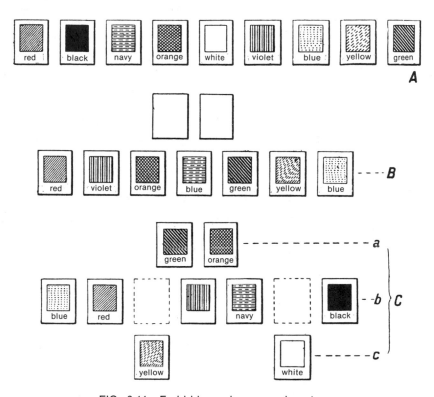

FIG. 3.11 Forbidden colors experiment.

the questions given to the child demand that he respond with a color, he does not answer directly, but first, glancing at the "forbidden" cards, he checks to see whether he is answering with the forbidden color. Only at this point does he select his answer, circumventing the forbidden color. It is clear that here the very structure of the process changes: Organized behavior and the way of thinking itself changes. Instead of answering "grass is green," the child, when forbidden to name the color green, answers, "grass can be yellow (in the fall)"—forbidding one color causes the inhibition of certain answers; turning to different, new situations a new, roundabout path of thought.

Moreover, the experiment does not end with the use of the cards: In order to complete the second task without repeating the same color twice, the child picks from the cards lying in front of him those that respond to the current question (e.g., yellow) and, in order to indicate that this color has already been named, he moves the card a little down and then looks at both rows of forbidden colors (C rows a and c). Only after this, once he has made the process indirect, does he successfully circumvent all the "dangerous places" in the experiment.

The process, however, does not end at this. If we allowed the child to run through such a game several times, we would in all likelihood notice a change in his behavior: He soon stops using the cards, begins to solve the problem with external auxiliary techniques, and seemingly returns to normal use of attention. But this impression only seems so; in fact, we see that the child successfully solves the problem that he earlier could not solve; he successfully maneuvers around all obstacles, conditioned by the instructions.

How are we to explain this change in behavior? Under close examination we are convinced that the process of attention still remained indirect; only instead of externally indirect, it became *internally indirect*. Having learned to use auxiliary tools with the outer material cards, the child works out a series of inner auxiliary techniques. Instead of spreading out the forbidden cards in front of him, *he fixes in his mind* (visually or, even better verbally) these two forbidden colors and then by means of these fixed colors gives all his answers. The method, which was worked out with the external operations, at the same time rearranges the internal structure of the process, developing a system of inner stimuli and techniques. Two major factors cause us to regard this picture of the transformation of outer processes into inner processes as most plausible: the analogous transformation of mnemonic memory observed in our experiments, and the behavior of the older child who, in solving the same problem, substitutes the external manipulation of the cards with an inner connection. Precisely these techniques, this mediated character and inner fixation [connection — J. K.], are also specific to the process of "cultural attention" that was for so long little understood.

Similar experiments resolved for us many of the uncertainties connected with operations involving attention. It becomes absolutely clear that we must look for specific features of attention precisely in operations with certain stimuli and signs that make the process mediated and that play a denoting, focusing, and differentiating role. These stimuli may be natural (e.g., in the case of the natural center of a perceived structure) but the development of these means first and foremost occurs through the development of new devices of cultural behavior, of new organizing signs and their further use. We picture certain guide-posts beyond which the human being must pass from primitive, natural forms of attention to complex, cultural ones and we think that further research will reveal to us new aspects and details of this process.

CULTURAL DEVELOPMENT
OF SPECIFIC FUNCTIONS: ABSTRACTION

Abstraction is one of the most powerful tools that cultural development fosters in the mind of a human being. It would be wrong to think that abstraction in the mind of a cultural adult is a kind of specific process or special function that is combined with other functions and together with them forms our intellectual life. It would be much more correct to say that, in the mind of the cultural person, abstraction is a necessary, integral part of any type of thought process, a technique fostered in the process of the development of personality, and a necessary condition and tool for one's thinking.

With the example of the development of abstraction—this pivotal condition of any thinking—it is possible, as in no other process, to show how a specific device in the operation of our nervous–psychological system, that is, a specific product of cultural development, is created and how, once created, it transforms a whole series of psychological processes.

The main goal of this book is to show the cultural genesis of a whole series of behavioral processes and its affect on the metamorphoses of nervous–psychological activity; there is no better way than a study of the processes of abstraction to better help us with this task.

Earlier (see sections on primitive perception and primitive thinking) we found it necessary to point out that the forms of educating a child are characterized by their concreteness. The child approaches each object as a unique concrete specimen. In this case he repeats the primitive man: He knows the birch tree, the pine, the willow, the poplar; he can name trees in general. If he, like the primitive man, is asked to count, he may ask what exactly he must count, because he can only count concrete objects. According to Stern, the child knows how many fingers are on his hand, but he cannot answer a question about how many fingers there are on the hand of another person.

In short, his thinking is concrete through and through; and abstract presentation of a quantity, quality, or sign is for him still in its most rudimentary forms. Piaget gave the following table that illustrates with concrete examples the development of these processes in a child:

A 5-year old child differentiates his left hand from his right.

A 7-year old child differentiates right from left with objects.

An 8-year old child differentiates between the right and left hands of a person standing in front of him.

An 11-year old child differentiates between right and left in relationship to three objects placed in a row.

We see that even such a concept as right and left requires only relatively little abstract processing which develops rather slowly in a child even in those not very complicated cases and that it reaches full development by around eight or eleven years of age.

All this clearly shows that it is difficult for the child to detach himself from the object being perceived in all its concreteness and to extract from it a corresponding sign common for the whole series of objects.

The process of abstraction develops only with the growth and cultural development of a child; his development is closely tied to the initiation of the use of external tools and to the working out of complex techniques of behavior. Abstraction itself can in this case be examined as one of the cultural techniques implanted in children during the process of his development.

We can observe the emergence of this process in a concrete example that especially reveals the relationship between primitive, whole perceptions of external objects and the beginnings of abstraction, necessary for any kind of "cultural" psychological process.

For this purpose, we would like to present our research on the development of counting operations in a child.

Counting or operating with numbers appears to be one of the most typical elaborated cultural devices, solidly imbedded in the psychological inventory of a cultural person.

The use of numbers is usually accompanied by maximum abstraction, and, when speaking of the ordinary counting processes, we are speaking of cultural functions, the condition of which is the maximum abstraction of objects from their concrete forms.

However, this cultural function did not develop immediately, and in the experiments with children, we can follow this whole process with sufficient clarity. In fact, we ask ourselves: What takes the place of abstraction in children in whom it has not yet developed?

We give three or four children sitting at a table small cubes; while playing, a 4- to 5-year-old child is supposed to divide the piles of cubes into equal piles and give them out to all those playing. Once the division is achieved, the child is asked the question: Did the number of cubes turn out to be equal for all the players? He (the child) must then compare the divided number of cubes and make a correction if the division turns out to be unequal.[28]

It is understood that an adult possessing sufficient counting techniques will simply recount the cubes and compare the resulting sum. A child does not possess this abstract method of counting. Our little experimental subjects solve this problem in an entirely different way. In order to compare the resulting sums of cubes with each other, they (the children) give them some kind of shape and afterward compare the divided piles according to the shape they have created. The shapes, by which the children compare the divided sums, vary. Sometimes there is a schematic representation of certain familiar objects. From the divided checkers (or cubes), our 5-year-old

---

[28](A. L.) These experiments were repeated and continued in our laboratory by E. Kuchurin.

children made "a bed," "tractor," and other familiar objects (Fig. 3.12), and if each of the participants in the games succeeded in rendering this "object," they thought that the division was correct. Sometimes they made a "tower" (c), and then several "towers" in a row and made them equal by feeling with the hand. Or they placed the checkers in an "arc," or in a "road," and, just as concretely, made them equal by shape.

In all these cases there is one common feature; in the child's operations, where indirect perception of the form plays the predominant role, the apparatus of abstraction — of counting — is not yet sufficiently developed and the child substitutes a primitive use of the natural perception process; a shape replaces counting as the means of comparison.

What we just discussed occurs both in children who often still have not yet completely mastered counting as well as in children still in the first stages of developing their counting skills. Immediate perception of shapes frequently continues to play a large role in determining the counting process.

A child who could already count (7 to 8 years old), was asked to recount randomly placed cubes and cubes placed in a row. Obviously, this second procedure went faster and more correctly; The child was not confused and did not count the cubes twice, as often happened when the cubes were randomly placed. The shape (a road) precisely determined the child's count. Then, in order to check the degree of the shape's influence on the counting process, we placed the cubes in such a way that the two efficient systems intersected, sharing common elements: In this way, we gave children crosses made from the cubes or two intersecting squares (Fig. 3.13) and suggested that they recount the number of cubes that composed each of the suggested figures. If the child's counting process was adequately developed, then we could expect that the counting procedure would be used correctly. This is exactly what we do not see in the child.

The proposed experiment provides a good opportunity to observe the

FIG. 3.12 Shapes made with checkers and blocks by a 5-year-old child — a "bed," "tractor," and other familiar objects.

FIG. 3.13   A cross and inter-secting squares made with blocks.

very structure of the counting process — its sequence and construction — (the child points his finger at each cube he counts); and while observing the structure of the process, we can record the whole series of steps in the cultural development of the child's mind.

In front of us is a 3-year-old child. He does not know how to count in sequence and is unable to point his finger at each cube one after another as he counts them (we of course pay no attention to the correctness of the counting accompanying these gestures). It is characteristic that for him the correct form apparently does not usually evoke any particular sequence; he begins to count from one end of the cross to the other, then once again returns to the starting point, pointing many times to the same elements. The process bears the character of elementary formlessness.

We had a chance to observe the same thing with a retarded child, a 13-year-old hydrocephalic. She counted just as chaotically, pointing her finger repeatedly at the same cube and returning to those already counted.

By the age of 6 to 7 years old the process takes on an obviously different form. At this age, shape renders a striking deductive influence on counting.

A child of this age counts out the squares of the cross in straight lines. In the second figure, he adheres to the form of the 2 squares. But what is particularly interesting is this influence of the shape. It appears to be so strong here and the numeric abstraction freeing the child from the laws of the visual field is still so inconsequential that he counts twice the cubes included in two systems (the middle cube in the cross, the two cubes in the intersection of the square). In other words, he counts them as many times as they appear in the system of shapes. In the first instance, the cross is counted as a system of two intersecting lines, in the second we have two intersecting squares. And each time, having come to the intersecting cube, our child counts it anew, as an element of that row. We see that here the cubes are still not counted abstractly but are recounted *as members of a given concrete system.*

The experiments we conducted showed that in the case of the relatively easy shape (the cross), errors caused by inadequately developed abstraction were made by 62% of the preschoolers in the middle group and by less than 6% of school-aged children in group I. In the more complex example (the square within a square) 100% of the preschoolers in the middle group and 12% of the school-aged children in group I gave the same incorrect count.

The experiments show that we have an opportunity not only to concentrate on the inadequate development of abstraction in childhood, but also to indicate the time (and in some instances the tempo) for its formation.[29]

According to our observation, only toward the age of 9 to 10 years old (this, however, depends on the intellectual age of the child) does the "cultural" process of counting develop to such an extent that it turns out to be able to free him from the visual field, from the laws of concrete perception, and the child begins to count shapes given to him relatively correctly without forgetting to disengage himself from the shape and without recounting the same shape. However, the same component, once in a different system, will continue for a long time to be perceived as another completely different component, and repercussions of concrete thinking conditioned by concrete situations remain for a long time in the child's mind.

We had the chance to observe this fact in grown-ups and in children under relatively difficult conditions of life. In the Berlin Psychological Institute the following experiment was conducted: The experimental subject — a grown-up or a child — was left alone someplace where several objects were laid out on a table; among them lay a small mirror. When in an unlimited time frame, the experimental subject began to look through the individual objects. He tried the pendulum and looked in the mirror. We saw that this mirror, when placed in a certain situation, was used according to its straightforward function. But it is interesting that when the experimenter offered the mirror to be used as a reflector to aim the beam at a determined spot on the wall, the mirror lost its previous function, and not one of the subjects tried to look into it, each treating it like an "instrument." It acquired a completely new function.

When, in accordance with the situation, one and the same thing assumes a new characteristic, this process represents an original step in relation to objects in the external world. Being guided by what we have observed already in young children (how, as they operate in two different systems, they perceive a cube twice in conjunction with the "context") and switching to complex "cultural" shapes, we were able to produce this relative character of thinking that bears distinct structural features thanks to the functional use of concrete objects in different situations. However, a considerable dose of abstraction is still needed in order to develop a lasting connection with the objects so that an "invariable" is produced, allowing us to recognize and evaluate the objects regardless of the surrounding environment.

Let us return, however, to the counting process in a child and we shall attempt to approach it from another angle that is characterized by a transition from primitive forms of perception to complex "cultural" ones.

---

[29](A. L.) This question has been worked out in greater detail in our laboratory by a series of students from the Academy of Communist Education. The [statistical] figures have been taken from the work done by the students Novitskii and Elmenev.

We ask a 7- to 8-year-old child who knows what is "even" and "odd" to determine "even" and "odd" numbers of proposed cubes. The first time, we offer him four cubes, forming a square (Fig. 3.14, *A*); the child immediately answers that in front of him is an "even" number. He does this with suspicious speed, and we note that he usually does not recount the individual cubes with his eyes, but fixes his mind on the figure as a whole. In order to check, we give him a second figure *(B),* composed of five cubes; the child just as quickly tells us that in front of him is an "odd" number. Naturally, we become suspicious when the child does not recount the cubes to determine evenness, but simply perceives the shape, being confident that the correct form always gives an "even" number, whereas an incorrect "unfinished" one gives an "odd" number.

In order to be certain of this, we give him the following provocative figure *(C):* here there are nine cubes arranged in a proper square; the child just as quickly answers that the number of cubes lying here is even; the inverse combination — 10 cubes, arranged in an incorrect form *(D)* — produces the child's confident determination that the number is odd. We tried to set up the experiment more abruptly, changing directly before our eyes the form in which the cubes have been put together, let us say changing *D* into *E,* and immediately we receive the answer from the child, that, if the first figure contains an even number of cubes, the second is a clear uneven number.

The judgments that seem strange to us were in no way explained by the fact that the child misunderstood our instructions: in a series of concrete examples, which we posed orally, we were able to become convinced that the child correctly understood the concept of even and a odd numbers (he always determined nine boots as an odd number, but ten as an even number). The results that we received can be explained by the fact that the child perceived the cubes presented him as a *whole concrete form,* and for him, precisely the perception of this form took the place of the process of counting, which is still difficult and somewhat foreign to him.

The process of performing abstract numeric operations develops rather late in a child; only under the influence of the effect of school and the surrounding cultural environment does the child work out for himself this specific cultural technique, and all the processes described earlier become markedly transformed.

With a child in his first years of schooling, we no longer see instances

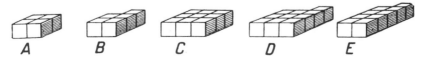

FIG. 3.14 "Odd" and "even" experiment with blocks.

where primitive perceptions of forms take the place of counting; the child masters abstract calculation, the decimal system, and this entails a notable liberation from the undivided primacy of the visual field's rules, which had made the child's thinking purely empirical, concrete, and dependent upon direct perception in the first years of development.

Thinking in the first stages of childhood is the function of perceiving forms; it gradually frees itself, working out its own new cultural techniques. As it transforms, it (thinking) evolves gradually into the type of thinking that we have become accustomed to observing in the adult cultural human being.

CULTURAL DEVELOPMENT
OF SPECIAL FUNCTIONS: SPEECH AND THINKING

We should make several concluding remarks about the paths that the development of child thought follows. After introducing thcsc materials, it would not be difficult for us to talk about this in brief terms. However, what we have said is not sufficient to sketch an outline of the development of child thinking. In order to do this, we must tie the question with a mechanism not yet touched upon — with the most important, if you will, means of thinking — with speech.

Recent psychological literature has established the opinion that speech plays an enormous, decisive role in thinking. Moreover, many authors believe that when reflecting, we inaudibly voice to ourselves what we are thinking. Thinking, in their opinion, is speech minus sound. According to this view, the development of thought turns out to be not very difficult to trace. To do this it is necessary only to properly study those paths along which speech develops. The wealth of vocabulary and speech forms testifies to the wealth of thought, and the study of thought itself boils down to a study of those speech habits that are characteristic for any given person.

It is absolutely clear that putting the question this way has immense pedological and pedagogical significance because the study of speech will help us solve a series of practical questions about school, upbringing, and the education of the child.

Therefore, let us ask ourselves, is this theory correct? Is it true that thinking is simple, inner, inaudible speech? Is it true that child thought is only speech, impoverished in material and forms, whereas adult thinking consists of soundless monologues, structured by all the logical rules?

Let us return to the development of thinking and speech. There is much evidence to make us think that in reality the situation is considerably more complicated than this theory suggests.

First of all, we may say that thought and speech have undoubtedly different roots and, at different steps of development, very often can exist without each other. For example, we know that forms of intellectual activity can exist without speech phenomena. If we define intellect as planned, organized behavior, directed at the solution of some complex tasks, then we will find its primitive forms in the absence of speech.

In chapter 1, we described behavior of apes that would be impossible to call anything but intellectual. The ape is placed in difficult situations and presented tasks that it can in no way solve by the natural, usual means it has at its disposal. The ape encounters a series of systematic, organized acts. If, for example, the target fruit lies too far away, the ape curtails its spontaneous endeavors and takes a stick. If the stick turns out to be too short, the ape places one stick inside another and gets the fruit this way. These acts cannot but be recognized as the result of a certain, albeit primitive, intellectual activity, even in the absence of speech.

We turn to another example. Let us remember small children who want very much to get something out of reach or too far away. They drag a chair in from another room and get up on it; they use a dozen primitive, yet clearly purposeful techniques. They reveal great "practical intelligence." However, the primitive forms of these acts can be observed even in that period when speech is still not completely or barely developed.

This opposite view carries weight here: We know many examples where developing speech has nothing in common with thinking, where it is apparent that speech originates from absolutely different roots and has a different functional significance.

We all know that the most primitive form of speech is the shout and other voiced reactions that accompany movements, strong emotions, and so forth. Here also belong exclamations or interjections while working, cries or laughter, and exuberant yells when victorious or terrifying cries when pursued.

Do these have something in common with the intellect, with thinking? Of course, not. They are rooted in the simple tendency to relieve tension built up in the organism; they can claim no greater role than simple, expressive movements. Their basis is emotional; they do not in the least help a person solve life's complex tasks in any organized way. They do not help an experimental subject plan his own behavior and they occur in an absolutely different sphere of intellectual activity. Hence, here, at its deep roots, speech may fail to converge with thinking, remaining a completely independent process with different roots.

However, this lack of correspondence between thinking and speech exists not only in the early, primitive stages of development. We are aware of instances of this lack of correspondence even at the highest levels of activity.

In fact, it has been shown that, in a number of cases, mediated acts occur without any apparent presence of speech, even inner speech. One of the German psychological schools, the so-called Würzburg school, has shown that intense mental work may occur not only without words, but also without images, often even unconsciously so that the person may not be able to account for how this or that thought came to mind. Such processes as reflection at the chess board may take place apparently also without inner speech, that is, exclusively with the help of a combination of visual images.

On the other hand, the cultural adult has many forms of speech that bear no direct relationship to thinking. For example, the emotional speech described earlier serves only as a means of expression; the same may be said about speech in its simplest communicative functions.

Consequently, speech and thinking may occur separately in an adult, but this in no way means that these two processes do not *meet* and influence each other. Just the opposite may be said: The convergence of thinking and speech constitutes the most important moment in the development of an individual, and precisely this connection places human thought at an unprecedented height.

We shall try to observe a small child and draw a series of conclusions that are very interesting for our topic. A child up to one year old represents a mute (in the precise meaning of the word) being. It is true that we may notice many vocal phenomena in the child, but one can hardly consider these to be even primitive forms of speech. A child yells when something bothers him, when he wants to eat, or when he suddenly wakes up from sleep. Any person dealing with children is familiar with the smacking of lips, groans, or series of inarticulate sounds that are impossible to convey here on these pages. Strictly speaking, the first sound we hear from the child is the first cry upon entering the world, the first cry at birth. Of course, this cry bears no relationship to speech. There is no relationship to an expression of some mental state. This is simply a reflectory act, and yet many such cries are sounds that mothers love to take as the first appearance of meaningful speech in the child; in fact, this is not yet speech, but simply reflexes of the voice box.

However, precisely these reflexes of the voice box lay the ground work for the "greatest discovery in the child's life" — for that moment when the child begins to understand that these sounds and their combination may *stand for* certain objects, that with their help a great deal can be achieved, that, if you say "am-am," you can get something to eat, and if you say "ma-ma," you can call mother.

Of course, even this discovery of the functional use of the word as a means for naming an object, for expressing a certain desire and so forth, does not take place immediately. When observing a child, we notice around the one year mark the appearance of the tendency to imitate the sounds he hears. This is how a dog gets the name "bow-wow," and a cow "moo" and how we get a whole series of imitative sounds that adults have introduced; precisely this tendency creates the first conditions for the beginning of the functional usage of words, causing an enormous turnabout in the child's life.

And there is absolutely no doubt that such a turnabout actually occurs. Primitive child thinking that until then had developed in halting, naive steps, "groping" its way along, suddenly acquires new possibilities. These possibilities are incorporated into speech as the child suddenly finds himself able to attach to his desires and urges a clear verbal form that enables him to fulfill them more easily. All observations indicate that precisely this function of speech is the primary and most urgent and persistent one. Having understood the meaning of a word, as a form of expression, as a means of getting control of those things interesting him, the child begins to tempestuously amass words and use them for this purpose. The word *nanny* in no way means only nanny for the child: It means "Nanny, come here," or "Nanny, go away," or "Nanny, give me an apple." Depending on the circumstances, it may acquire different meanings, but always appears in its active form that expresses in a single combination of sounds the child's whole wish. The first period of meaningful speech use is always a period of one word sentences. Words actively express the child's wish or singles out certain elements on which the child has focused. Other complex speech phenomena are differentiated precisely from this root.

One simple and striking phenomenon makes it possible for us to see the child actually switching from sound to speech, from simple voiced reflexes to the intelligent use of words, that is, a "concretization"—to use Stern's term[30]—of sounded out reactions and thought: The child begins to quickly acquire more and more new words, entering into a period of rapid, active enrichment of vocabulary. This is actually a period of primary accumulation in the child's life. After discovering the value of words and learning how to control them, the child begins within the parameters of his circumstances to search for new words; the child asks again and again how something is called, chattering nonstop; he repeats more and more new words, acquiring a greater and greater word inventory. Finally, after a certain period he starts to actively create words, beginning to expand his insufficient stock of words with new words invented impromptu.

For the observer, this is truly the most curious period in the child's life; for the child himself, this is the most important period without which his thinking could neither advance further nor develop.

Chukovsky (1925/1968) recently came out with an interesting book,

---

[30](J. K.) A. Luria does not make it clear here which research he had in mind, that done by W. Stern (1914, 1924b) or C. Stern and W. Stern (1927). (For Luria's discussion of the contributions of these child language psychologists, see also A. Luria, 1981 pp. 34, 50.)

dedicated to child language of precisely this period. We find in it many examples of how a child in this period of active word accumulation does not stop at the accumulation of already existing words; in addition to the material he already possesses, he produces more and more new words that give him the possibility of mastering more and more new concepts. Thus, if something belongs to everyone and everyone may use it, the child designates it as "all-body's" [*vsekhnuju*] (Chukovsky, 1925/1968, p. 51).[31] What he uses to dig with, he calls a "divel" [*kopatka*, i.e., "dig" combined with "shovel" — J. K.] and what fastens (a button hole) — a "floop" [*tseplei*, i.e., "fasten" combined with "loop" — J. K.]. If the little child must give more precise meaning to the expression "drown" in order to indicate that the doll did not completely drown in the bath but can appear again, she will say that the doll "drowns-in" [*Vot pritonula*] or "drowns-out" [*Vot vytonula!*].[32] One child, upon pondering his future profession, decided that he ought to fix his mother's sewing machine and that he absolutely will become a "machiner" [*mashinnik*][33] [from the word "machine" — J. K.]. We will not bring in examples from the materials introduced in this book. They all very graphically indicate the active character of a child's ability to create words and the intensive, rapid process of acquiring and enriching vocabulary.

Such a process actually takes place. Thus, according to Tracy, (1894) the vocabulary of a 12-month-old child is confined to 4 to 10 words. By 2 years, there is already an average of about 300 words, and by 3 years — more than 1,000 words.

This stage in child development illustrates an enormous fundamental significance: For the first time, speech begins to be used as a technique for expressing the specific contents (of thought). For the first time, thinking becomes verbal and receives a great push forward in its development. If the child finds himself in a position to use the word "all-body's" [*vsekhnuju* — J. K.], then with this he masters a new concept. Saying "drowns-in" and "drowns-out," the little girl clearly formulates a new nuance of thought and masters it.

The fact that speech and the word represent the most important fulcrum in the progression of thought and in the formation of new ideas has been

---

[31](J. K.) Here the child combines the pronoun "everyone" [*vsekh*] with the suffix *"nyj,"* which the child has learned as a rule for forming adjectives.

[32](J. K.) Here the Russian child attaches well-known prefixes such as "pri-," which can convey the meaning of an *incomplete action or one of short duration as well as the action of arriving at,* and, in the second example, the prefix "vy-," which in the case of a verb of motion signals that an object or person has disappeared only momentarily. Again, we chose to use M. Morton's translations of these newly created expressions (Chukovsky, 1925/1968, p. 7)

[33](J. K.) Here the child has attached the suffix *" 'nik,"* which he has learned that as a rule means someone who does something. This suffix can be equated with the English suffix " =er."

brilliantly shown by a number of experimental research endeavors by several different psychologists. It is natural that studying the process of new concept formation is very difficult because concepts that are new for one (child) are already well-known to another. Therefore, Ach (1905, 1921)[34] decided to develop in children absolutely new nonexisting concepts not previously known by the children and to do this by means of using words as auxiliary tools. He succeeded in his experiments, and in fact had the opportunity to observe in the laboratory how a child works out new concepts with the help of auxiliary words (Ach, 1905, 1921).

The experiments were set up as follows. A row of figures is placed before the child, which differ from each other by three or four distinctive features: They consist of various shapes (cubes, cylinders, pyramids, and so forth), sizes (large or small), and weights (heavy and light). Included in the task of the experiment was the elaboration of some new concept not yet existing for the child (for example, the concept of large and light objects, small and heavy objects, and so-forth). Ach developed such concepts with the help of artificially created words. The child took one object (let us say a large and heavy cylinder) and with this he read a label that contained a nonsensical syllable such as "ras." He pronounced this word as he lifted up other objects that had different forms but similar features. Another object (for example small and light ones) he called "gatsun" and repeated this word as he lifted objects possessing the same features. Finally, he gave the provisional name "fal" to large and light objects, and "taro" to small and heavy ones. The child's task entails first diverting his attention from the object's individual attributes and then learning with the help of the proposed words to select from the general lot of objects the shapes possessing a particular combination of these attributes.

In such artificial conditions, it was possible to investigate to what degree the child was able to work out new concepts and to what degree words helped him with this task.

Ach's experiments fell into two series: First the child learns the name of each individual object, then the inscription with the "names" are removed and the child must select from the series the objects with the names "ras," "fal," "taro," and "gatsun." To be sure, reinforcing all these combinations by means of purely mechanical memory turned out to be impossible, and the successful resolution of the task demonstrated that an appropriate new concept really had been worked out.

The experiment showed that far from all of the children were able to

---

[34](J. K.) Cf. also Vygotsky (1986, pp. 97–101) and A. Luria (1976, pp. 48, 50) where Ach's experiments to develop concepts and classifications in young children by means of artificially created words is also discussed.

master this task and, on the other hand, far from all were able to master it with equal ease.

These experiments, which at times may seem very artificial and removed from life, made one thing clear: They showed how the child, with the help of a conventional word, could build a new concept and master a task that he would not have been able to without this artificial tool. Language here becomes the tool of thought, and even more it is a reinforcement tool, a mnemotechnical tool.

This last process plays a significant role in the life of the child. School training that provides intense stimulation for speech development[35] also produces, at the same time, a series of essential changes in the child's mind. Enriching vocabulary, speech that was learned and by means of which concepts were built, also changed the child's thinking; it gave him greater freedom; it allowed him to operate with a series of concepts that were previously inaccessible to the child. Speech made possible greater development of a new logic that until then existed in the child only in beginning stages. Moreover, even such functions as memory sharply changed from the moment speech began to dominate the child's behavior. It has been established with sufficient accuracy that at school age visual pictographic memory develops into verbal memory. If at the preschool age the memory of visual objects was not weaker but even stronger than the memory of words, now the picture changes radically and the school-aged child usually begins to acquire a memory of verbal nature. Words and logical forms begin to play the role of decisive tools for remembering. By this time, the type of miraculous visual pictographic memory that was known by the term *eidetism* and that dominates the early years (about which we spoke earlier) fades out.

Speech takes a commanding height; it becomes the most used cultural tool; it enriches and stimulates thinking, and, through it, the child's mind is restructured, reconstructed. Speech mechanisms, which previously were vividly expressed in the first period of active speech (in this "period of initial accumulation") now change into inner, inaudible speech, and the latter becomes one of the most important auxiliary tools of thinking. In fact, how many complex and subtle intellectual tasks would remain unresolved if we did not possess inner speech, thanks to which thinking is able to adopt precise, clear forms, and thanks to which preliminary, verbal (or sooner — intellectual) probes of individual decision as well as their preliminary planning become possible.

---

[35](A. L.) I dwell on this aspect elsewhere: A. Luria, *Speech and Intellect in Child Development.* (1928) and *Speech and Intellect of the Peasant, Urban and Homeless Child.* (1929a)

If, according to Marx's classic analogy, the architect, unlike the bee, builds his structure by first thinking it out and composing a plan and computation for it, then to a large degree we owe this enormous superiority of intellect over instinct to the mechanism of inner speech. In the human being, speech mechanisms far from play only a role of expressive reactions. These (mechanisms) differ from all other reactions in that they play a specific functional role: Their action is transformed into the organization of future behavior of the personality. And indeed the highest cultural forms of intellectual activity are achieved by human preliminary verbal planning.

Turning from outside inward, speech formed the most important psychological function, representing the external world within us, stimulating thought, and, as several authors believe, also laying a foundation for the development of consciousness.

Those primitive forms of the child's speech activity that we have already mentioned—this entire period of child chatter and "collective monologues,"—all this is the preparation for those stages of development when it (speech) becomes the pivotal mechanism of thinking. Only in this last period does speech turn from a taught, external device into an inner process, and human thinking acquires new and enormous perspectives for further development.

THE STAGE OF CULTURAL DEVELOPMENT OF A CHILD

The observations that we have just put forth convince us that it is absolutely impossible to reduce child development to meer growth and maturation of innate qualities. As we said earlier, in the process of development, the child "rearms himself," changes his most basic forms of adaptation to the external world. This process expresses itself first and foremost in a change from direct adaptation to the world using "natural" abilities endowed by nature, to another more complex stage: The child does not immediately enter into contact with the world, but first works out certain devices and acquires certain "skills." It is necessary to state that the child begins to use all types of "tools" and signs as a means and accomplishes the tasks encountered far more successfully than before.

However, it would be a mistake to think that this entire process boils down to a gradual, evolving accumulation of complex techniques and practices, to the growth of skills, and that the difference between a 4-year-old and an 8-year-old boils down only to the latter's culturally acquired ability to functionally control both the tools of the external world and his own behavioral processes in a better and more developed way.

Having observed the child in the process of his natural development, then placing him in artificial experimental conditions and "feeling out" in as much detail as possible all his individual manifestations, we are convinced that a child's behavior represents significant qualitative differences at different ages. As we have already mentioned, these differences are rooted not only in purely physiological changes, but also in a different ability to use various cultural forms of behavior. To put it more briefly, we may say that a child goes through certain stages of cultural development, each of which is characterized by the different ways the child relates to the outside world; by a different way of using objects; by different forms of invention and different cultural techniques, be it some sort of system worked out during the cultural process, or a technique invented in the course of growth and personality adaptation.

Let us remember how a child gradually learns to walk. As soon as his muscles are strong enough, he begins to move across the floor in the same primitive way in which an animal does, in the way endowed to him by nature. He crawls around on all fours, and one distinguished modern psychologist has said that a very young child outwardly reminds us of a small four-legged animal, something similar to a "monkey-like cat" (Blonskii, 1926, p. 96). This animal continues to move around in such a primitive manner for some time. However, a few months later, he begins to get up on his feet and begins to walk. Usually, this does not happen immediately. At first, he makes use of surrounding objects to hold himself up; he forces his way along, holding onto the edge of the bed, an adult's hand, the table, dragging it behind him and leaning on it. In short, his gait is not steady; it is still [linked], as it were, "to the woods" of external tools that facilitate its development. Yet another month passes, and the child, having surpassed this "woods," discards it. Outside help becomes less and less necessary for him; external objects are replaced by evolving inner neuro-dynamic processes. He has developed strong legs, sufficient sturdiness, and motor coordination. He has reached the stage of a completely formed gait.

We already see here that the development of a certain function goes through several phases that, as we will see, may be tracked in almost any process, from the simplest to more complex ones.

Development begins with the mobilization of the most primitive (innate) functions, with their natural use. It then goes through a training phase, where, under the influence of external conditions, it changes its structure and begins to convert from a natural process into a complex "cultural one," when a new form of behavior is formed aided by a series of external devices. Development finally arrives at a stage when these external auxiliary devices are abandoned and rendered useless and the organism comes out of this evolutionary process transformed, possessing new forms and techniques of behavior.

Our experiments with little children give us the opportunity to trace this process in great detail and to note certain more or less clear stages through which child development inevitably passes.

We pose some task to the child, one which is sufficiently difficult to complete. For example, we present the child with a simple experiment requiring a selection response. In the conditions of these experiments, the child will receive stimuli in response to each of which he will have to perform an appropriate conditional response — let us say — press this or that key on a piano. We produce here in artificial circumstances those conditions requiring a different reaction to each object in life's existing environment and constituting a significant part of our behavior. We set up experiments with the child that show how he masters choice in a series of possibilities, how he ends up being able to differentiate between one action and another.

Let us imagine that we give the child several pictures one after another — an ax, an apple, a letter, a chair, and so forth; in reaction to the first one he is supposed to press one key on a children's toy piano, to another a second key, then the next one, and so forth. Of course, the task of remembering these instructions and successfully carrying them out, differentiating one key from another, is not an easy task for a child, particularly if we supply a choice of eight different stimuli.

If we take a child of 5 to 6 years and present him with this task, he will try to tackle it with all the means he has at his disposal. In the strict sense of the word, he still does not use any particular "techniques." Usually, he decides to remember the instructions and complete the task. If, after a few tries, the child still does not succeed in remembering the instructions and correctly complete the selection response, then he rejects the task and despairs of success, announcing that he cannot do it.

If we propose to the child the use of some artificial device that will facilitate the execution of the task, we will become persuaded that our little subject not only can not devise some helpful artificial device, but even turns out not to be able to master any means proposed to him. The phase in which the child is found may be characterized as the phase of *natural forms of behavior,* or as the primitive phase. Its basic feature is that in any situation, the child adapts exclusively by means of those natural functions that he possesses (e.g., the natural imprinting of separate actions); the thought that he may solve a given task by a more complete means using some kind of technique, functionally using the stimuli as signs, is a thought that is alien to him.

In fact, we try to make his task easier. We give the child a second series of propped up pictures and we suggest that he use them as markers placed on the piano before the appropriate keys. We may pick this second row so that each of them (the pictures) will call to mind one of the pictures of the first series, which serve as a conditional stimuli (the first series presents an ax and the second a boy cutting wood; then an apple and a pear; a letter and a steam ship; a bug and a butterfly; and so forth). By arranging them in a definite order, placing the appropriate marker before a definite key, the child may substitute his natural, yet still very complex selection response with an artificial process of adaptation that involves a mediated mnemotechnic operation. In this way he successfully solves the task. For this he need only understand that the propped up picture cards offered him may play a functionally different role as auxiliary signs and he must only establish corresponding connections between them and the first series of stimuli.

A child of the earliest developmental phase can not perform this last task. It will in no way occur to him that the proposed auxiliary cards can really play some role, that they may bear some sort of relationship to the picture cards of the first series, that between them one may artificially establish some connection, which would help solve the proposed task, that it is possible to use them as a means to execute a psychological operation.

A child of this phase may act only using the simplest means; like many animals even the higher ones, the child does not know how to functionally control tools, to use them to solve complex psychological problems, and this has a decisive influence on his behavior.

In order to develop further, the child must pass from this natural stage to a more complex stage of behavior: He must expand his natural abilities; once he has learned to use tools, he should pass from the natural stage to the cultural one. We shall try to set up such an experiment with a slightly older child. We pose an analogous problem to a 6- to 7-year-old child. Without remembering our instructions directly, he readily turns to the auxiliary signs, if we offer them. It is true that with the use of these auxiliary pictures, he decides, without understanding precisely why they help him, that it is sufficient to externally perform a successful operation — to place any sign in front of the keys so that the problem would be solved and so that he would remember automatically when he needs to press this key. Having placed some marker, he no longer worries about remembering; he is naively convinced that "the marker itself will remember for him." After appropriately placing a nail before a key, one of our young test subjects even assuredly announced to us that "the nail would remember" and there is no point in completing the task.

This disparity between the use of a particular device and the understanding of it, this naive trust in the efficiency of such a sign in and of itself and comprehension of its meaning without a knowledge of its use are characteristic features of this stage in the child's cultural development. We had the chance to observe how the child takes an object having no connection with the stimulus and places it in front of himself "in order to remember." Moreover, the child often takes a number of identical objects (nails, pens, and so forth) and arranges them in advance before each key without any attempt to connect each mark with the stimulus presented. He naively believes in the adequacy of this purely external action.

All this gives us reason to believe that the child experiences a particular phase of cultural development — a phase involving a naive attitude toward all external cultural operations: "Magic." In certain respects, this phase reminds us of several traits in the thinking of a primitive man who is beginning to master individual techniques but does not know their limits and who develops an entire naive strategy based on an insufficient understanding of those mechanisms of the operations that really helped him adapt to the external world.

In our experiment, we were able to produce this phase of development in child thought in a relatively pure form. However, in life we are able to observe echoes of this naive phase rather extensively. If we tried to gather all the techniques widely used among young children, we would be convinced that this "naive psychology" in children is frequently very rich. We would see that, along with the techniques that really help the child master certain tasks, there also exist those devices that only appear to have the form of adequate devices, but in fact are based on the primitive judgement of the child's unique logic and blind faith in any external device for which he still does not know the meaning.

One may suppose that this primitive, inadequate, naive attitude toward objects and toward one's own mental processes will be found in other areas of child evolution (the development of drawing, writing, counting) as well, and that this attitude characterizes an entire phase in the history of behavior. However, let us make one more step forward and examine what characterizes the next evolutionary stage in a child's cultural behavior.

If in this phase of development that we have just disclosed, children still did not know to use external devices efficiently, then, as they gradually develop, they very quickly begin to understand the very mechanisms of their actions. They begin to use these mechanisms intelligently. It becomes clear to them that auxiliary pictures and marks can only help them when they somehow connect these signs with the presented stimulus. The child begins to understand that not every mark can render him help, but only certain ones with which a connection with the stimulus can be established. Children stop examining the marker as an element that acts independently; they evolve to a new, complex form of behavior where an auxiliary object begins to occupy a unique, functional "secondary" place.[36]

The "natural" means of solving difficult tasks gradually evolve into complex tool use; the cultural phase of behavior matures. When analyzing child memory and conducting the experiments just set forth, we can trace

---

[36](J. K.) In other words, it becomes part of a "Second signal system," to use the words of Pavlov's later works.

how the ability to use such auxiliary signs gradually forms. A 6- to 7-year-old child turns out to be able to establish only the most primitive connection; he can make use of only that sign that in real earnest closely and directly reminds him of the stimulus. Therefore, he easily remembers the picture of the apple by connecting it with the picture of the pear ("because they taste good"). Before the appropriate key, he puts the picture that in real life experience is directly connected with the stimulus to which he must respond by pressing this key. However, even with all this he has still not gone very far in learning how to use auxiliary signs. It is enough to give him two pictures, which are very remote from each other in content in order that he not to be able to use one as a tool to remember the other. Only later does he prove able not only to use the given connections directly, but to actively picture the auxiliary structures. We have already introduced an example of such structures (see section on cultural development of memory); the child remembers the word "shovel" with the help of a picture portraying chicks and explains that they "dig with their nose, like a shovel." Even very removed things are transformed by children with surprising ingenuity into tools for remembering.

We introduce here only one example of how a 9- to 10-year-old child can manage to use such external devices. We give the child the following task: At the pronouncement of individual words, he is supposed to press the same key each time. To help him remember, we give him a small box filled with nails, ribbons, feathers, pieces of rubber tubes, and other such small odds and ends. The child immediately examines these things and we begin our experiment:

> The word "night" is given; the child places a piece of rubber tube (explanation: "here in the tube it's dark like at night"); at the word "mother," the child places a feather crosswise in front of the key ("This is mother laying down and sleeping"); at the word "woods" the child takes a nail and places it obliquely ("they cut down the tree in the forest — and here it is lying here"); at the word "school" the child takes a filled up tube ("here it is like a house, and here the children are studying"). In this way eight words are given, at each one the child must press a new key. After an instantaneous presentation of the word stimuli and an appropriate placement of the signs the child responds with his selection without a single mistake and in a time interval that is almost neglible for such a task.

> In the following experiment the child is given other words, and these same signs are used in a different context, they acquire a new meaning (the rubber pipe reminds him of the word "smoke" "because smoke can come from it," "a feather is used as a sign for the word "oar" and so forth, and the child again, it turns out, is able to decide the given task without an error.

Of course, all the experiments about which we are new talking sometimes possess a very artificial character, but we think that they help us explain those mechanisms by which both the schoolchild's and the cultural adult's minds work. Indeed, in these experiments, albeit very artificial and primitive, we only brought to the surface those devices that each of us use and that become organically embedded in the behavior of each cultural adult.

In the experiments that we introduced, one interesting feature is observed: The child, who repeats the experiment many times, remembering with the help of external secondary notes, begins at a certain step of development to refuse to use them. He does this, however, not because he has not grown mature enough for them, but because he has already outgrown them. What he did earlier with the help of external signs, he now begins to do with the help of inner signs that replace for him entirely those external signs that he learned. The child who remembered earlier with the help of external pictures, now begins to remember with the help of an inner system, planning and connecting the material to his former experience so that the inner images that are hidden to the outsider's eye and that remain perpetually in the memory, begin to play a functional auxiliary role: They serve as an intermediate link for remembering.

In this way, the nervous psychological processes, while developing and transforming, begin to build according to an entirely new system. From natural processes, they are transformed into complex ones, formed as a result of a cultural influence and the effect of a series of conditions, — first of all, as a result of active interaction with the environment.

A small child cannot solve complex real-life problems by means of natural direct adaptation; he begins to use indirect paths to solve these problems only after school and experience have refined the adaptation process, after the child has acquired cultural techniques. In an active encounter with the environment, he develops the ability to use things from the external world as tools, or as signs. At first, their functional use bears a naive, inadequate character; subsequently, the child little by little masters them and, finally, outgrows them while working out the ability to use his own nervous psychological processes as techniques for achieving certain goals. Natural behavior turns into cultural behavior; outer techniques and cultural signs learned from social life become inner processes.

To use a metaphor, we may say that we have here the same process that occurs during the transition from the natural crawling stage to the cultural stage. At first, the earth produced as much as the natural conditions (its properties, weather, germination of random seeds) permitted; with cultural management and new conditions — fertilizer, development of better tools and maintenance — it began to yield a far greater harvest, and gradually (under prolonged cultural) the earth itself changed and proved to have adapted to maximum production.

If this is so, if even agriculture, so interminably dependent on natural factors, must be approached from the transforming influence of cultural economy, then all the more attention must be paid to this process when we begin to speak about human behavior.

Given the contemporary state of our knowledge now, examining man as a creature who remained entirely with the same essential qualities that he acquired from nature—even if they are multiplied—means making an enormous mistake.

Man is a social creature, and social cultural conditions profoundly change him, developing a whole series of new forms and techniques in his behavior: A conscientious study of these characteristics constitutes the specific task of the science of psychology.

DEFECTOLOGY AND PSYCHOLOGY

The position that we have tried to develop allows us to approach from completely new points of view those children whose physical deficiencies have placed them in particularly disadvantageous conditions and who are called "physically defective."[37]

When studying the physically defective, psychologists have usually tried to answer the question: To what degree has their mental capacity been damaged and what precisely have they retained from the usual inventory of the healthy child? These psychologists have usually limited themselves to "the negative characteristics" of the physically defective child, and they were partially correct in as much as the issue at hand was a study of the fate of those functions with which a child is born into this world and that turn out to be adversely affected in the physically handicapped child—in a blind or deaf-mute child.

But to remain on the level of such "negative characteristics" is, of course, impossible: This would mean to overlook the most essential, to overlook what is particularly interesting for a psychologist. Along beside "negative characteristics" of a defective child, it is also necessary to create his "positive characteristics."

In fact, the blind or deaf-mute could not live if he did not compensate his deficiencies with something. His physical defect prevents him from being well adapted. At this point, a special and unique mechanism comes into its own right: *Compensation of the defect* takes place. In the course of

---

[37](J. K.) The term *defective* is commonly used in the former Soviet Union even today as a label for children whom in the United States would be called physically handicapped or physically impaired. At the beginning of the 20th century when this term was used among certain psychologists and specialists, it was not felt that it was a derogative term. To be true to Soviet cultural and social practice, it was decided to keep this term (see also Vygotsky, in press).

experience, the child learns to compensate for his natural deficiencies; on the basis of defective natural behavior, cultural techniques and skills come into existence, masking and compensating for the defect. These make it possible to cope with an unmanageable task using new, different paths. Compensatory cultural behavior overlays defective natural behavior. A specific "culture of the defect" is created: In addition to his negative characteristics, a physically handicapped person acquires positive characteristics.

This then, in our opinion, is what the psychologist should primarily study. Recently, due to a whole series of research projects, the picture of these "positive characteristics" of a handicapped condition and its basic mechanisms are beginning to become clearer and clearer for us.

Already in 1905 the German psychologist Alfred Adler laid the foundation for a unique thesis on personality, which we only now are beginning to interpret objectively enough and the individual aspects of which clarify for us much about the development of the mind and behavior of a physically defective child.

Adler, at that time a doctor in internal medicine, was struck by the fact that patients suffering from a serious defect of some organ were in spite of this able to overcome their defect. A simple phenomenon and well-known fact supports this observation: When one of the paired organs (the lungs, kidneys, even a hand) becomes diseased, its functioning is taken over by the other "stand-in" organ.[38] However, in an enormous number of instances, this occurs according to a much more complicated schema. Indeed, many of the organs of our body are not paired; many are totally affected and their total function proves to be affected. This occurs particularly in those cases when the organ's function is not totally interrupted but turns out only to be weak from birth. Thus, we often have a congenital weakness of vision or sight, a congenital defect of the speech apparatus (a weakness of the vocal cords, confused articulation, and so forth), and congenital defects of the muscle, sexual, nervous, and other systems.

On the other hand, as Adler has shown, people not only cope with these defects, compensating for congenital weaknesses, but often even "over compensate:" people born with weak hearing become musicians, people with vision impairments become artists, and people with speech defects become orators. A defect may be overcome just as in the case of Demosthenes who transformed from a tongue-tied person into a well-known orator, having compensated for his natural shortcomings many times over.

---

[38](A. L.) In a number of works, it was established that such a "substitution" can take place even in respect to brain hemispheres. When the centers of speech in the left hemisphere are damaged, the function of speech may be restored as a result of the development of the given function in the right hemisphere. It is natural that this occurs with significantly great difficulties, because a simple "switch" is not sufficient.

What course does "over compensation" take?

The basic mechanism of compensation and overcompensation of a defect proves, apparently, to be the following: The defect becomes the center of the individual's attention and on top of it is built a certain "psychological superstructure," which attempts to compensate the natural shortcoming with persistence, practice, and above all with a certain cultural use of this defective function (if it is weak) or of other substituting functions (if it is completely absent). A natural defect organizes the mind, it arranges it in such a way that maximal compensation is possible. And what is most important, it nurtures an enormous persistence in practicing and developing everything that might compensate the given defect. As a result, a unique unexpected picture emerges: A person with weak vision that does not allow equal footing with others, which renders him inferior, puts this defect at the center of his attention and directs his entire nervous psychological activity at the defect. This weak vision develops a particular ability to make maximum use of the information that he receives visually so that he becomes a person whose vision stands at the center of his work — an artist, a draughtsman, and so forth. We know that in history there are many such half-blind artists, musicians with organic hearing defects who toward the end of their life became deaf (such as Beethoven), and great actors with weak voices and poor diction. All these people were able to overcome natural defects and rearrange their psychological make-up so that they became great people precisely in that area where the path was almost entirely obstructed. It turned out that a defect that first of all deflates one's psychological state of mind, making it weak and vulnerable, may serve as a stimulus for its development, even boistering it up and making it stronger.

From this dynamic point of view, a physically defective person obtains not only his negative passport, but also his positive characteristics.[39]

Let us ask, however, what constitutes the mechanism of this compensation of a defect? Is it simply a mechanism for switching the function, as is often the case with illnesses involving one of the paired organs?

One phenomenon pushes us toward a correct answer to this question: the psychology of the blind is this very phenomenon.

Psychologists studying the life of the blind have long been interested in the question of how precisely a blind person compensates his natural weakness. An entire series of legends has been created about how unusually refined the senses of touch and hearing are in the blind. It has been said that

---

[39](J. K.) Although this metaphor and terminology may seem rather strange to Western ears, the internal passport plays such an enormous role in every Soviet citizen's life, particularly if it contains some negative characteristics, that again we have chosen to give a literal translation of Vygotsky's text.

they develop a new, unusual, finely tuned "sixth sense," however, an accurate experiment has rendered unexpected results: It turned out that neither the sense of hearing nor touch, nor any other sense organ in the blind represents any exceptional phenomena, that they are in no way developed better than the average sighted person (Bürklen, 1924). However, at the same time, it is no secret to anyone that a blind person achieves in the realm of hearing, touch, and so forth, significantly better results than a sighted person.

The majority of authors studying the blind resolve this seemingly contradictory position with the following explanation: Although a blind person possesses sense organs that are identical to those in the sighted, he develops for himself an ability to use these organs in a way that far surpasses that ability in the sighted. Those audio and tactile sensations that in a seeing person lie dormant under the dominance of his sight are mobilizes by the blind person and used with an unusual degree of fullness and sensitivity. A blind person's surprisingly developed activity of hearing and touch, is not the result of an innate or acquired physiological acuity of these receptors, but is a product "of the culture of the blind," the result of an ability to use the remaining sense organs culturally; in this way, compensation of the natural deficiency occurs.

We may say that the blind often possess dozens of developed skills and techniques that we do not see in the sighted. One only has to examine the subtle and agile nature of movement often displayed by the blind and the unusually refined analysis of the sensations perceived through touch and hearing, in order to understand the paths that allow them to compensate at least partially for their natural inability to adapt. Hearing and touch become the center of attention for the blind person who masters the development of a number of techniques for the maximal use of these senses — for the blind person, these devices merge with the very function of the perceptions. Remembering with the aid of these devices and even thinking with them restructures the perceptions. As a result of this process we have blind people who, by means of the Braille alphabet, quickly read a text that analyzes geographical maps and who, following their own paths, prove able to become full members of society. We have only to remember the well-known story of how Helen Keller, deaf and blind from birth, achieved a high level of education, in order to understand that a rational influence and the introduction to cultural devices can restructure the mind, even when development is severely handicapped by a physical disability.

Similarly, we encounter a circle of "cultural superstructures" in the presence of other forms of physical defects. We often see how, with a specific congenital defect, a particular function begins to perform a completely different, new role, becoming a tool that compensates the existing disability. Thus, we know that in the case of deaf-muteness,[40] mimicry begins to acquire a completely new function. It [mimicry] ceases to be simply a channel for expressing emotions and becomes a most important means for communicating, until new, more complete techniques—lip reading and finger reading [dactylology—J. K.]—take the place of this more primitive means of expression and contact.[41]

Moreover, this example can convince us how much each "tool" used by a deaf person perfects, develops, and changes his psychological make-up. We are certainly convinced that a particular psychological structure corresponds to each of the techniques used. It is absolutely clear that each deaf person using exclusively mimicry for conversations with others possesses limited possibilities for communication, for exchange of experience and information, and consequently, has very few possibilities for the further development and perfection of his intellect. How much these possibilities will increase if he switches to the language of signs,[42] making it possible for him to convey any word, any combination of sounds! How incredibly does his psychological inventory expand! What a huge stimulus is given to the development of his intellect, now enriched not only by a significant number of new concepts, but above all by a new and significantly more encompassing method of interaction with other people! Finally, maybe a similarly important leap forward is made in the deaf person's development when he learns lip reading and from there even ordinary speech, which he may often perfect, although

---

[40](J. K.) Deaf people in the Soviet Union were until very recently referred to as "deaf-mutes," although many deaf people do learn some speech—the major goal of contemporary Soviet education of the deaf. *Mimicry,* the term used for the natural sign language developed among the deaf, has been discouraged in the Soviet classroom and, although there is now some interest in reinstating its position in the educational system, the controversy between oralists and those propagating sign language is as heated in the Soviet Union as it has been in the United States. Vygotsky himself changed his position on sign language, first considering it detrimental to the growth of abstract thinking, and later considering it a vital tool for communication and thus for the full psychological development of a deaf child (cf. *Fundamentals of Defectology,* vol. 2, of Vygotsky, in press, and Galina L. Zaitseva, 1990, "L. S. Vygotsky and Studies of Sign Language in Soviet Psycholinguistics,"

[41](A. L.) It is interesting to note that all the previously indicated forms of speech are often preserved by the deaf and used for various areas of material being conveyed: Thus, deaf-mute children most often use lip-reading in communication with adults, and finger-reading in communication with each other, and mimed speech [sign language] for expression of emotional experiences [sign language].

(J. K.) This view is radically changed in Vygotsky's later works where he begins to promote "polyglossia"; a more positive opinion of "mimicry" (sign language of the deaf) is expressed, for example, in the later articles of deaf education in *Fundamentals of Defectology* (in press).

[42](J. K.) Although the word "sign" is used by these authors elsewhere in reference to any symbolic act, here it refers primarily to written and spoken language; it does not refer to the sign language of the deaf. Both Vygotsky and Luria use the word "mimicry" for sign language of the deaf.

he himself never hears it. Once having mastered these "tools," the deaf person enters the world of normal, hearing and speaking people. He gains the possibility of entering into a conversation with and understanding anyone. Not to mention the immense psychologically therapeutic significance of this conquest, which brings him out of his isolation, changing his entire personality, making him a socially complete being. This inclusion into a wide social strata immediately opens up new possibilities for his intellect. Of course, in an intellectual sense, one can hardly compare the deaf-mute, who is able to read lips, with that primitive being who uses only the imperfect tools of mimicry and inarticulate sounds for interaction with others.

There is still another simple example that illustrates how physical defects may be compensated with artificial means. We have in mind the numerous cases of wounds and amputations during the war.

All these cases are characterized by the common feature that a person is suddenly knocked out of commission, deprived of an extremity, and then restored his normalcy only with the help of an artificial limb—with a prosthesis. Learning to use a prosthesis in place of a hand or a leg essentially reshapes the character of this subject's behavior, and the "psychology of a prosthesis" that grew up during the war pointed out a series of traits associated with the use of these artificial hands or legs.

The Braille alphabet of the blind, finger spelling and lip reading of the deaf, the prostheses of invalids, all now become the object of study for psychology on the same footing with such processes as instincts, habits, attention, and affect. Such a broadening of psychology becomes essential when turning to the history of human behavior and the study of its cultural forms.

William James once pointed out that the personality of a human being ends not with the tip of his finger, but with the toe of his boot, and that his boots, hat, and clothes enter the make-up of his personality just as his head, hair, and fingernails.

This position is absolutely indisputable if we also decide to study the cultural forms of the behavior of personality. The notion of a cultural personality goes beyond the boundaries of the organism, and a study of cultural habits and clothes provide us most valuable material for understanding human behavior.

The entire history of clothes and fashion tells us about how one of their essential purposes was always to set off aspects of the figure, to conceal physical shortcomings, and—where necessary—to compensate them. One only has to glance through 16th- and 17-century memoirs in order to find a number of examples of this kind of fashion and individual dress pieces. Ruffles on the sleeves were introduced in order to hide unattractive hands of courtiers; ladies' fillets, introduced into fashion as a must at the beginning of the 19th-century, fitted tightly around the neck in order to conceal ugly scars there. In order to increase one's height, high heels were worn, and, on the contrary, large feet were concealed by long dresses. A thin figure or an undeveloped form is compensated by corsets, bustles, petty coats, and so forth (particularly widespread in the late Middle Ages and the Renaissance). It would be difficult to enumerate all the instances when physical defects were compensated by "the strategy of dress," when it was used in a systematic way to embellish and improve someone's identity. It is enough to remember all the military outfits, which increase the height and the figure, rendering a frightening or threatening appearance. These began with the war dress of indians and are still seen in modern military uniforms. It is enough to remember this in order to be convinced that clothes really do make up part of the personality and are frequently organized by its overall set.

We cannot pass over yet another external device used successfully in 18th- and 19th-centuries' fashions to compensate shortcomings and to distract attention from one part of the body, directing it at another. We have in mind "beauty spots," that were used by fashionable ladies in the past centuries and that served accordingly as a wonderful artificial device to attract attention.

All the techniques enumerated above can be summed up as external tools for compensation of natural shortcomings. In order to be logical, we should mention that inner compensatory techniques also supplement these external ones. What we have said about the formation of character traits applies precisely here. Compensating for a natural weakness by speaking unusually loudly, by behaving provocatively and rudely, is common and serves as the origin of a number of characteristic traits in a difficult child, in a trouble maker, and so on. We know that people who seem to be unusually cruel, upon close examination turn out to be gentle; their cruelty is only a compensatory mask, their lack of will is often camouflaged by stubbornness.

Physical shortcomings as well as certain psychological defects are often compensated not only by external methods, but also by the organization and orientation of the character of the entire personality.

We cannot look at a defect as something static and forever stuck in place. It sets into action and organizes a number of devices that may not only weaken the impact of the defect, but may sometimes even compensate (and even overcompensate) it. A defect can function as a powerful stimulus toward the cultural reorganization of the personality, and the psychologist must only know how to discover the possibilities for compensation and how to make use of them.

RETARDATION AND GIFTEDNESS

The view expressed on these pages forces us to reexamine our relationship to the all important question of modern pedology,[43] the question of "re-

---

[43](J. K.) A. Kozulin (see Vygotsky, 1986, p. xlv) has translated this term as roughly meaning "interdisciplinary educational psychology," which was condemned by a special degree of the

tardation" and "giftedness." In fact, this type of exploration in psychological studies began long ago. However, modern views about the retarded[44] child have little in common with the current opinions to which we have become accustomed.

In fact, the picture given of a retarded child is usually very simple. To be retarded means to be "stupid." A retarded child, or more precisely, a *debile, imbecile, or idiot,*[45] is one who possesses a deficient psychological inventory, who does not possess the necessary memory, adequate perceptibility, or adequate intelligence. A retarded person is psychologically impoverished from birth.

More accurate investigations of retardation, however, do not completely confirm this view.

Is it really true that a retarded child in all respects functions at a lower level than a normal child of the same age?

Let us consult statistics. One German author (Gelpke, 1904, cited in Troshin, 1915) conducted a detailed examination of vision in children with varying degrees of retardation. The results were astonishing; The best vision was found in the group of idiots. Here is a short summary of these findings:

TABLE 3.2
Vision of Mentally Handicapped Children

Group	Occurances of normal vision (in %)	Occurances of above normal vision (in %)
Idiots	57.0	87.0
Imbeciles	54.7	54.7
Retarded	43.0	54.3
Normal	17.0	48.0

According to these data, the percent of normal vision in the group of idiots is 3 times above that of a normal child, and their above-average vision is 2 times above the norm (plus standard deviations in both cases).

Communist Party in 1936 because of its association with the IQ tests then gaining prominence in Western Europe and the United States. Even though Vygotsky often used the term *pedology,* as Cole points out, he was very scornful of this practice (Cole et al., 1978, p. 10). For more discussion of this term, see the Introduction to *Fundamentals of Defectology* (Vygotsky, in press).

[44](J. K.) This word in Russian is literally translated as "backward," a term that was often used at the beginning of the century in reference to the mentally retarded. We have chosen, however, to use the more contemporary term *retarded.*

[45](J. K., V. G.) There are three generally accepted categories of retardation in Soviet defectology — debile, imbecile, and idiot, listed by degree of severity. For more explanation of these categories, see the introduction to L. S. Vygotsky's (in press) *Fundamentals of Defectology, Collected Works,* vol. 2, and James Gallagher's (1974) *Windows on Russia.*

Moreover, the percent of normal vision regularly decreases when crossing from the group of idiots to groups with lesser degrees of retardation and to groups of normal children.

Consequently, in regard to vision, we see the reverse process of what we expected: the greater the retardation, the better the basic physiological function of vision.

Roughly the same can be said about other organs of perception, in particular hearing. On the basis of numerous examinations, specialists have reached the conclusion that keen hearing in retarded children is not any lower than the norm. Thus, an interesting and somewhat unexpected conclusion has been reached: We expected to find in retarded children a degradation of all psychological physiological functions, and at the same time we see that their basic natural base — the activity of the sense organs — is not in the least diminished, but in several instances is actually higher than the norm.

The same surprise awaited us in subsequent investigations of the mind of the retarded child.

We have become accustomed to thinking that all "intellectual" functions are without a doubt lower in all retarded children. Frequently, however, retarded children and imbeciles strike us with their surprisingly keen memory. We are aware of incidents when a retarded child was found to be able to mechanically remember sufficiently large excerpts from a text without exhibiting any comprehension of it.

This, however, was far from always the case. In cases when the proposed material was interesting and comprehensible to the imbecile but not sufficiently imprinted in a natural manner, when some energetic exertion was required in order to master this material, the memory of it turned out to be exceedingly poor, almost nonexistent. According to Troshin (1915), a leading authority in the study of retarded children:

> The border line for active memory falls between retardation and the norm. . . . Natural memory is above average while artificial memory is almost zero. Anything that is colored by feeling, that has a relationship to the personality and interests of the retarded child — anything immediately pertaining to his every day experiences and not demanding any effort, everything which the retarded child really needs — all this he will recognize as normal; his memory refuses to work, if there is something unusual and incomprehensible, requiring an unpleasant exertion. . . . (pp. 683, 687, 688)

It would be difficult to better express this duality in the activity of a retarded child's memory. We are only able to understand it from one point of view: We suppose that a retarded child's natural memory (just as in the case of his vision, hearing, and other natural functions) can often remain unaffected by his disability. The difference lies only in the fact that a normal child rationally uses his natural functions and the more he advances, the more he is able to devise appropriate cultural devices to aid his memory. Such is not the case with the retarded child. A retarded child may be endowed with same natural talents as the normal child, but he does not know how to use them rationally. Thus, they lie dormant, useless, like dead weight. He possesses but *does not know how to use* these natural talents, and this is the basic defect of the retarded child's mind. Retardation consequently is a defect not only in the natural processes themselves, but also in their cultural use. To combat this, the same auxiliary cultural measures are required.

Earlier researchers understood this very well and more than once pointed it out, saying that defects in a higher functioning retarded child first and foremost consist of an inability to use his own natural resources:

> Not one of the intellectual abilities of an idiot can be considered completely absent, but he does not have the ability to freely apply these abilities to phenomena of a moral and abstract nature. . . . Physically he *is unable,* intellectually he *does not know how,* psychologically he *does not want to.* He would both *be able and know,* if only he *wanted to,* but the tragedy lies in the fact that he *does not want to.* (Seguin, 1903/1971, pp. 35–37)

So said Sequin in his book entitled, *Traitement moral, hygiene et education des idiots et des autres enfants arrieres.*

First and foremost we see a fundamental, correct position underlying these profoundly true, although somewhat naive statements. The phenomenon of retardation is not only a phenomenon of natural deficiency, but also, to a greater degree, a phenomenon of cultural deficiency–an inability to desire and to know how.

We attempt to prove this through an experimental study of memory in normal and retarded children.

Earlier (see section or acquisition of tools) we cited the example of a retarded child who, in contrast to a developed or a mature child, does not know how to adequately use the tools of his inner world, or how to use objects fundamentally as a means for the systematic realization of some goal, preferring to exert his own natural efforts. We also see the same thing with the child's memory. We examined the natural memory of children of different ages from preschoolers to elementary school children with different levels of development (from gifted to varying degrees of retardation). From all the analyzed data, we are under the impression that natural memory (the mechanical imprint left from a suggested series of words) varied only very insignificantly depending upon age and overall giftedness. On the average, retention of the material fluctuates between 4.5 and 5.5 words out of 10. Moreover, we do not see a significant distinction here between gifted and retarded children.

What accounts, therefore, for the difference in the memory of the retarded and of the gifted child? We had the opportunity to convince ourselves that this difference lies in an unequal ability to culturally use one's memory.

If a normal (and likewise, gifted) child turned out to be able to use a series of artificial devices to help his memory and strongly increase its activity, then a retarded child, when left to himself, was almost incapable of using these methods. We became convinced of this on the basis of the experiment we have already described: We gave a child a series of cards with pictures on them and proposed that he utilize them to remember, while we selected each word that corresponded to one of the pictures (experiment described in section on cultural development of memory).

The results give us an interesting picture of the difference between the mind of a retarded child and that of a gifted child.

In order to illustrate this, we look at three children between the ages of 10 and 11 years old. All three children are gifted: their IQ, according to the Binet, is significantly above average. Three tests for memory were given to each of the three children. First, they were simply asked to remember a series of words that were read (natural memory). In two other experiments, pictures were offered in connection with words designed to help the child remember the word. The last two series differed in the following way: in the first, the children were offered pictures, among which they could find those close to the content of the given words. The final series was somewhat more difficult, that is, the words suggested to the subject had a more definite connection with the pictures, and the child had to devise an artificial connection between them.

Here are the results of the research done with these three children:[46]

TABLE 3.3
Memory of Gifted Children

Name	Age	IQ	Natural Memory	I	Cultural Memory II	Average	Coefficient of Natural Memory (in %)
Aleks T.	20:6	1.23	5	10	8	9	180
Grinia L.	10:2	1.27	6	10	9	9.5	159
Kostia D.	10:9	1.36	4	8	6	7	175

What does this data on all these children mean?

We see that all these children posses an average natural memory (4, 5, and

---

[46](J. K., V. G.) Here we have introduced several cases only to show the quality of the illustrated material. Detailed statistical data were given in the work by A. M. Leontiev, which came out in the studies of the Psychological Laboratory of the Academy of Communist Education.

6 words out of 10). However, when we offer them the assistance of pictures, that is, when we examine their active ability to use their memory with the help of appropriate devices, we see that the number of remembered words increases almost twofold — now they remember 9 to 10 words. (If the number of given words were larger, we would have been able to come up with still more significant results.) Using artificial techniques, a child strongly improves the natural ability of his memory: the increase here averages 170% to 200%. 'We introduce here a sample of a report in this series:

Grinia L.

| | Second Series: | | | Third Series | |
Word	Picture	Impression	Word	Picture	Impression
snow	sled	+	woods	mushroom	+
lunch	basket	+	house	washroom	+
learning	pencil	+	rain	sponge	+
young	saw	+	meeting	table	+
dress	hat	+	flowers	cherry tree	+
father	boots	+	wing	beet;e	+
field	onion	+	fire	bell (ring)	+
bird	dove	+	truth	watering can	−
horse	horse shoe	+	roof	barrel	+
			worker	turner	+

When examining this sample, we see that the child does not pick the pictures accidentally, but each time chooses the image that is in some way connected with the given word, sometimes artificially linking them.

We now take a more extensive look at how these children connect the words with a specific picture and how they themselves explain this connection:

> Al T.
> The word given is "dress:" he chose the picture of a "purse." To the question "why?" he answered, "because you put a purse in a pocket."
> The word given is "field:" he chose the picture of wild strawberries ("They grow in fields").
> The word given is "meeting:" He chose a "little bell." ("They ring it at a meeting, when it gets too noisy."
> The word given is "truth:" He chose the picture "letter" ("In letters you can write everything and no one will open it [because] there is a sealing wax").
> Kostia D.
> The word given is "dress." He chose the picture with a brush. ("You can brush the dress off.")
> The word given is "horse." He chose the picture of boots. ("There were no hooves so it took some boots.")
> The word given is "dinner." He chose the picture of a knife. ("You can cut bread with this knife.") etc.

We see that the child makes successful use of the pictures as auxiliary devices. Wishing to remember the given word, he most often choose the picture that represents the subject that falls within the same category as the given word (dinner-knife, dress-brush, meeting-bell). Moreover, he sometimes constructs a highly artificial and complex connection; he in no way [mechanically] reproduces previous experience, but intentionally combines individual elements. (Truth goes with letter: because no one can open it, you may write the truth; a horse goes with boots, etc.)

A gifted child proves to be able to actively use his previous experience by putting to use a number of methods that perfect his natural psychological processes.

This is not what we see in retarded children.

We now look at four children from the same children's institution, who are noticeably retarded: Katya K. with severe oligophrenia and three others with debilitation.[47] We lead them through a series of analogous experiments and examine the results:

TABLE 3.4
Memory of Retarded Children

Name	Age	IQ	Natural Memory	Cultural Memory			Coefficient of Cultural Memory
				I	II	Average	
Katia K.	12,0	0.58	6	5	4	4.5	75
Vera B.	10,5	0.69	4	3	3	3	(75)
Kolia Sh.	11,4	0.56	5	4	0	2	40
Vania Ch.	11,4	0.71	5	5	3	4	80

We see that the outcome differs with these children. It is true that natural memory turns out to be the same for both groups of children. Neither retardation nor giftedness affect their natural memory. If, however, we compare the numbers that characterize their cultural memory, we see great discrepancy. If, in the first case, we had a sharp increase in memory with the transition to cultural forms of memory, then in the case of the retarded children the reverse is true. The pictures given to them as aids not only did not help them, but actually interfered, causing a deterioration in the activity of their memory. Instead of the coefficient of 180% to 200%, which we saw in the gifted children, we obtained a 40% to 70% to 80% coefficient for cultural memory. In other words, the child with the help of pictures remembers less than without them. The proposed cultural devices turn out to be beyond the the retarded child's capability. He is able to use them, but

---

[47](J. K., V. G.) The milder form of retardation, which might be considered to be a category of learning disabled. These children were taken from the Medical–Pedagogical Clinic of NARKOMPROS (Peoples Committee on Education).

they only distract him from direct use of his memory. Thus, the major difference between retarded and gifted children seems to be a difference not in the natural processes themselves, but in the use of them with cultural devices.

Indeed, let us now take a look at how each child relates to the pictures offered for his assistance. Here is a summary from the original report of several of the participants:

Vania Ch. 'debile:

Word	Picture	Reproduce
snow	pencil	−
dinner	boots	+
learning	grater	+
hammer	butterfly	−
dress	sled	+
father	basket	−
field	strawberries	+ "They grow in fields."
game	hoop	−
bird	knife	−
horse	horseshoe	+ "Horseshoes are on a horse."

Katia K., oligophrenic

Word	Picture	
snow	sled	+
lunch	boots	+
learning	strawberries	−
hammer	tongs	+
dress	basket	+
father	butterfly	−
field	onion	+
game	horseshoe	−
bird	watch	−
horse	knife	−

We see that these children often choose the picture accidentally, not making any connection with the given word. Therefore, naturally we do not see an increase in their memory capabilities. In the introduced data, we do not see the structures that were used by the children mentioned earlier. A retarded child most often is unable to understand how he may use a picture to remember a word. "Snow is snow—yes, but there is no snow in any picture." Not being able to actively make a connection between a word and a picture, he searches for an easier representation and, not finding it, most often chooses a picture mechanically, independently of the assigned task of matching it with the word given. To the question, why did he choose that picture, he most often responds, "because I like it." He does not relate to it as a goal, does not see its functional role, and does not use it as a means. Therefore, it is completely understandable that in the majority of cases he resorts to his own natural memory and recalls the mechanical imprint on his memory by what he read. In short, pictures do not help him, quite the opposite, they distract him so that the results are worse than they were initially.

We have introduced examples of the research conducted on natural and cultural memory and we have discovered what constitutes the difference between retarded and gifted children. One may assume that this also applies to other areas. The major difference is rooted not in the inherent natural processes alone, but in a deficiency of the cultural devices, in the inability to create and use them.

In all these instances, purely biological defects appear together with this factor that can limit and inhibit the cultural adaptation of a child.

It turns out that the difference between the normal and retarded child often has nothing to do with the natural abilities of one or of the other, but stems from a different use of these natural abilities in conjunction with the varying degrees of the child's cultural development. In both the debile and the imbecile, this cultural development is hindered by actual defects in the development of the brain, whereas the backward[48] child lacks sufficient influence from his cultural environment. But if in the first group we see that education does not have a significant influence, if this influence often encounters considerable constitutional difficulties, then with respect to retarded children in a normal school, we maintain a healthy optimism: By instilling in the child certain cultural techniques of behavior, we can successfully cope with the child's retardation not as a biological fact, but as a phenomenon of cultural underdevelopment.

What we take for exceptional inherent giftedness in one area is often not in the least the result of some inherent qualities, but rather the product of rational employment of cultural devices and considerable ability to maximize the use of one's own natural resources.

These natural abilities themselves may not even differ from the average abilities of a normal child.

The research on counters[49] that Binet conducted may serve as an example of this. Binet subjugated people known as outstanding counters to psychological tests; these people were known for the phenomenal speed with which they completed mathematical operations and for their ability to memorize long series of numbers.

What we find so striking in these people, Binet called "the simulation of an outstanding memory" and he showed that it constituted a series of

---

[48](J. K., V. G.) Here what is meant is perhaps closer to the modern understanding of learning disabled or developmentally delayed children.

[49](J. K., V. G.) Here Luria has in mind, of course, *idiot savants*.

techniques, which the just-mentioned people mastered and by means of which they succeeded in obtaining fantastic results with only an average memory.

The use of rational cultural techniques makes it possible for the activity of any given function to achieve greater success and to create, as it were, an illusion of great natural giftedness.

All these facts compel us, of course, to re-evaluate our attitude toward inherent and acquired forms of giftedness and raises the question of "cultural giftedness" as one of the most important problems concerning modern psychology today.

EVALUATION OF GIFTEDNESS
AND THE PROBLEMS
OF CULTURAL DEVELOPMENT

Over the past several years, measurement and evaluation of giftedness has become a matter of great practical importance. The idea voiced in America and France at the end of the 19th century that it is possible to express in numbers the degree of a child's giftedness, has managed over the past 10 years to find specific forms of application; now not only do we have a series of elaborated systems of texts, but we have successfully employed them in schools, clinics, and on the job.

The idea underlying modern tests in assessment of giftedness briefly is the following: If we give the subject a series of tasks, each of which concerns one activity connected with a definite function and if we then arrange these tasks in an order of increasing difficulty, then it is natural for the person more gifted with respect to the given function to be able to solve a greater quantity of such problems or to complete them more successfully. This provides us with the opportunity to express the degree of giftedness in relative numbers.

All tests of giftedness are based on this fundamental position. The individual systems of application differ only in the details and techniques of the implementation of this basic idea.

Thus, Rosilimo's[50] famous system for a "psychological profile" emanated from a study of the peaks in the development of individual functions (attention, memory, will, quickness, etc.), these peaks being expressed in conditional units—the number of accomplished tasks. The result of such an investigation is the "Psychological Profile" that indicates the peak of each individual function. Another famous system of testing—Binet's system—attempts to give a summary estimate of the degree of development for a child of a certain age. Noticing that not every task can be solved by children

---

[50](J. K., V. G.) See also Vygotsky (in press) for further discussion of these testing systems.

of different ages, Binet chose a group of empirical test series, each of which was easily completed by a normal child of a certain age. Such a series of problems was worked out for 3-, 4-, and 5-year-olds, and so on. If a child of a given age turns out to be retarded, then he usually does not solve all the problems of the corresponding age group. If, however, we conduct this experiment with an advanced, gifted child, then in addition to the problems prescribed for his age group, he is also able to solve several problems at the next age level. Thus, the degree of his development or retardation is empirically calculated.

However sound and reliable this theory may in essence seem, measuring giftedness by means of tests raises more complex questions, if we take a closer look.

Indeed, what characteristics are we to look for when giving different tests of giftedness? What exactly produces giftedness and what is generally understood by this term?

When examining more closely the different systems for testing giftedness, we are persuaded that they often test completely different functions from completely different areas. One can also say that almost all modern tests of giftedness examine either the conditions of innate psychological, physiological functions or something completely different, namely the development of skills and the extent of a person's informedness. The first cycle of processes, as is presupposed, is not subject to development, not even on a very low level. Therefore, it is often important to test a person's natural memory, his vision, his hearing, the speed of his movements, reflexes, and so on. On the other hand, a person's level of knowledge is, of course, subject to most powerful fluctuations and is the result of more or less rich experiences, of successful and prolonged contact with the environment. If we analyze the data, received, for example, as a result of the Binet texts, then we must recognize that what we obtained, strictly speaking, is highly heterogeneous material and that the sum total, which seemingly reflects a child's intellectual growth, conceals the undifferentiated merging of those evaluated natural abilities with school-acquired knowledge. Indeed, can naming monetary signs, naming the months in order, finding rhythms for words, and so on, be evidence of a school child's giftedness? On the basis of this data we can judge not how great, strictly speaking, is the degree of giftedness, but how much school knowledge a child has acquired, how large or small is his vocabulary, and so on. Of course, this all may enter into the widely understood notion of giftedness, but it nevertheless far from exhausts this conception. After all, we know instances and aspects of giftedness that are not accompanied by large amounts of knowledge. Along with an investigation of the wealth of a child's information, we must also study his other capabilities that have no direct connection with his knowledge, but play a large role in his cultural development.

On the other hand, we believe it to be far from sufficient to evaluate only the natural, innate characteristics of personality.

Can we, without further analysis, reject the intellectual work of a person with a very poor natural memory? Can we consider him to be not very gifted if, along with having a poor natural memory, he gives us low scores with respect to other processes: speed of reaction, precision of movements, attention, and so on? It seems to us that it would be wrong to draw such a conclusion. We cannot forget that some people, who are without question gifted, often have poor natural abilities, that a natural deficiency does not necessarily remain a gaping hole all one's life, and that it can be filled in and compensated for in the course of life by other artificial devices. Even with a poor natural memory, cultural giftedness, as we have shown earlier, means knowing how to maximize the use of this shortcoming. At the same time, there are other instances where good natural abilities remain untapped.

When ascertaining the state of a person's inherent abilities, we determine only his "starting point" which with cultural development can yield dissimilar results.

What constitutes cultural development and how should we set out to establish and evaluate it with specific psychological tests? If you consider this entire account, our answer to these questions becomes self-evident. We think that the degree of cultural development expresses itself not only in acquired knowledge, but also in the ability of a person to use objects in his external world and, first and foremost, to rationally use his own psychological processes. Culture and environment remake a person not just by giving him certain knowledge, but by transforming the very structure of his psychological processes, by developing in him certain techniques for using his own abilities. Cultural giftedness means first of all to rationally use one's endowed capabilities, be they average or poor, to achieve the kind of results that a culturally undeveloped person can achieve only with the help of considerably stronger natural abilities.

Cultural giftedness, in essence, means the ability to control one's own natural resources; it means the creation and application of the best devices for using these resources.

It is not necessary to think that cultural giftedness is a single, static phenomenon; it may have absolutely different manifestations. Giftedness in one area is not necessarily evident in another. A musician who develops unusual cultural activity in one area might possess none of the resources that we suppose a scientist to have. Here again, a person with great practical talents possesses a completely different set of abilities. In place of the abstract and little used term *overall giftedness,* the new concept of a whole realm of special "exceptional capabilities" is being advanced.

However, in all these cases, there is one common factor. It boils down to the maximum ability to use one's inherent abilities for the invention of ever newer internal and external, structurally simple and complex, techniques that convert the natural processes into mediated, artificial cultural processes. There is something in common in the wealth and activity of these devices that gives us the notion of "cultural giftedness."

Of course, this notion assumes a dynamic character when acquired in live contact with the social environment: These psychological formations are a product of social influence on the human being; they are the representation and fruit of the external cultural surroundings in the life of the organism. Each person has these forms, but, depending upon the history of each person and on the varying plasticity of his initial constitutional abilities, they are richly developed in one person and are in embryo in another. The task of the psychologist is to study them with sufficient precision and to determine the coefficient of this "cultural development" in each of the individuals under examination. The program of study of individual giftedness should consist of the following: First, the degree of natural inclinations, the age level of neuro-psychological activity, the entire basis of natural neuro-dynamics, and then the stage and structure of the cultural process, the degree of informedness and the wealth of skills.

It is possible to count on further experimental psychological investigations in the not so distant future that will give us both ready-made systems to test cultural development and the standards to identify the features of cultural development in children of different social, biological age groups.

Studying not only man's inherent characteristics, but also those forms of nervous psychological activity that owe their existence to the cultural influence of the environment will make it possible for us to better understand the child in our kindergartens and our schools. More precisely, it will allow us to evaluate the character of his development and to learn to advance his development further and further ahead by using rational cultural influences.

References

Ach, N. (1905). *Über die Willlenstätigkeit und das Denken* [Activity of the will and thinking]. Göttingen, Germany: Vandenhoeck and Ruprecht.

Ach, N. (1921). *Uber die Begriffsbildung* [Development of concepts] Bamberg, Germany: Buhner.

Arsenev, V. K. (1936). *Dersu Uzala.* Moscow: Molodaiia gvardiia.

Arsenev, V. K. (1986). *Selections.* Moscow: Sovetskaiia Rossiia.

Blonskii, P. P. (1911). *Studies in scientific psychology.* Moscow: State Publishing House.

Blonskii, P. P. (1926). *Pedologiia* (Pedology). Moscow.

Bonte, T., Leifman, E., & Rössler, F. (1928). *Untersuchung ber die eidetische Veranlagung von Kindern und Jugendlichen* [Study of eidetic memory in children and adolescents]. Leipzig, Germany: J. A. Barth.

Bühler, C. (1930). *The first year of life.* New York: Day.

Bühler, C., Hetzer, H., & Tudor-Hart, B. (1927). *Sociologische und psychologische Studien über erste Lebensjahr* [Sociological and psychological study of the first year]. Jena, Germany: Fischer.

Bühler, K. (1927). *Dukhovnoe razvitie rebenka* [Mental development of the child]. Moscow.

Bühler, K. (1929). *Die geistige Entwicklung des Kindes* [Mental development of the child]. Jena, Germany: Fischer. (Original work published 1919)

Bühler, K. (1930). *The mental development of the child.* New York: Harcourt, Brace. (Russian ed., 1927, original and complete version published in 1919)

Bürklen, K. (1924). *Blinden Psychologie* [Psychology of the blind]. Leipzig, Germany: Barth. (Russian trans. published in 1924)

Chukovsky, K. (1968). *From two to five.* (M. Morton, Trans; rev. ed.). Berkeley: University of California Press. (Original work published under the title *Little children* in 1925/1928)

Clodd, E. (1905). *The story of the alphabet.* New York: D. Appleton and Company.

Cole, M., Scribner, S., John-Steiner, V., & Souberman, E. (1978). *L. S. Vygotsky. mind in society.* Cambridge: Harvard University Press.

Comte, A. (1853). *A course in the philosophy of positivism* (Vol. 2). London: J. Chapman.

Corsini, R. J. (Ed.). (1984). *Encyclopedia of psychology.* (Vols. 1-3). New York: Wiley.

Cushing, F. H. (1979). *Zuni: Selected writings of Frank Hamilton Cushing.* Lincoln, Nebraska: University of Nebraska.

Cushing, F. H. (1990). *Cushing at Zuni.* Albuquerque, NM: University of Mexico.

Danzel, T. W. (1912). *Die Anfänge der Schrift* [The beginning of writing]. Doctoral dissertation, Leibzig, Germany: Voigtländer.

Engels, F. (1960). *The dialects of nature.* New York: International Publishers.

Frazer, Sir James G. (1890). *The golden bough: A study in comparative religion.* London: Macmillan.

Gallagher, J. (1974). *Windows on Russia. A report of the United States-USSR seminar on instruction of handicapped children.* Washington, DC: DHEW Publication No. OE 7405001

Gatschet, A. (1890). *The Klamath Indians of Southwestern Oregon. Contributions to North American Ethnology: Vol. 2, Part 1. The Klamath language.* Washington, DC: Government Printing Office.

Gelpke, T. (1904). *Über die Beziehung des Sehorgans zum jugendlichen Schwachsinn* [Assessment of sight in adolescent feeblemindedness]. Halle an der Saale, Germany: State Publishing.

Groos, K. (1907). *The play of animals.* New York: Harper. (Original work published 1898)

Groos, K. (1916). *Dushevnaia zhizn' rebenka* (The mental life of a child). Kiev.

Helmholtz, H. (1924-1925). *Helmholtz's treatise on physiological optics* (T. Southall, Trans.) Rochester, NY: Optical Society.

Jaensch, E. R. (1927). *Über die Aufbau der Wahnehmungswelt* [The construction of the world of perception]. Leibzig, Germany: J. A. Barth. (Original work published 1911)

Jaensch, E. R. (1930). *Eidetic imagery.* New York: Harcourt, Brace. (Original work published 1925)

Khoroshikh, P. P. (1926). Birki irkustskikh buriat [The tallies of the Irkutks Buryats]. *Sibirskaja zhivaja starina, 1,* 97-112.

Klein, M. (1925). *Razvitie odnogo rebenka* [Development of one Child]. St. Petersburg.

Knox, J., & Stevens, C. (Trans.). (in press). Introduction to *L. S. Vygotsky's Fundamentals of defectology, Collected works.* New York: Plenum.

Koffka, K. (1928). *The growth of the mind* (R. M. Ogden, Trans; 2nd. rev. ed.). New York: Harcourt Brace. (Original work published 1925)

Köhler, W. (1921). *Intelligenzprüfungen an Menschenaffen* [Testing the intelligence of anthropoid apes]. Berlin: Julius Springer.

Köhler, W. (1926). *The mentality of the apes* (E. Winter, Trans.). New York: Harcourt Brace. (Original work published 1921)

Kozulin, A. (1990a). The concept of regression and Vygotskian developmental theory. *Developmental Review, 10,* 218-238.

Kozulin, A. (1990b). *Vygotsky's psychology.* Cambridge: Harvard University Press.

Leibniz, G. W. (1991). *Monadologie.* Pittsburgh, PA. University of Pittsburg. (Original work published 1714)

Leontiev, A. N. (1930). *Issledovanie oposretsvennogo vnimaniia u detei* [Investigation of Mediated Attention in Children]. In *Works of the Psychological Laboratory of the Academy of Communist Education.* Moscow: Moscow State University.

Leontiev, A. N. (1931). *Razvitie pamiati u detei* [Development of child memory]. Moscow: Uchpedgiz.

Leontiev, A. N. (1965). *Chelovek i kultura* [Man and culture]. In *Problemy razvitiia psikhiki* [Problems of the development of the mind] (2nd ed.). Moscow: Mysl. (Original work published 1905)

Leontiev, A. N. (1981). *Problems of the development of the mind.* Moscow: Progress. (Original work published 1959)

Leroy, L. (1927). *La raison primitive* [Primitive reason]. Paris: Librairie orientaliste.

Lévy-Bruhl, L. (1923). *Primitive mentality.* New York: The Macmillan. (Russian ed., 1930). (Original work published 1922)

Lévy-Bruhl, L. (1926). *How natives think*. London: George Allen & Unwin LTD. (Original work published work 1910)

Lewin, K. (1935). *A dynamic theory of personality* (D. Adams, Trans.). New York: McGraw. (Original work published 1926)

Lipmann, O., & Bogen, H. (1923). *Naive Physik* [Naive physicist]. Leipzig, Germany: J. A. Barth.

Lipps, T. (1907). *Rukovodstvo k psikhologii* [Manual for psychology]. St. Petersburg: O. N. Popov.

Livingstone, D. (1865). *Narrative of an expedition to Zambesi and its tributaries*. London: John Jurray.

Luria, A. R. (1928). Speech and intellect in child development [Rech' and intellekt v razvitii rebenka]. In *Works of the Psychological Laboratory* (Vol. 1). Moscow: Academy of Communist Education.

Luria, A. R. (1929a). Rech' i intellekt krest'ianskogo, gorodskogo i besprizornogo rebenka [Speech and intellect of the peasant, urban and homeless child]. In *Works of the Psychological Laboratory* (Vol. 2). Moscow: Academy of Communist Education.

Luria, A. R. (1929b). Puti razvitiia detskogo myshleniia [Paths of development of child thought]. In *Estestvoznanie i marksizm* (Vol. 2). pp. 97-130 Moscow: Institute of Marx and Engels.

Luria, A. R. (1963). *Mozg cheloveka i psikhicheskie protsessy* [The human brain and the psychological processes]. Moscow: APN RSFSR.

Luria, A. R. (1974). *Ob istoricheskom razvitii poznatel'nykh protsessov* [Historical Development of the Cognitive Processes]. Moscow: Nauka.

Luria, A. R. (1976). *Cognitive development: Its cultural and social foundations*. (M. Cole, Ed.). Cambridge: Harvard University Press.

Luria, A. R. (1981). *Language and cognition* (J. Wertsch, Trans.). New York: Wiley. (Original work published 1979)

Major, D. (1906). *First steps in mental growth*. New York: Macmillan.

Mallery, D. G. (1971). *Sign language among North American Indians*. The Hague, Netherlands: Mouton.

Marx, K. (1981). *Das Kapital. Kritik der politischen ekonomie* [Capital. Criticism of political economy]. Berlin: Dietz.

Meyers, C. S., & McDougall, W. (1903). Hearing, taste, smell, variation of blood pressure, and reaction time. In A. Haddon (Ed.), *Report of the Cambridge anthropological expedition to Torres Straits*. (Vol. 2, No. 2, pp. 72-150). Cambridge, England: University of Cambridge Press.

Norsworthy, N. (1906). *The psychology of mentally deficient children*. Unpublished doctoral dissertation, Columbia University, NY.

Peiser, I. (1914). Prüfungen höheren Gehirnfunktionen bei Kleinkindern [Testing higher brain functions in small children]. *Jahrbuch für Kindernheitkunde, 91*.

Piaget, J. (1923). *Le language et la pensee chez l'enfant* [Language and thought in a child]. Paris: Neuchatel, Delachaux & Niestle S.A.

Piaget, J. (1924). *Le judgement et la raisonment de l'enfant* [Judgement and reasoning in the child]. Paris: Neuchatel, Delachaux & Niestle S.A.

Piaget, J. (1928). *Judgement and reasoning* (M. Warden, Trans.). New York: Harcourt, Brace.

Piaget, J. (1957). *The language and thought of the child*. (M. Gabain, Trans.). New York: Meridian Books.

Powers, S. (1976). *Tribes of California*. Berkeley: University of California.

Prokhorov, A. M. (1985). *Bolshaia sovetskaia entsiklopediia* [Great Soviet encyclopedia]. Moscow: Soviet Encyclopedia.

Raspe, C. (1924). *Kindliche Selbstbeobachtung und Theroiebildung* [Children's self observation and theory building]. In Stern, W., & Lipmann, O. (Eds.), *Zeitschrift für angewandte Psychologie* (Vol. *23,* pp. 302–328). Leipzig, Germany: J. A. Barth.

Rivers, W. H. R. (1901). Primitive color vision. In A. Haddon (Ed.), *Reports of the Cambridge anthropological expedition to Torres Straits* (Vol. 2, pp. 10–5). Cambridge, England: The University of Cambridge Press.

Rivers, W. H. R. (1926). *Psychology and ethnology.* New York: Humanities.

Roth, W. E. (1897). *Ethnological studies among the N.W. Central Queensland aborigines.* London: Brisbane E. Gregory.

Schmidt, F. (1904). *Untersuchung über die Hausaufgaben des Sculkindes* [Examination of home work of school children]. Leipzig, Germany: Quelle & Meyer.

Seguin, E. (1971). *Idiocy and its treatment by the physiological method.* New York: A. M. Kelley. (Russian edition published in 1903, Petersburg.) (Original work published 1846)

Spencer, H. (1871). *Principles of psychology.* New York: E. Appleton.

Stern, C., & Stern, W. (1927). *Die Kindesprache: Eine psychologische und sprachteoretische Untersuchung* [Child speech: Examination of psychology and speech theory]. Leipzig, Germany: Quelle & Meyer.

Stern, W. (1914). *Psychologie der frühen kindheit bis zum Sechsten Lebensjahre* [Early child psychology up to six years]. Leipzig, Germany: Quelle & Meyer.

Stern, W. (1924a). *Methodensamlung zur Intelligentprufung von Kindern und Jugendlichen.* [Methods collecting intelligence testing of children and adolescents]. Leipzig, Germany: J. A. Barth.

Stern, W. (1924b). *Psychology of early childhood up to the sixth year of age.* New York: Holt, Rinehart & Winston. (Russian ed., Petrograd, 1915.) (Original work published 1914)

Stratz, C. H. (1922). *Der Körper des Kindes und seine Pflege* [The body of a child and hygiene]. Stuttgart: Enke. (Original work published 1909)

Taylor, I. (1899). *History of the alphabet.* New York: Scribner.

Thurnwald, R. (1922). *Psychologie des primitiven Menschen.* In G. Kafka (Ed.), *Handbuch der vergleichenden Psychologie* (*Band 1,* pp. 147–320). Munich: Ernst Reinhardt.

Thurnwald, R. (1935). *Black and white in East Africa.* London: G. Poutledge.

Tracy, F. (1894). *The psychology of childhood.* Boston: D. C. Heath.

Troshin, G. Ja. (1915). *Sravnitel'naia psikhologiia normal'nikh detei* [Comparative psychology of normal and abnormal children] (Vol. 1). Petersburg: G. Ja. Troshin Shkola Lechebnitsa.

Tylor, E. B. (1964). *Early history of mankind and the development of civilization.* Chicago: University of Chicago.

Tylor, E. B. (1874). *Primitive children.* London: J. Murray.

Tylor, E. B. (1877). *Primitive culture* (2nd ed.). New York: Henry Holt.

Ukhtomskii, A. A. (1945). Ocherki fiziologii nervnoi sistemy [Essays on physiology of nervous system]. In *Collected works* (Vol. 4). Leningrad: Leningrad State University.

Viner, O. (1909). *Rasshireniie nashikh zhuvstv* [Extension of our senses]. St. Petersburg.

Volkelt, H. (1930). *Eksperimental'naia psikhologiia doshkolnika* [Experimental child psychology]. Moscow: Gosizdat. (Original work published 1926)

Volkelt, H. (1962). *Fortschritte des experimentellen Kinderpsychologie* [Advances in experimental child psychology]. In F. Sander & H. Volkelt (Eds.), *Ganzheitspsychologie* (pp. 201–246). Munich: Beck. (Original work published 1926)

Von den Steinen, K. (1897). *Under den Naturvölkern Zentralbrasiliens* [About the primitive people of Central Brazil]. Berlin: D. Reimer.

Von den Steinen, K. (1969). *Die Marquesaner and ihre Kunst* [The Marquese and their art]. New York: Harcker Art Books.

Vygotsky, L. S. (1928). Problema kul'turnogo razvitiia ù rebenka [Problem of cultural development of the child]. *Pedologiia, 6,* 58–57.

Vygotsky, L. S. (1929a). *Geneticheskie korni myshleniia i rechi* [Genetic roots of thought and speech]. *Estestvo i Marksism* (Vol. 1). Moscow: Institute of Marx and Engels.

Vygotsky, L. S. (1929b). *Pedologiia podrostka* [Pedology of the adolescent]. Moscow: Bureau of Extension Education at Moscow State University.

Vygotsky, L. S. (1982). *Sobranie sochinenii. Tom pervyi: Voprosy teorii i istorii psikhologii* [Collected works. Vol. 1. Problems in the theory and history of psychology]. Moscow: Pedagogika.

Vygotsky, L. S. (1984). *Sobranie sochinenii. Tom chetvertyi: detskaia psikhologiia* [Collected works. Vol. 4: Child psychology]. Moscow: Pedagogika.

Vygotsky, L. S. (1986). *Thought and language* (A. Kozulin, Trans.). Cambridge: MIT.

Vygotsky, L. S. (in press). *Fundamentals of defectology.* In *Collected works* (Vol. 2, J. Knox & C. Stevens, Trans.). New York: Plenum.

Werner, H. (1900). *Einführung in die Entwicklungspsychologie* [Introduction to developmental psychology]. Leipzig, Germany: Engelmann.

Werner, H. (1961). *Comparative psychology of mental development.* New York: Science Education.

Wertheimer, M. (1912). *Über das Denken der Naturvölker Zahlen und Zahlengebilde* [Thought in primitive folk: Counting and figures]. *Zeitschrift für Psychologie, 1,* 60.

Wertheimer, M. (1966). *Productive thinking.* London: Associated Book.

Whipple, G. (1914). *Manual of mental and physical tests.* Baltimore: Warwick & York.

Zaitseva, G. (1990). L. S. Vygotsky and studies of sign language in Soviet psychololinguistics. In S. Prillwitz & T. Vollhaber (Eds.), *Sign Languages Research and Application* (pp. 271–290). Hamburg: Signum.

Author Index

Subject Index

Pitta-Pitta, 121
Zūnis, 129
Borneo villagers, 126, 138
North Americans, 95, 106, 109, 112, 116
Californian Indians, 109
Minnesota Indians (Ojibwa), 106
North Dakota Indians, 102
Maoris (New Zealand), 110
Papuans (New Guinea), 91, 92
Peruvian tribes, 102–104
semiliterature, illiterate peoples of the
former Soviet Union
Buryats, 129, 131
Kurds, 131
in Uzbekistan, 13, 14
Nanaitsy (the Golds), 88
Udegeians, 107
Evolution, 36–37
biological, 79–80
Darwin's theory of, 1, 41, 45, 80
Engel's theory of, 75–78
from animals to humans, 140
higher stage of cultural development, *see*
Two lines of development
missing psychological link in evolutionary
chain, 44
Vygotsky's notion of, 16
Expeditions (in Soviet Asia), 13–15
persecution of, 15, 16
Experiments and methods, 42–60, 64–70,
79, 83, 153, 166, 193
Pavlov's experiments, 42–43, 64, 70, 79,
83, *see also* Pavlov's theories
Piaget's tests and observations, 153, 166,
193
Köhler's experiments, 45–60
with apes, 19, 20, 44–59, 66–68
with dogs, 47, 51, 65, 66
with chickens, 55–57, 64–66, 69

F

Fantasy, 11, 125
egocentrism in child fantasies, 154–155
of primitive man, 101
"naive psychology," 138
"naive physics," 100, *see also* Magic
Formalists, Russian, 9

G

Genetic Analysis, 18–19, 140
biogenetic law, 140

genetic psychology, 19
ontogenetic, 2, 18, 38
phylogenetic, 38
Gestalt psychology, 19, 56, 60, 63, 67, 70
altering spatial structures, 60
independence of structures, 63
law of structures, 19, 67, 70
visual perception of a structure, 56, *see
also* Visual fields, Thinking in complexes
Gestures, *see* Auxiliary devices, Sign types,
Writing
Gifted Children, 219–231
and retarded children, 219–228
cultural giftedness, 231
evaluation of, 228–231
natural versus cultural, 228
overall giftedness, 230

H

Hand, 40
functions and transformation of, 75
development of, 170
hand as a tool, 106
influence on mind, 115, *see also* Sign
types
Handicapped children, 10, 26, *see also* Auxiliary devices, Defectology, Defects
Higher mental processes, *see* Higher psychological processes
Higher psychological processes, 10, 26
abstract numeric operations, 198, *see also*
Numeric operations
cultural attention, 18, 192, *see also* Attention
cultural memory, 18, *see also* Memory
evolution of, 17
in primitive people, 10
mediated mental process, 11
volution (will), 18
Hyperkinesis, 64

I

Imagination, *see* Fantasy
Inner Speech, *see* Speech
Instincts, *see* Development
animal, 79
differentiated, 57
instinctive adroitness, 88
Institute of Defectology, *see* Defectology
Institute of Psychology, 15